DATE DUE

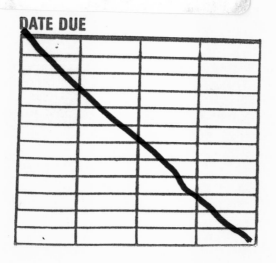

Israel-Palestine

Recent Titles in
Contributions in Political Science
Series Editor: Bernard K. Johnpoll

ISRAEL-PALESTINE
A Guerrilla Conflict in International Politics

Eliezer Ben-Rafael

CONTRIBUTIONS IN POLITICAL SCIENCE,
NUMBER 161

GREENWOOD PRESS

NEW YORK • WESTPORT, CONNECTICUT • LONDON

Library of Congress Cataloging-in-Publication Data

Ben-Rafael, Eliezer.
  Israel-Palestine : a guerrilla conflict in international politics.

  (Contributions in political science, ISSN 0147–1066 ; no. 161)
  Bibliography: p.
  Includes index.
  1. Jewish-Arab relations. 2. Fedayeen. 3. Guerrillas—Israel.
4. Guerrillas—West Bank. 5. Munaẓẓamat
al-Taḥrir al-Filasṭīnïyah. I. Title. II. Series.
DS119.7.B38343 1987 327.5694017′4927 86–12096
ISBN 0–313–25553–9 (lib. bdg. : alk. paper)

Library of Congress Catalog Card Number: 86–12096
ISBN: 0–313–25553–9
ISSN: 0147–1066

First published in 1987

Greenwood Press, Inc.
88 Post Road West, Westport, Connecticut 06881

Printed in the United States of America

The paper used in this book complies with the
Permanent Paper Standard issued by the
National Information Standards Organization (Z39.48–1984)

10 9 8 7 6 5 4 3 2 1

Contents

Part II: In the Field

List of Exhibits

Acknowledgments

This work draws from a variety of sources. Among them are scores of informants—both Israelis and Palestinians, officials as well as ordinary citizens, including hundreds of PLO members—and dozens of documents revealed to the public in the aftermath of the 1982 Israeli invasion of Lebanon.

This work is my responsibility. However, numerous colleagues have read parts of the manuscript and have discussed its themes with me. I am particularly indebted to Ephraim Yuchtman-Yaar, Yonathan Shapiro, and Shaul Mishal. I also recall my fruitful discussions with Seymour M. Lipset, Louis Kriesberg, William Goode and Annie Kriegel. The research was supported by the Project for Peace and the Faculty of Social Sciences of the Tel-Aviv University.

Special gratitude is due to Shelly Shenhav, my research assistant, and to the students of my advanced research seminar on the PLO in the occupied territories. Tami Berkowitz and Alisa Lewin spared no effort in their work on the text, and Roslyn Langbart and Sylvia Weinberg invested their best in the typing of the manuscript and the numerous corrections. At Greenwood Press, Loomis Mayer and Anne Hebenstreit were of the greatest help in the creation of this book. Finally, I owe much to my wife, Miriam, for her patience and encouragement.

Part I Theory and Background

1 Guerrilla Conflict: The Theory and Its Implications

A. THE STORY

Hundreds of books and articles have been written about the Israeli-Palestinian conflict. Some have investigated historical developments; others have analyzed social aspects. Many have focused on structural, political, or strategic issues.

In brief, it was during the British Mandate over Palestine (1921–48) that local Arab notables, confronted with the scheme of a Jewish homeland, began to emphasize an Arab-Palestinian nationalism, which grew in popular appeal during the 1936–39 Arab revolt. This revolt broke out in reaction to the mass immigration of Jews fleeing Nazism.[1]

At the same time, in the atmosphere of Pan-Arabism prevailing in the area, the neighboring states became increasingly involved in the struggle against Zionism. This confrontation reached its peak in the 1948 war, which culminated in the creation of the state of Israel in one part of what had been Palestine. The West Bank was then occupied by Jordan and the Gaza Strip by Egypt. Since that time, most Palestinians have been living in Arab countries, about half a million of them as refugees from Israeli territory.

Because of the relative stability of Jordan's Hashemite regime, the leaders of those Palestinians who were now considered Jordanians collaborated with their new rulers. In the other major Palestinian concentration, the Gaza Strip, Egypt maintained a military government over semiautonomous bodies. Many of the Palestinians, including most of those in Lebanon and Syria, were confined to refugee camps. Although adopting the Palestinian Cause as their own, those host countries took no specific responsibility for it.[2]

The situation was altered when President Gamal Abdel Nasser's political shift toward the USSR opened the door to Russian penetration of the area. The influence of the USSR grew as it developed the image of supporter of the "progressive" Arab states. In 1964, this group imposed the creation by the Arab League of a Palestinian Liberation Organization (PLO) as one indirect means of delegitimizing the Hashemite Kingdom. The new organization was an umbrella for all Palestinian groups that subscribed to its call for the liquidation of the Zionist entity. In 1969, the fedayeen (i.e. the combatants) took over the leadership of the PLO from the politicians who had been appointed by the sponsors of the organization.[3]

The 1967 Six-Day War between Israel, Egypt, Syria, and Jordan, however, reunited the Palestinians of Gaza and the West Bank—under an Israeli military authority. Protest multiplied, but the new rulers, who deployed a determined military force, did not hesitate to use drastic means of deterrence. Among their strategies was the creation of Jewish settlements in given areas, representing the intention of a permanent presence. In spite of the friction between the inhabitants and their rulers, the occupation generated economic progress, as a result of the availability of new jobs in Israel and of bridges to the Arab world. The Israeli juridical system, moreover, was accessible and responsive to the complaints of the inhabitants.[4]

Economic and social progress did not hinder the infiltration of the PLO. The PLO succeeded in strengthening its influence among the population, and in 1978, subsequent to the Camp David Agreements, a Committee for National Guidance was created by pro-PLO elements and was supplied with millions of dollars from external sources in order to prevent any form of cooperation with Israel on the part of Palestinians.[5]

Throughout this entire period, the major Arab states were generous to the PLO. "Mini-Palestines" existed until 1970 in Jordan (where a wide majority of the population is of Palestinian origin) and until 1982 in Lebanon (where about 8 percent of the inhabitants are Palestinians). Financial aid came primarily from Saudi Arabia, while other countries supplied weapons or training.

Since the late 1960s, at least fourteen distinct groups have coexisted within the PLO. The Fatah, the center-oriented party of Palestinian nationalism, was the dominant faction, owing to its pragmatic relations with almost all the Arab countries.[6] In the aftermath of the Six-Day War, according to Rosemary Sayigh, "the Resistance movement now had a specific usefulness in diverting public opinion from the defeat and giving it new hopes."[7] However, when the PLO became stronger and aspired to some freedom of action, any attempt to affirm its independence provoked repression (as, for example, in Jordan in 1970 and in Lebanon in 1976).[8]

Within these limits, PLO assets multiplied while the movement also gained respectability on the international scene. Terrorist activities, which had taken place not only within Israel and the administered territories (the West Bank and the Gaza Strip) but also all over Western Europe against Israeli or Jewish targets, became less frequent.[9] Nevertheless, a leading Palestinian scholar, E. Q. Said, stated in 1979, "the PLO gathers support every minute now . . . [but] the present [political] situation is essentially at an impasse."[10]

The 1982 Israeli invasion of Lebanon and the rout of the PLO have had drastic consequences.[11] The present weakening of Palestinian nationalism explains the recent indications of more serious consideration of peace plans. At the same time, the acute divisions within the Arab world, as well as in the Palestinian movement, are also generating a restructuring of the conflict, by strengthening those actors who share a realistic perspective. Only the future will tell whether the end is in sight for this conflict, which has entered its third—even fourth—generation.

However, the coherence of this overview notwithstanding, it by no means answers all the questions that this case raises. Most commentators neglect the distinction between the Israeli-Palestinian conflict and the conflict between the Jewish state and its neighbors. Both conflicts, to be sure, overlap and intermingle, but they are not one. The latter has witnessed wars and even one peace treaty; the former subsists without any direct contact. I suggest this distinction as the key to understanding the extent and limits of the international support received by the PLO and Israel's ability to withstand military and political setbacks. When focusing on the Palestinian conflict exclusively, few scholars acknowledge the additional distinction between the forms and the dynamics of the confrontation "in the field"—that is, within the administered territories—and the rules of the game that dominate the conflict elsewhere. Hence, many researchers make do with descriptions or, at most, with categorizations that have no explanatory power.[12]

These difficulties, I contend, result from the absence of a clear definition of the conflict and of the type of conflict it exemplifies. For this reason, no appropriate conceptual framework is presented and systematically utilized. However, only within such a framework can difficult issues be explained, and in this case such issues are central. For instance, (1) it was under Israeli rule that the PLO became the genuine representative of the Palestinian population, (2) political power in this case inversely correlates with military strength, and (3) enormous political assets of insurgents are hardly ever converted into concessions by incumbents who often find themselves isolated from the world community. I propose to define the Israel-Palestinian confrontation as a guerrilla conflict and to use this definition to try to explain the issues at hand.

This approach is justified by the conspicuous presence of the major characteristics of any guerrilla conflict. Specifically, (1) an unconventional military confrontation is being waged within a given territory—

the administered territories—and (2) the regime is engaged in a political contest with segments of the population whose loyalty is sought by the incumbents' clandestine opponents—the PLO. Moreover, as has been the case in almost all guerrilla conflicts since World War II, (3) the conflict within the administered territories is extended transnationally by external terrorist and antiterroristic warfare, and (4) for both sides, the conflict has had serious international diplomatic effects. It is my contention that this theoretical viewpoint may provide new insight into this conflict and that such an analysis will promote further elaboration of guerrilla-conflict theory.

B. GUERRILLA CONFLICT AS AN INDEPENDENT SUBJECT OF SOCIAL SCIENCE RESEARCH

Numerous labels appear in the social science literature in connection with guerrilla conflict. The definitions overlap widely, and their common denominator is the notion of protracted violent conflict. The terms most frequently used in the 1960s were *insurgency, revolutionary war, rebellion, subversion,* and *guerrilla war;* in the 1970s and 1980s, one more often finds *microviolence* and *transnational* or *multinational terrorism.*

Although their own works address numerous theoretical considerations that should be a part of any overall discussion, the researchers who use these labels are aware of the theoretical weakness of the field.[13] Following Mao Tse-tung, many emphasize that significant protracted violence grows mainly in societies confronting acute social crises.[14] Because of the small number of fighters (who may even be recruited from the social margins) and the minimal resources needed to start such a conflict, however, this kind of activity is also appropriate for the implementation of a subversive policy initiated by foreign elements. For the same reasons, according to contemporary scholars of terrorism, this type of conflict may be sustained by international connections among underground organizations.[15]

In order for dissenters to become a significant political factor, they must have appropriate leadership possessing charisma, a practical and impassioned mind, and a good knowledge of the "field" and its inhabitants. Such individuals may be able to attract intellectuals, declassés of all kinds, and the underprivileged.[16]

The initial structure of the movement—whether strongly centralized or dispersed throughout the territory—is a reflection of the population's characteristics, the political regime, and communication conditions. The expansion of the movement will be enhanced by (1) its ideological slogans and the length of its political arms, (2) the probability that members of the revolutionary camp will be leading citizens in the future, and (3) the extent to which coercive means may be used freely by this camp.

The strengthening of a guerrilla movement depends on its ability to control new inner nexi of power. This is the role of such phenomena as the "politruks" (party officials) in paramilitary units and the establishment of ideological identification.[17]

The paramilitary activity itself begins with the securing of hideouts from which conspicuous violent acts in populated centers are carried out. This type of violence may remain the major one throughout the conflict (as in contemporary Western European cases), if the movement is unable to achieve a sufficient hold in the population. In the contrary case, the movement evolves into an organization oriented toward fighting in rural areas. It then aims at the domination of communication channels and geographic areas in order to establish territorial bases and more conventional military units.[18]

The success of the insurgency is contingent upon the antiguerrillas' inefficiency. As far as the political regime is concerned, because the outbreak of the conflict involves violence regarding given political disputes, it constitutes both an illegitimate phenomenon, endangering social order as such, and an alteration of political realities.[19] A regime that first defines the conflict with respect to the former aspect also defines the need for an uncompromising struggle against its opponents; a regime that emphasizes the latter aspect leaves more room for maneuvers and for alternative approaches toward the rebels.

In any event, most commentators agree that an efficient antiguerrilla policy requires a regime to develop new orientations toward the population. It should formulate its goals in ideological terms, in order to strengthen its legitimacy, and it should initiate administrative, social, and economic reforms to isolate the insurgents from their social constituency.[20]

At the level of military response to the conflict, the antiguerrilla campaign represents a particular mode of action. Defensive targets include public institutions, officials, commercial centers as well as national borders. Offensive means consist mainly of small, highly mobile units using appropriate technologies to detect, chase, and liquidate barely observable enemies. These means are eventually sustained by unconventional antiguerrilla formations, such as "quasiguerrillas," or militia.[21]

The purpose of political action within the population is to "clear" it of hostile elements—that is, to bring the inhabitants to detach themselves from the insurgents; of military action, to extinguish them—that is, to suppress the insurgence physically. Both dimensions need to be fully integrated into a consistent, overall antiguerrilla policy. Once the guerrilla movement has been weakened on both fronts, it becomes a small, isolated terrorist organization such as exists in some Western countries today. Then, as many specialists suggest, the regime's reaction to violence is to emphasize the continuation of the "normal" functioning of institutions, the creation of appropriate instruments of action (such as special antiterrorist units) and the creation of frameworks of legal disposition and international conventions.[22]

C. TOWARD A DEFINITION OF GUERRILLA CONFLICT

These descriptions, when taken as a whole, hardly satisfy the criteria for a well-crystallized theory. Yet R. Tanter shows that this type of conflict is statistically distinct from all others.[23] Moreover, the theoretical justification for this position resides in the particular role assigned to violence in this type of conflict. While violence is a means of measurement of power relations in war (between states) and in revolution (between social entities and a regime), here, in the context of a confrontation within a society that is initiated by a weaker contender, it constitutes a means of changing power relations over time.[24] This type of conflict will be referred to as "guerrilla conflict."

From this definition, it is possible—the views to the contrary of many scholars notwithstanding—to derive a specific theoretical approach to this subject. The center-periphery perspective, sociopolitical concepts borrowed from the exchange approach, and non-zero-sum game theory are most useful for this analysis.[25] The various sequences include, as in any social conflict, (1) conditions accounting for growth, (2) models of reaction, (3) patterns of development, (4) broader implications, and (5) conclusions and results. Moreover, consistent with this definition— though, again, contrary to the position widely accepted by scholars in this field—the political center, as the stronger party at the start of the conflict, should be seen as the major codifier of the confrontation.[26] This view is taken at least as far as "in-the-field" aspects are concerned, notwithstanding the fact that the guerrilla movement compels the center to react to its deliberate assaults. Thus, a theoretical approach primarily implies analysis of those factors pertaining to the center which underly this codification. In the following, these theoretical assumptions are elaborated and are illustrated through a brief comparative analysis of four cases: Vietnam, Algeria, Cyprus, and Cuba.

D. A THEORETICAL APPROACH TO GUERRILLA CONFLICT: A COMPARATIVE ANALYSIS

1. Conditions Accounting for the Growth of Guerrilla Conflict

For the weaker contender, violence as a political tactic constitutes not only dangerous hardship as such but also a gamble on overcoming the center. Generally considered illegitimate, violence may well provoke negative reactions rather than advancing the insurgents' cause. The rationale behind protracted violence in general becomes clearer, however, when, following Talcolt Parsons' distinction of two components of power,[27] one indicates a particular type of situation:

First the power of the center is embodied in practical means of coercion such as police [or] army . . . usually supervised by governmental agencies. . . . Second, in society, the ability to exploit force is dependent on legitimate authority and social support which are "power proper.". . . . As power constitutes the basis of force, the less a regime enjoys support, the weaker the deterrent effect of its force and the greater the amount of force necessary to its survival.[28]

When such a discrepancy exists, it exemplifies what Parsons calls an "inflation of power," whereby the undermining of the legitimacy of the social order is a function of the level of coercion in center-periphery relations. Situations of this kind are empirically correlated with the growth of historically significant guerrilla conflicts.[29] Moreover, within this context and not discounting the political risks and real sacrifices involved, guerrilla conflict is most likely to emerge in the absence of two further conditions: (1) less expensive legal or semilegal alternatives on the part of the opposition party to further its cause and (2) efficient structures of control capable of rapidly detecting any attempt at crystallizing power autonomously from the center.[30]

In these circumstances, an "initial capital" may be accumulated. Its investment in the form of violence becomes "profitable" when, activated in a clandestine manner from within the population, it compels the center to intensify the coercion it exerts over the latter.[31] Consequently, the use of violence hinders the center's ability to increase its power assets, that is, the support of elements in the population that it requires for its ever-increasing employment of force. Previously committed groups, either in the process of breaking away or already alienated from the center, may even channel their sympathy toward the guerrillas, and their support may be converted into elements of anticenter force.

The initial capital of the guerrillas involves militants ready to become fighters, appealing ideological tokens, and organizational links that will assure the enlistment of further resources.[32] Some of the components of this capital may, it is true, be provided by an external "benefactor,"[33] but in order to constitute more than a mere disguise for an interstate conflict and to present an internal challenge to the center, at least some of these must be acquired by the guerrillas in the local setting itself, such that they alter the center's relations with the population. Within the framework of the general conditions for significant guerrilla conflict, as discussed above, the variety in the initial capital of guerrilla movements may be accounted for by the specific nature of the center's inflation of power in each particular case.

In *Algeria,* for instance, the country's inclusion in the *metropole* signified the subordination of the local population to the expanding European sector at the hour of decolonization of the rest of North Africa. Most of the Algerian upper strata were absorbed by the French, so, the guerrilla force—The National Liberation Front (FLN)—recruited from the periphery, mainly from among the new lower class in cities, within the European Sector, and the Villagers. This composition was expressed in the Arab-Muslim formulation of the struggle and in the FLN organizations called willayahs, which respected the population's geosocial structures.[34]

In French *Vietnam,* guerrilla conflict began in the late 1930s with a handful of Communists. The sudden end of World War II, which immobilized the troops of both Vichy France and Japan, was rapidly exploited to establish a new regime under the flag of a National Front of Liberation (Vietminh). Numerous military and political networks were promptly recruited to oppose the French, whose return, for most sectors, was an unbearable regression to their prewar colonial status.[35]

In colonial *Cyprus,* Britain's rule had always been undermined by the *enosis* (union with Greece) orientation of the Greek-speaking community. After World War II, which further shook the regime, leftist forces made progress in the cities and weakened the political status of the church, which had always been the traditional voice of the *enosis* movement. *Enosis* being definitely ruled out by the center, Archbishop Makarios, by basing his efforts on parochial frameworks and the more traditional groups, "ordered" the formation of an underground organization to "specialize" in violent activity against the British.[36]

In *Cuba,* where Fulgencio Batista's coup on the eve of elections inducted a caudillo regime and ousted middle-class politicians, it was a group originating among the latter that turned to the remote periphery in order to draft power. While oppositionists in Havana were demonstrating against the abolition of democracy, the Barbudos in the Sierra Maestra had to weave new webs on the basis of distributive slogans— mainly for land reform—in order to "revolutionize" the lower-class peasants, who were indifferent to and loosely controlled by the center.[37]

In sum, these cases manifest diverse initiators of violence who represent the wide variety of conflictual situations; yet beyond these differences, the superiority of power of the center and its exercise of coercion over elements of the population are common to all. Moreover, the center is able to effectively rule out the insurgents' claims, although it is not strong enough to prevent the accumulation of some power assets in the hands of the guerrillas.

2. Models of Reaction: The Antiguerrilla

The initial capital of any guerrilla force, regardless of its particular features, serves, by the very definition of this type of conflict, as a means of changing power relations. Both to gain control over the population and to assault the center. Thus the center, in its reaction to such a force, cannot avoid aligning itself on two distinct fronts: on the one hand, it has to define and implement a policy toward the population, and, on the other, it must counter the guerrillas' military attacks. By the very essence of the concept of inflation of power, the center's choices are limited. The first possibility is to strengthen its assets by acquiring or reacquiring the commitments of various elements in the population in return for commodities, political moves, or ideological tokens of its own making. This strategy may be termed a "penetration model" since, by promoting greater penetration of the population by the center, it intends to prevent the guerrillas from capitalizing on their investments by causing their isolation.[38]

In an alternative strategy that is less comprehensive and hence requires fewer resources, the center may continue to make use of the deterrent value of its force. The strength of this element may be preserved, provided that unconditional internal or external sources of support are at the regime's disposal. This policy, which may be termed a watching-over model, aims not at competing with guerrilla influence over the population but at impeding the insurgents' capacity to convert power assets into elements of force, that is, into active involvement in paramilitary guerrilla activity. This policy is implemented by the use of such coercive means as collective punishments, curfews, and pass permits that facilitate the center's surveillance of the population.[39] Although the two policies may reinforce each other, beyond a certain point the intensification of coercion necessitated by the second is counterproductive to the commitments sought by the first.

In all events, in view of the differences in cost, the respective emphasis of each model on antiguerrilla activity depends on the significance attached to the conflict by the center in terms of its aspirations to political authority over the population. Indeed, the greater these ambitions, the more the center will be particularly sensitive to the fact that the guerrilla movement is a challenge to its legitimacy. In such a case, the penetration model is most appropriate. On the other hand, the lower the center's ambitions in this respect, and the more it grounds its rule on mere coercion, the more sensitive it will be to the fact that the guerrilla movement represents an alteration of a given political reality. The more likely, then, is it that a watching-over model will prevail.

In either case, however, a guerrilla conflict requires that the center employ augmented resources. Although these resources vary in scope from one model to another, the question of their availability points to another crucial factor in the shaping of antiguerrilla policy. In particular, if the authority tends to the more expensive penetration model, and the necessary resources are unavailable, the antiguerrilla effort will inevitably have to combine the least expensive patterns of buying commitments with accentuated coercion. Moreover, if the means are so limited as to be insufficient even for application of the watching-over model, the center will be compelled to indulge in maximum coercion despite its ever-decreasing deterrent value.

The question of availability of means, however, is relevant mainly to the second aspect of antiguerrilla activity, namely, the unavoidable military confrontation with the guerrilla forces themselves. As in any military confrontation, the means available determine the extent to which the incumbent is limited to a defensive posture or may also indulge in offensive moves. In a guerrilla conflict, the former involves the protection of people and institutions while the latter may include large-scale campaigns against guerrilla strongholds.

In this military sense, the means differ from those bound to the center's policy toward the population. For the sake of simplicity, however, it is convenient—and not implausible—to assume that there is a positive relation between the center's ability to draft both kinds of means (that is, those required for implementation of its policy toward the population and those related to its military capacity against the guerrillas). Furthermore, one may also assume, even in reference to the watching-over model, that sufficient means of the first kind imply sufficient means of the second kind for the development of an offensive military strategy. Thus, by considering the two kinds of resources as essentially one, and by treating means and aspirations toward the population as dichotomies, we obtain four profiles of antiguerrilla activity, as outlined in exhibit 1.1.

Algeria provides an illustration of profile 1. France, regarding Algeria as an integral part of itself (high ambitions), mobilized enormous resources (sufficient means) on the outbreak of violence. The army was followed by the penetration of the population by social workers, teachers, and officials, while extensive administrative and economic reforms were introduced. On the military front, huge forces were posted throughout the country while paratroopers were sent to the most remote spots and pro-French irregular units of Algerians formed.[40]

In *Vietnam*, France was again moved by high ambitions to regain preeminence in Asia. Yet it was not prepared this time to invest all its energy (insufficient means); its contingent numbered a mere 120,000 (see profile 2). Thus, on the one hand, the center's antiguerrilla strategy involved increasing its control over the population, but on the other, the regime maintained economic prosperity by means of an artificial

Exhibit 1.1
Profiles of Antiguerrilla Models

	Perspective of Center in the Conflict	
Availability of Means	High Ambitions vis-a-vis the Population	Low Ambitions vis-a-vis the Population
Sufficient Means Available	Profile 1 penetrative model vis-à-vis population; defensive and offensive alignment against guerrillas	Profile 3 watching-over model vis-à-vis population; defensive and offensive alignment against guerrillas
Insufficient Means Available	Profile 2 penetrative model vis-à-vis population; defensive alignment only against guerrillas	Profile 4 watching-over model vis-à-vis population; defensive alignment against guerrillas

monetary rate, accepted an allied Vietnam's independence (Bao Dai was recalled), and bribed castes and parties with privileges. On the military front, French troops were scattered in a defensive posture while offensive moves were sporadic.[41]

In *Cyprus,* which illustrates profile 3, the EOKA's (Ethniki Organosis Kipriakov Agonos, or the National Organization of Cypriot Struggle) first attacks led to concessions by Britain, which by then had lost interest in its imperial scheme anyway (low ambitions). Its major concern, besides continuing military presence in Cyprus, was the avoidance of a Greek-Turkish clash over *enosis.* Thus, the center did not indulge much in the manipulation of commitments. On the other hand, despite its lack of popularity on the island, it was able to enlist its force directly from the *metropole* (sufficient means). The EOKA's men were thus vigorously sought out and attacked.[42]

In *Cuba* (see profile 4), Batista, himself a former putschist, was unable to react to the guerrillas on the grounds of legitimacy (low ambition), while the poorly equipped troops (insufficient means) could not adapt to the vicissitudes of antiguerrilla warfare. They made do with fierce repression in the cities and attempts to prevent the insurgents' expansion outside the Sierra.[43]

3. Patterns of Development

The guerrilla "arsenal" also includes well-defined courses of action associated with the logic of the profitability of violence. Thus, acts of terrorism, particularly if selective, challenge the center's claims to represent security and order and may provoke it to impose more constraints on the population. Beyond this phase, the guerrilla camp may increase its own political assets[44] by propagating slogans, setting up communication channels, and using its own means of coercion.[45] Such assets, if converted into fighters, funds, or intelligence information, enable the development of instrumental fighting, that is, fighting aimed at specific goals such as the "liberation" of towns and rural areas. Needless to say, actual empirical instances differ from one another in terms of the means most dominant in the guerrilla activity. This variance explains the lack of agreement among specialists over the characterization of the process as a whole.[46] It may now be suggested that in fact this diversity is accounted for by the actions of the center, which delineate where, if at all, the rebels may hope to invest most profitably. To be more precise, in first addressing the nature of the military confrontation, it is evident that the guerrilla camp, when confronted with a combination of offensive and defensive alignments (sufficient means), can hardly hope of developing beyond the terrorist stage of microviolent actions. Such conflict develops into instrumental fighting only in the event that the antiguerrilla campaign is restricted to a defensive posture as a result of limited means at the center's disposal (insufficient means). In this case, the incumbents may be incapable of preventing guerrilla forces from concentrating in large units in remote areas and from launching attacks on the weaker links of the center's alignment.

On the other hand, as far as control over the population is concerned, a center that adopts the watching-over model for antiguerrilla action, refrains from the manipulation of commitments and relies heavily on its deterrent force, leaves the population open to political infiltration. This process is eventually sustained by the guerrillas' own means of coercion. Infiltration may be prevented or at least hindered only through application of the penetration model, the efficiency of which is a function of the means available for such an investment. Accordingly, each antiguerrilla perspective entails a corresponding profile of guerrilla development in terms of military structure and activity and linkage with the population, as summarized in exhibit 1.2.

In *Algeria*, initial response to the guerrilla appeal was enthusiastic. However, the casbah of Algiers was rapidly cleared of the FLN's political apparatus, and the willayahs were so severely hit that their activity was limited mainly to indiscriminate acts of terrorism by small gangs.[47]

In *Vietnam*, the French regained influence with many elements in the South (religious castes, the Catholics, the traditional elites). In the North, however, they were unable to dismantle the Vietminh's political structures among the dense population. Nor could they impede the Viets'

Exhibit 1.2
Profiles of Antiguerrilla and Guerrilla Organizations

Characteristics of Incumbents		Profiles of Antiguerrilla Alignment		Profiles of Guerrilla Movement	
Ambitions Regarding Population	Availability of Means	Model toward Population	Military Alignment	As Political Party	As Military Organization
high ambitions +	(1) sufficient means	(1) penetrative model +	defensive and offensive	(1) marginal group	+ terrorist network
	(2) insufficient means	(2) penetrative model +	defensive	(2) group competing with incumbents +	quasi-military organization
low ambitions +	(3) sufficient means	(3) watching-over model +	defensive and offensive	(3) important political factor	+ terrorist network
	(4) insufficient means	(4) watching-over model +	defensive	(4) important political factor	+ quasi-military organization

building of a typical rural guerrilla army, which was able to launch attacks against the incumbents' strongholds.

In *Cyprus,* endless anti-British demonstrations constituted the major expression of the EOKA's struggle, in which the political hierarchy played the leading role. Militarily, the EOKA was unable to maintain its hold in the rural areas and was soon compelled to subsist with small cells in the cities. It was more active against moderate Cypriots than against the incumbents.[48]

Cuba is the only example in which guerrilla activity was directly responsible for the collapse of the regime. Encouraging protest in the cities, the cohorts of rebels gradually spread out among the villages while new recruits arrived from Havana.[49]

Thus, the FLN developed into a type 1 profile, the Vietminh a type 2, the EOKA a type 3, and the Castro movement a type 4.

4. The Non-Zero-Sum Character of the Conflict

An additional dimension of any guerrilla conflict is its non-zero-sum character. This concept means that the sum of the resources at the disposal of both contenders is not fixed from the beginning. As a result of the conflict's development, "additional costs" or "profits" from various sources influence both sides' behavior.[50]

The means employed by guerrillas in order to demonstrate their presence are totally out of proportion to those which incumbents must use for their defense and public safety. Thus dissenters may often hope to achieve their aims more as a result of exhausting the regime than through their own expansion.[51] Because it challenges the regime of a sovereign state, the conflict must also be considered within its wider international context.

Incumbents representing a *metropole* may rely on the steadfast support of foreign allies and may be able to maintain the deterrent value of their "imported" force regardless of their power (or lack of power) in the conflict setting. On the other hand, as a rule, a guerrilla conflict weakens the international standing of the state involved.[52] It encourages unfriendly countries to support the insurgency and to aggravate international conjunctures in ways that are detrimental to the regime and its allies. The conflict itself becomes a valuable source of profit for the guerrillas. It is particularly beneficial if additional assets include facilities to set up "in-exile" political structures and military bases. This accumulation of assets may help the insurgents in their internal struggle and may expand the conflict to both diplomatic campaigns and transnational terrorism. The limit is the point where external assets are the major means of overcoming the incumbents and the guerrilla conflict becomes essentially an interstate confrontation between the incumbents and the guerrillas' benefactors.

Yet even within this limit, that is, as far as the concept of guerrilla conflict remains relevant, external assets may raise the problem for the insurgents of their autonomy of action vis-à-vis their benefactors. Most crucially, benefactors who disagree among themselves about relevant issues may cause internal schisms and disorganization. New possibilities of action made available to the insurgents may have little effect on the incumbents if used mainly against targets abroad. Furthermore, incumbents might fight back on the diplomatic scene with unexpected moves or strike at the insurgents' external strongholds themselves. This could provoke a new international juncture, resulting in vast changes in the additional profits and costs that the conflict represents for each contender.

Beyond such general statements, obviously, the numerous international contexts in which guerrilla conflicts may occur make a meaningful a priori formulation of their possible modes and scopes of interference impossible.

International dimensions played a determining role in only one of our four cases. In *Algeria*, outside assistance was of crucial importance in bringing the Gaullist regime to accept the independence of this "integral part of France." The FLN's alliance with the Arab world, the in-exile army set up in Tunisia and Morocco, and the active backing of the Soviets and the Third World were all major factors in the French turnabout a few years after the Pieds Noirs and the army had, from Algeria, put Charles de Gaulle into power in Paris.[53] The prospect of international isolation caused by the conflict was even more unbearable to this rightist regime than to any former French government.

In contrast, in French *Vietnam*, the incumbents' impatience in the face of an endless confrontation drove them to set up the offensive base of Dien Bien Phu in the heart of the Vietminh zone.[54] Because the military means were insufficient, this enterprise led to a humiliating defeat; this precipitated France's readiness to negotiate and to concede North Vietnam to the insurgents. In *Cyprus*, the EOKA's weakness was feebly compensated for by Greece's limited help. Britain's superiority forced Makarios to finally accept an independence compromised by the exclusion of *enosis*.[55] In *Cuba*, there was an almost total absence of external resources. Castro achieved the collapse of Batista in Havana after capturing a provincial town without any support from the outside.[56]

5. Impacts and Outcomes

In those cases in which the guerrilla movement "inherits" the position of the political center, the issue of the impact of the conflict on society arises. This is consistent with the starting point of the present analysis, which questions the nature of the new regime's relations with the population. These relations, culminating in the retreat of the formerly stronger contender, imply more than a mere "resorption of inflation." Indeed, they constitute a new dynamic political reality related to both the type of conflict that has engendered it and the unique features of each particular case. Here we come to the limits of the concept of inflation of power as an interpretive scheme.

We turn first to those features common to all regimes resulting from guerrilla victory (which are hereafter called "postguerrilla regimes"). It may be said that the special nature of these features resides in the juxtaposition of resounding myths on the one hand and powerful forces for their routinization on the other. The former arise as the protracted struggle over commitments and control necessitates the amplification of ideological slogans. When the new rulers devote their attention to the legitimization of their authority, they cannot but rely on these myths. At the same time, the forces of routinization are also of the greatest strength, as these new rulers have achieved their authority by prolonged domination of organizations built on manipulative principles and imbued with the "ethics" of political responsibility. This juxtaposition has long-term effects on the postguerrilla regime that are beyond the scope of the present discussion. Its impact, however, is already evident at the time of the resolution of the conflict.

Thus, in *Cyprus*, the myth of *enosis* dominated the entire struggle and was to continue to cause grave tensions between communities; yet the church leaders were nevertheless able to impose a partial solution on their supporters.[57] In North *Vietnam*, the rulers, who had replaced the Vietminh with the Communist party at the height of combat, were able to conclude an interim agreement with their enemy and to impose it on their followers.[58] This was achieved despite the influence of the myth of the national challenge, which would later prove forceful enough to justify a further war. In *Algeria*, although the new regime soon joined forces with the radical Arab camp, substantial concessions to France were provided by the Evian Agreements which concluded the conflict between the French and the FLN. In *Cuba*, Castro's victory was presented as the triumph of liberty, while in actual fact, the measures taken by the new center were based on precise political considerations including the suppression of political rivals.[59]

In light of these remarks, our focus turns to the unique aspects of the new political reality of each particular case. The specific legacy of the guerrilla conflict—and thereby the print of the antiguerrilla models—may be discerned in this phase of the process in the nature of the assets held by the new rulers. Specifically, a prior accumulation of power or force is significant in determining whether (1) the new regime rapidly gains a high degree of control over the population, (2) it remains at the authoritarian stage, or (3) it has to compromise with autonomous foci of power. This variable strength of the new center also determines the extent to which it has to be generous toward groups whose support was sought during the conflict.

Thus, in *Algeria*, where the willayah leaders and local FLN emerged weakened by the struggle, it was the external military structures that served as the new regime's major asset. In the absence of a firm political apparatus, consolidation of power took the form of land reform (European-owned land had now become available). Nevertheless, several years later, radical administrative reorganization was required in order to strengthen the new center's control over the population.[60]

In North *Vietnam*, the expansion of the political apparatus was concurrent with the impressive development of military frameworks. Once in power, the new regime was able to further the liquidation of its enemies and of every potential threat to its position.[61] Moreover, it was able to implement an agrarian reform intended more to tighten its control over the peasants than to gratify them. This resulted in a revolt, which was firmly suppressed after two years.

In *Cyprus*, the political assets acquired during the conflict were more important than the achievements of the military branch.[62] Related to this, the continuing presence of an autonomous Turkish community as well as the Communist sector demanded compromises.

Throughout the conflict in *Cuba*, military units gained importance alongside political frameworks. After the victory, the first task was to increase control over the numerous organizations still insubordinate to the "July 26 movement." For this purpose, generous—and not always economically rational—measures were soon taken in favor of the peasants.[63]

In brief, even in the postguerrilla regime, antiguerrilla measures and the resultant development of the conflict continue to make their mark. The same is true of the additional gains, whether political, military, or both, accumulated by the guerrillas, which eventually become components of the new social order. It is with this conceptual framework in mind that we now turn to the thorough analysis of the Israeli-Palestinian conflict. In contrast with the other cases mentioned above, the solution of this case has not yet been found. It thus represents a challenge for the theory.

E. STRUCTURE OF THE ANALYSIS

In accordance with the foregoing, our analysis of the Palestinian case must confront the following issues.

1. The Historical, Social, and Political Background of the Israeli–Palestinian Conflict

The beginning of the conflict may be traced to June 1967, when Israeli rule was established in the West Bank and the Gaza Strip. The conflict, however, is not merely the direct result of the new circumstances but has deep roots in the past. Hence, the discussion of inflation of power is to be based on historical material concerning (1) the Mandate period, (2) the Palestinian issue from 1948 to 1967, and (3) the essential characteristics of the post-Six Day War situation. The first stage of the formation of Palestinian guerrilla movements is to be introduced in this sociopolitical and historical context.

2. The Regime's Policy toward the Inhabitants

The regime's definition of the struggle, the administration, and its policy vis-à-vis the population concerns which model—"penetration" or "watching-over"—has dominated the regime's policy over the years. This analysis has to include examination of the regime's ambitions with regard to the administered territories and their inhabitants and the scope of means at the incumbents' disposal.

3. The Military Aspect of the Antiguerrilla Campaign

The investigation of the means at the regime's disposal should then attempt to delineate the basic characteristics of the military antiguerrilla alignment, including both defensive and offensive goals and tactics.

4. The Guerrillas as a Political Power in the Administered Territories

It is in the context of the above that the evolution of the guerrilla movement into a political force, the patterns of linkage between the guerrillas and the population, and the scope of their influence as well as their conflicts, rivalries, and competitions are now to be considered.

5. The Guerrillas as a Military Force in the Administered Territories

The next subject is the organizational structures of the PLO as it has crystallized since 1967. This analysis is to deal with the local paramilitary networks, the patterns of recruitment of fighters, the tactics utilized, and the intensity of the action over time.

6. The International Issue: Blessings

In terms of the non-zero-sum character of the conflict, no less commanding issues are the PLO's links to the interests of the Arab states, the Soviet bloc, the Third World, and other parties. Similarly, the implications of the conflict for Israel's foreign relations are a central concern of the discussion.

7. The International Scene: Curses

The analysis of the evolution of the conflict on the international scene should clarify the rules of its dynamics, the vicissitudes of the PLO's dependence on benefactors, and the events that have transformed its relations with Israel.

8. Israel and the PLO: Where to Now?

The solution of the Israeli-Palestinian conflict is still in the future. However, at this point, one may consider the probable decisive factors: the evolution of power relations in the field, the external gains and costs involved in the continuation of the conflict, and the interactions between these two factors. Accordingly, scenarios of possible endings of this conflict can be discussed.

This comprehensive analysis of the Israeli-Palestinian conflict should emphasize aspects of the case that have been neglected by alternate approaches. Furthermore, locating this case within the realm of the theoretical possibilities defined by guerrilla-conflict theory should contribute to the elaboration of this theory.

In keeping with this scheme, this historical sociopolitical work relies on a variety of methods, with a number of different kinds of data. The historical information is based on secondary sources, while the sociological findings were collected by the author during 1983 and 1984. A first project was a survey of PLO political activities in the administered territories, based on interviews of informants—Arabs and Jews—of all camps. Another operation involved the analysis of the legal files of a random sample of about five hundred persons tried in military courts (Gaza, Nablus, and Ramallah). These files contain data concerning the social characteristics of PLO activists, the organization of PLO networks, and their motivational aspects. A media research project was carried out during 1982–83, after the Israeli invasion of Lebanon. This study contributes to our understanding of the development of the conflict in the world context. Finally, extensive PLO documents seized by the Israeli Defense Force (IDF) in Lebanon during the Peace for Galilee campaign (summer 1982), and recently disclosed by the army's spokesman, con-

stitute another very reliable source of information about the development
of the PLO outside the field.

NOTES

1. Y. Porat, *From Riots to Revolt: The National Arab-Palestinian Movement, 1929–1939* (Tel Aviv: Am Oved: [Hebrew], 1978), 349–56; G. Furlonge, *Palestine Is My Country: The Story of Musa Alami* (London: John Murray, 1969), 104.

2. For more on this period, see L. W. Holborn, "The Palestine Arab Refugee Problem," in *The Arab-Israeli Conflict,* ed. J. N. Moore (Princeton, N.J.: Princeton University Press, 1977), 152–66; E. Beeri, *The Palestinians under the Jordanians* (Jerusalem: Magnes Press [Hebrew], 1978), 50–51; Y. Harkabi, *The Palestinians: From Quiescence to Awakening* (Jerusalem: Magnes [Hebrew], 1979), 48; and P. A. Jureidini and W. E. Hazen, *The Palestinian Movement in Politics* (Toronto: Lexington Books, 1976), 92.

3. See G. Golan, "Soviet-PLO Relations," *Jerusalem Quarterly* 16, (1980):121–36; E. O'Ballance, *Arab Guerrilla Power, 1967–1972* (London: Archon Books, 1974), 45–63; Y. Harkabi, *The Palestinian Covenant and Its Meaning* (Jerusalem: Information Center [Hebrew], 1977); S. Hadawi, *Bitter Harvest: Palestine, 1914–1967* (New York: New World Press, 1967), 307; and R. El-Rayyes and D. Nahas, *Guerrillas for Palestine* (London: Croom Helm, Portico, 1976), 71.

4. See M. Nissan, *Israel and the Territories: A Study in Control* (Ramat Gan: Turtledove, 1978), 101–2; W. B. Quandt, "Political and Military Dimensions of Contemporary Palestinian Nationalism," in *The Politics of Palestinian Nationalism,* ed. W. B. Quandt et al. (Berkeley: University of California Press, 1973), 121–22; A. Perlmutter, "Types of National Movements, Progressive and Fascist," in *The Palestinians and the Middle East Conflict,* ed. G. Ben-Dor (Ramat Gan: Turtledove, 1978), 491; O'Ballance, 191–204; Nissan, 124; and S. Teveth, *The Blessing's Curse* (Tel Aviv: Shocken [Hebrew], 1969), 315.

5. See H. Cobban, *The Palestinian Liberation Organization* (Cambridge: Cambridge University Press, 1984); D. Pirhi, "Speeches and Works," *Ten Years of Israeli Rule in Judea and Samaria,* ed. R. Israeli (Jerusalem: Magnes [Hebrew], 1980), 164–65; J. Tsuriel, "The Troublemakers in the Territories, *Maariv,* 1/5 (Hebrew); A. Susser, "The Palestinian Organization," *Middle East Contemporary Survey,* ed. C. Legum et al., Vol. 3 (New York: Holmes and Meier, 1979), 285–305; M. Maoz, "Processes and Tendencies in the Territories," *Skira Khodshit,* May 1980 (Hebrew), 3–9.

6. See A. Yariv, "The Support of Arab Terror by Arab States," *Skira Khodshit,* July 1980 (Hebrew), 19–20; J. W. Amos, *Palestinian Resistance: Organization of a Nationalist Movement* (New York: Pergamon Press, 1980); I. Rabinovitch and M. Zamir, *War and Crisis in Lebanon, 1975–1981* (Tel Aviv: Hakibbutz Hameukhad [Hebrew], 1982), 32–33; S. Bar-Haim, "The Palestine Liberation Army: Stooge or Actor," in Ben-Dor, 173–92; Quandt, 66; and Cobban, 195–244.

7. R. Sayigh, *Palestinians: From Peasants to Revolutionaries* (London: Zed Press, 1979), 144.

8. W. Khalidi, *Conflict and Violence in Lebanon: Confrontation in the Middle East* (Cambridge: Harvard Studies in International Affairs, 1979), 67–91.

9. See A. Y. Yodfat and Y. Arnon-Ohanna, *PLO, Strategy and Tactics* (New York: St. Martin's Press, 1981), 48–67; and P. Wilkinson, "Terrorist Movements," in *Terrorism and Practice*, eds. Y. Alexander et al. (Boulder, Colo.: Westview, 1979), 102.

10. E. Q. Said, *The Question of Palestine* (New York: Times Books, 1979), 238.

11. H. Cobban, 119–38.

12. G. Ben-Dor, "Nationalism without Sovereignty and Nationalism with Multiple Sovereignties: The Palestinians and Inter-Arab Relations," in Ben-Dor, 143–72.

13. See O. Heilbrunn, *La Guerre de partisans* (Paris: Payot, 1964); R. H. Schultz, Jr., "The State of the Operational Art," in *Responding to the Terrorist Threat*, ed. R. H. Shultz and S. Sloan (New York: Pergamon, 1980), 18–58.

14. Cf. Mao Tse-tung, *La Guerre révolutionnaire* (Paris: Union Générale d'Edition, 1955), 40; J. S. Pustay, *Counter-Insurgency Warfare* (New York: Free Press, 1965), 49, 83.

15. See P. W. Blackstock, *The Strategy of Subversion* (Chicago: Quadrangle Books, 1964); P. Wilkinson, "Terrorism: International Dimensions," *Conflict Studies* 113 (1979):1–22; B. M. Jenkins, *The Study of Terrorism: Definitional Problems* (Santa Monica, Calif.: Rand Corp., November 1980 [Mimeo]); and Y. Alexander, "Terrorism in the Middle East: A New Phase?" *Washington Quarterly* 1, no. 4 (1978):115–17.

16. C. W. Thayer, *Guerrilla* (London: Michael Joseph, 1964), 87; B. Crozier, *The Rebels* (London: Chatto and Windus, 1960), 18; and Pustay, 54–60.

17. See V. Ney, "Guerrilla Warfare and Modern Strategy," in *Modern Guerrilla Warfare*, ed. F. M. Osanka (New York: Free Press, 1962), 25–28; D. Galula, *Counter-Insurgency Warfare* (New York: Praeger, 1966), 29; Pustay, 65; R. Trinquier, *Modern Warfare: A French View* (London: Pall Mall, 1964), 5; P. Paret and J. W. Shy, *Guerrillas in the 1960's* (New York: Praeger, 1966), 21.

18. See M. W. Browne, *The New Face of War* (Indianapolis: Bobbs-Merrill, 1968), 1–13; J. R. Corsi, "Terrorism as a Desperate Game," *Journal of Conflict Resolution* 25, no. 1 (1981):47–85; Jenkins; N. Leites, "Understanding the Next Act," *Terrorism* 3, nos. 1–2, (1979):1–46; K. Knorr, "Unconventional Warfare," in *Unconventional Warfare*, ed. J. K. Zawodny (Stanford: Annuals of the American Academy of Political and Social Sciences, 1962), 53–64; and J. K. Zawodny, "Guerrilla and Sabotage," in Zawodny, 9–18.

19. L. M. Pye, "Roots of Insurgency and the Commencement of Rebellion," in *Internal War*, ed. H. Eckstein (New York: Free Press, 1964), 157–79.

20. See R. Thompson, *Defeating Communist Insurgency* (New York: Praeger, 1966), 50–55; and C. T. R. Bohonnan, "Anti-Guerrilla Operation," in Zawodny, 19–29.

21. Trinquier, 57.

22. See J. J. McCuen, *The Art of Counter-Revolutionary War* (London: Faber & Faber, 1966), 55; Marine Corps School, "Small Unit Operations," *The Guerrilla and How to Fight Him*, ed. C. P. Greene (New York: Praeger, 1967); Wilkinson, "Terrorism"; J. B. Motley, "International Terrorism: A New Mode of Warfare," *International Security Review* 6, no. 1 (1981):93–123; C. C. Aston, "Restrictions Encountered in Responding to Terrorist Sieges: An Analysis," in R. H. Schultz

and S. Sloan, 59–92; E. Mickolus et al., "Responding to Terrorism: Basic and Applied Research," in Schultz and Sloan, 174–89.

23. R. Tanter, "Dimensions of Conflict Behavior within Nations, 1955–1960," *Peace Research (International) Papers,* vol. 3 (1965), Chicago Conference, 176–77.

24. Cf. N. S. Timasheff, *War and Revolution* (New York: Sheed and Ward, 1965); C. Johnson, "The Third Generation of Guerrilla Warfare," *Asian Survey* 6 (1968):439; and Heilbrunn, 216.

25. E. Shills, "Center and Periphery," *The Logics of Personal Knowledge* (London: Routledge & Kegan Paul, 1961), 117–30; T. Parsons, "Some Reflections on the Place of Force in Social Processes," in Eckstein, 33–70; and M. Shubick, *Game Theory and Related Approaches to Social Behavior* (New York: Wiley, 1964).

26. Cf. Crozier, 107; Marine Corps School, 270–307.

27. Parsons, 33–70.

28. E. Ben-Rafael and M. Lissak, *Social Aspects of Guerrilla and Anti-Guerrilla Warfare* (Jerusalem: Magnes, 1979), 8–9.

29. T. Gurr, *Why Men Rebel* (Princeton, N.J.: Princeton University Press, 1970), 147–48.

30. Tanter, 176–77; T. Gurr, "Comparative Study of Civil Strife," in *The History of Violence in America* (New York: Times Books, 1969), 580, 628–30.

31. W. A. Kerstetler, "Terrorism and Intelligence," *Terrorism* 3 nos. 1–2 (1979):109.

32. Thayer, 87; Pye, 157–59; and Pustay, 54–60.

33. Blackstock.

34. J. Duchemin, *Histoire du FLN* (Paris: La Table Ronde, 1962), 55; Paret and Shy, 22.

35. See R. Levy, *Regards sur l'Asie du Sud-Est* (Paris: Armand-Colin, 1952), 97; M. N. Katz, "Origins of the Vietnam War," *Review of Politics* 42, no. 2 (1980):131–51; and E. J. Hammer, "Genesis of the First Indochinese War," in *Vietnam,* ed. M. E. Gettleman (New York: Fawcett, 1965), 63–86.

36. See W. Byford-Jones, *Grivas and the Story of the EOKA* (London: Robert Hale, 1959), 46–7; G. Grivas-Dighenis *Guerrilla Warfare and EOKA's Struggle* (London: Longmans 1962), 28–30.

37. J. Dubois, *Fidel Castro* (Buenos Aires: Eudeba, 1959), 105; and E. C. Guevarra, *Souvenirs de la Guerre Révolutionnaire,* vol. 1 (Paris: Maspero, 1967), 164.

38. Thompson, 50–5.

39. Heilbrunn, 201.

40. See F. Fanon, *Sociologie d'une révolution* (Paris: Maspero, 1965), 20; MacCuen, 101–3; and J. Baechler, "Revolutionary and Counter-Revolutionary War," *Journal of International Affairs* 25 (Winter 1971):85.

41. See L. Bodard, *La Guerre d'Indochine* (Paris: Air du Temps, 1963), 1: 11–19; A. Saurel, *La Guerre d'Indochine* (Paris: Rouff, 1966), 128–29.

42. J. Paget, *Counter-Insurgency Campaigning* (London: Faber & Faber, 1967), 121–25.

43. See Dubois, 105; and E. Gude, "Batista and Betancourt: Alternative Responses to Violence," in *The History of Violence in America,* 740.

44. G. Fairbairn, *Revolutionary Warfare and Communist Strategy* (London: Faber & Faber, 1968), 100–102; Thompson, 25.

45. Pustay, 65; Heilbrunn, 16–19; and Trinquier, 5.

46. Galula, 50–61; MacCuen; Crozier, 127–30.

47. J. Bedjoui, *Law and the Algerian Revolution* (Brussels: PIADL, 1961), 66; S. Bromberger, *Les Rebelles algériens* (Paris: Plon, 1958), 187–90.

48. Paget, 140; D. Barker, *Grivas: Portrait of a Terrorist* (London: Macmillan, 1959), 161–90.

49. A. Karol, *Guerrilleros au pouvoir* (Paris: Laffont, 1970), 576–80; Guevarra, 205–8.

50. Shubick.

51. Wilkinson, "Terrorist Movements," 105.

52. R. Clutterbuck, *Guerrillas and Terrorists* (London: Faber & Faber, 1977), 17.

53. M. and D. Bromberger, *Les 13 Complots du 13 Mai* (Paris: Fayard, 1959).

54. B. Fall, "Dien Bien Phu: A Battle to Remember," in Gettleman, 107; A. Eqbal, "Revolutionary War and Counterinsurgency," *Journal of International Affairs* 25, no. 1 (1971):22.

55. Barker, 161–90.

56. Guevarra, 205–8.

57. Barker, 166.

58. Saurel, 94.

59. L. Sauvage, *Autopsie du Castrisme* (Paris: Flammarion, 1962), 189–227.

60. Quandt; G. De Villiers, "L'Etat et la révolution agraire en Algérie," *Revue Francaise de Science Politique* 30, no. 1 (1980):112–39.

61. Bodard, 1–43.

62. Barker, 161–65.

63. N. Drogat, *Les Pays de la faim* (Paris: Flammarion, 1963), 99.

2 The Historical Background

A. THE BRITISH MANDATE: CONTEXT AND FIRST STEPS

Palestine first appears in Herodotus's writings during the fifth century B.C.. The term never referred to a political entity. Except for the short "Kingdom of Jerusalem," Palestine has always been divided into several administrative areas: *Palestina Prima* and *Palestina Secunda* during Roman rule, *Gund Palestina* and *Gund Elourdon* during the Moslem conquest. Rome, Damascus, Baghdad, Cairo, and Istanbul successively ruled the country, the latter for no less than four hundred years, until 1917.

At the beginning of the twentieth century a great majority of the population in Palestine was, as in the neighboring countries, Sunnite Moslem and Arab-speaking; the elite knew and used Turkish. The population numbered some 365,000, 75 percent of them villagers (the main cities were Jaffa, Haifa, and Jerusalem). Christians accounted for only 10 percent, and Druzes 1 percent. This population was among the best educated in the Arab world, with 48 percent of the children at school, 5,000 secondary pupils, and 1,000 university students. Among other factors, this was the outcome of the work of the numerous churches and missions in the Holy Land.[1]

The crumbling of the Ottoman Empire, the rising nationalist fever in Europe, and the creation of an Egyptian nation were to account for a new spirit of Arab nationalism in the Middle East. This nationalism had two faces: Pan-Arabism and local patriotism. Grounded in the Islamic concept of the Arab nation (*ummah*) and the community of religion and language, Pan-Arabism was turned against Turkish domination. Local patriotism was embedded in the political, economic, and social interests of elites and larger groups bound to local political and administrative institutions.

Exhibit 2.1
The Balfour Declaration (November 2, 1917)

Foreign Office
November 2, 1917

Dear Lord Rothschild,

I have much pleasure to conveying to you, on behalf of His Majesty's Government, the following declaration of sympathy with Jewish Zionist aspirations which has been submitted to, and approved by, the Cabinet.

"His Majesty's government view with favour the establishment in Palestine of a national home for the Jewish people, and will use their best endeavours to facilitate the achievement of this object, it being clearly understood that nothing shall be done which may prejudice the civil and religious rights of existing non-Jewish communities in Palestine, on the rights and political status enjoyed by Jews in any other country."

I should be grateful if you would bring this declaration to the knowledge of the Zionist Federation.

Lord Arthur James Balfour

The conquest of Damascus in October 1918 and the creation of a Sherifian authority under the protection of the British inflamed Pan-Arabism all over the area. In Palestine, the idea of a "Greater Syria" was propagated by two newly created associations, the Literary Club and the Arab Club. Both advocated Arab independence and a Syrian-Palestinian union; this spirit was expressed in the decisions of the first Congress of Palestinian Arabs, in Jerusalem in January 1919. The movement sent representatives to the Syrian Congress on July 2, 1919, and in 1920 created a Supreme Committee of Palestinian Associations. However, the arrival of the French in Damascus and the defeat of the Sherifian regime subdued the Palestinians' Pan-Arabist enthusiasm. Later, Palestinian Arab nationalism developed, now nourished by the unique experience of this population.[2] Indeed, the British Mandate, as confirmed by the 1920 San Remo Congress and the 1922 convention of the League of Nations, endorsed the Balfour Declaration of 1917, which favored the creation in this land of a homeland for the Jews. This scheme contradicted promises made by Britain to Arab parties during World War I (exhibit 2.1).

Apparently, a Western-oriented Jewish homeland in Palestine represented the possibility of maintaining a long-term British presence in the area, although good relations with the Arabs were also seen as an immediate imperative. The difficulty of compromising between these two contradictory aims was first experienced by Herbert Samuel, the pro-Zionist governor from 1920 to 1925. The Jewish population of the country doubled during his term, from 55,000 (1919) to 108,000 (1925), and the number of settlements rose from 44 to 100. A Jewish National Assembly, a National Committee, and local councils were instituted. As early as 1920 and 1921, however, the Mandate authorities indicated their intention to limit Jewish immigration, according to the interests of the existing population and the "absorptive capacity" of the country. British officials played an important role in the creation of the First Moslem Association, which led an active campaign against Zionism from 1919 on. This association, however, turned against the government during the 1920 anti-British wave that spread from Iraq to Egypt following the French takeover in Syria.

In this general atmosphere, anti-Jewish riots and terror also erupted in Palestine. This was the case on May 1, 1921, on the occasion of the Jewish labor demonstration in the streets of Jaffa. During the following weeks, the acts of violence spread to major Jewish agricultural settlements. In reaction to such tensions, the British issued the first White Paper in 1922, drastically reformulating the Jewish homeland scheme as a program intended to create only the "foundation" of such a homeland. Furthermore, Amin al-Hussaini, one of the most extreme anti-Zionists, was appointed by the British in 1921 to serve as mufti of Jerusalem and in 1922 as the chairman of the Supreme Muslim Council and its Executive Committee. These institutions became the centers of the anti-Zionist and, later, anti-British struggle.[3]

B. IDEOLOGY AND POLITICS

Among the various clubs and associations created in the aftermath of the Turkish defeat, a Moslem-Christian Association (MCA) was established in November 1918 in Jaffa. It was to play an important role in the anti-Zionist struggle. In Jerusalem, notables like Musa Kazim al-Hussaini and Raef al-Nashashibi were the dominant figures of the MCA local branch. The MCA was an important element in the general Palestinian-Arab movement then evolving, the outlooks and claims of which were intended to be the counterparts of Zionism. As expressed by an Arab intellectual in the 1960s:

The fundamental reason for Arab opposition to Zionism is based upon the fact that the Moslem and Christian inhabitants of the country could not be expected to yield to an ideology which sought to wrest their homeland from them. The Arabs absolutely and unanimously rejected any attempt to destroy the Arab character of Palestine. They still do. The Arabs claimed the right of a population to decide the fate of the country which they had occupied throughout history. To them it was obvious that this right of immemorial possession is inalienable;

and that it could not be overruled either by the circumstances that Palestine had been governed by the Ottomans for 400 years, or that Britain had conquered the land during World War I.[4]

It was thus emphasized first and foremost that Arabs had been continuous settlers of the country since the Moslem conquest of 634. Their language and culture had given the country its character for thirteen hundred years. Moreover, in 1918 Jews represented less than 10 percent of the population. By no means, then, were they entitled to the country by the principle of self-determination guiding the League of Nations. This is a Holy Land for three religions in the world; among them the Jewish religion had the smallest number of followers. In short, as reported at that time:

Palestine is a pure Arabic country surrounded from all parts by Arab countries. The national feeling has awakened and has become stronger and stronger in the Arab Nation which settles this continous territory . . . [and which] knows but Arab nationalism and all speak but one language. . . . There is no room for another nation with another language and other customs. . . . we live now in the era of nationalism and the historical development in Turkey, Russia, Austria, and England demonstrates that different nations cannot live together.[5]

The presence of the Zionists and the Mandate's commitment to them were also accused of impeding the creation of self-rule institutions, such as those which existed in surrounding protectorates and were gradually claiming national independence. It was also frequently contended, in legal terms and according to the 1909 Hague Convention, that the British, as conquerors of Palestine, were not allowed to alter in any way the administrative or juridical status quo ante until new international arrangements were agreed upon. (Such a change did, in fact, take place at San Remo in 1920.) The Arabs also claimed that the terms of the Mandate contradicted promises made by Britain to the Arabs during World War I, as well as various articles of various international conventions.[6] They saw the Jews as a religion only, not a people or a nation. They might live in the country but only if they recognized its Arab character and nature. "If the Jews are a Nation with rights to the country, why would not the Arabs claim rights with no less justification over Spain or Cyprus, . . . Italy, Brittany, Turkey, the Balkans?"[7] Other arguments held that because the Jews spoke a German language (Yiddish) they were the potential ally of Britain's enemy, or that they were dangerous leftists identifying with the USSR. Above all, the Jews were said to demonstrate moral corruption by their lack of respect for family traditions.

The pamphlets made a distinction between Zionists and non-Zionists; in this context, only the former were blamed. In practice, when violence broke out, the non-Zionist, orthodox neighborhoods were usually among the first attacked—as exemplified in Hebron and Safed in 1929.

It was on the basis of these views that the MCA became the major vehicle of Palestinian Arab nationalism in the 1920s. The nine members of the Executive Committee of the Arab Palestinian Congress were usually recruited from its ranks. In the following years, the two parties most active were the Arab Palestinian party and the Party of National Defense, dominated by the Hussaini and the Nashashibi, rival Jerusalem families, respectively. A third party, the Istiqlal (Independence), was created by Awni Abd al-Hadi with the support of younger and educated people residing outside Jerusalem; this group renewed the Pan-Arabic allegiance by claiming union with Syria and the whole Arab world. The strongest party was the Hussainis', which emphasized the specific Palestinian issue as such, as well as the more general Palestinian version of Arab nationalism. Amin al-Hussaini was the one who strengthened the ties of Palestinian nationalism with the Arab world and called on the latter to back the anti-Mandate struggle.

Among the Palestinians, however, rivalry was intense, and the weaker Nashashibis were gradually excluded from Palestinian institutions. They created various frameworks of their own and sent numerous messages to the British government about the lack of representativeness of the Hussaini-dominated bodies.

C. THE FLOOD OF EVENTS

Because they did not recognize the Mandate, the Arabs, unlike the Jews, did not create official institutions that could cooperate with the governor. Yet, though they had no constitutional status, the Palestinian Arab Congress and its Executive Committee were the Arab sector's counterpart of the Jewish bodies. In the beginning, the British did not recognize these institutions, but this attitude changed over time. In the late 1920s, the Executive Committee was even solicited to appoint representatives to various governmental commissions.

This same body, however, served as the leader of the Palestinian Arabs' anti-Zionist and anti-Mandate struggle, sending petitions, organizing demonstrations, and inciting riots. In August 1921, it organized a mission to Britain to meet public figures and journalists and to explain their anti-Zionist feelings. Winston Churchill, who headed the Colonial Office, received the delegation and negotiated with it (to no avail) for the creation of constitutional institutions.

Other delegations reached London in the following years. Nevertheless, the situation in Palestine was quite calm in 1925, when Lord Plumer replaced Herbert Samuel. This calm atmosphere remained undisturbed even when Lord Balfour visited the country for the inauguration of the Hebrew University of Jerusalem.

Tensions began to rise in spring 1928, when Jewish immigration from Eastern Europe increased. The Arab demand for restrictions on immigration became an increasingly acute issue. These tensions reached their peak in August 1929, when the Jews demanded new arrangements at the Western Wall, the most sacred Jewish site. This provoked Arab demonstrations, which soon degenerated into riots. Word spread among the Arab population that the Muslim Supreme Council had called for all believers to wage war against the Jews. Dozens of Jewish victims were murdered all over the country, often in isolated places such as Motza, Hartuv, Beer-Tuvia, and Kfar Etzion.

These events strengthened the power of the Jerusalem mufti and focused Arabic leadership on the Islamic institutions.[8] The British reacted with moderation vis-à-vis the Arabs. Their official response, the Shaw Report, recommended an understanding of Arab fears and limitation of Jewish immigration. Furthermore, a constitutional body composed of a majority of Arabs and a minority of Jews was suggested. These proposals were published in the 1930 White Paper.

At the same time, Jewish attempts to achieve rapprochement with the Arabs were checked by the British authorities. The "Worker Brotherhood," for instance, was banned because it united Jewish and Arab leftists. The same difficulties confronted a similar attempt at organization initiated by the left-wing Hashomer Hatzair and the Socialist League in 1942.

The publication of the White Paper caused the first profound crisis between Britain and the Zionist organization. Chaim Weizmann resigned from his position as chairman of the latter. Sensitive to this kind of pressure, Prime Minister Ramsay MacDonald issued a letter to Weizmann reiterating the British commitment to the Balfour Declaration. This move, in turn, generated vehement Arab reactions. In March 1931, a large public meeting in Nablus called openly for an armed struggle. Another general meeting in the same city in September attracted most of the recognized leaders, who repeated the appeal for arms. In 1931, the first wave of anti-British riots erupted. In December 1935, however, the governor invited both sides to accept new constitutional proposals.[9] These were rejected by the Jews as well as by the Arabs.

The Jewish community numbered more than 400,000 at that time, and many were still arriving from Hitler's Germany. In April 1936, the Arab Revolt finally broke out. Strikes, riots, and armed attacks against persons and property created a climate of civil war throughout the country. On August 7, 1936, the Peel Committee, appointed by MacDonald, met in Jerusalem to hear the testimony of dozens of witnesses. It concluded on July 7, 1937, that the Mandate could not continue and proposed that the country be divided into a Jewish state (5,000 square kilometers) and an Arab one (about five times as large) alongside an area that would remain British (Jerusalem and its surroundings, the Jaffa shore, Safed, and other sites).

The Jews, represented by the Zionist Congress of August 1937 (Zurich), rejected the proposal by a majority but left the door open to negotiation and fully endorsed the intention to establish a Jewish state. Rejection was much more total on the Arab side, where the revolt was renewed with still more violence.

The greater the violence, however, the sharper the inner rift among the Arab leadership. The Nashashibis withdrew their participation, thereby becoming a target for terrorism. In turn, the antimufti party in Nablus collaborated with the British in the capture of several important gang commanders. The Hussainis' opponents even cooperated with the Jewish Agency and the semilegal Jewish army, the Haganah, in the establishment of a network of their own, the "peace gangs," under the leadership of a former pro-Hussaini officer.

In the same period, the British launched strong attacks against the mufti's men and undertook cooperation with the Jews. Orde Wingate's "special night units," composed mostly of Haganah fighters, learned offensive antiguerrilla methods from British officers. Heavy penalties were imposed on Arab villagers who had helped Hussaini gangs: several terrorists captured by the British were even sentenced to death; houses where terrorists had been lodged were blown up; new identity cards were issued to facilitate further control over the population.

The Executive Committee was banned, as were the "national committees" created by the revolt in every town and village.[10] Amin al-Hussaini was dismissed from his official functions. In July 1937, with his arrest imminent, he found a way to escape, reaching Lebanon in October. The revolt gradually lost its impetus and died out. In one respect, it had been a complete success: it had interested the neighboring Arab countries in the conflict. These countries were now involved in permanent diplomatic contacts and talks with the British on the behalf of the Palestinian cause.

In the meantime, with World War II on the horizon, London was occupied with new problems. Guided by considerations of the general balance of power, new statements issued during 1938 diminished the future Jewish state to a small strip. Britain, sorely in need of Arab allies and seeking a definite settlement, called for a conference to be held in London in February 1939.

The British held talks with the representatives of the Arab states and separately with the Zionists. Although no solution was achieved, the most tangible result of these talks was the 1939 White Paper, which essentially represented a British break with the Balfour Declaration. The acquisition of land by Jews was restricted to a small strip, immigration was almost totally banned, and the national rights of the Arab population were explicitly given priority.

By this time, however, the Jewish community had already become a viable entity. It numbered almost half a million people compared to 12,000 in 1914; there were 254 settlements compared to 44; and its industrial production had reached 10 million pounds sterling, compared to half a million. When World War II broke out, it was clear to all that the conflict in Palestine had reached a pause, not an end.

During the war, Jewish immigration ceased totally, but it was renewed in 1945, even though the British opposed it more vigorously than ever. Despite the discovery of the scope of the Holocaust, the British arrested thousands of immigrants, survivors of the Nazi camps, and sent them to Cyprus. Those who managed to escape the authorities raised the Jewish population of Palestine to 630,000 by 1948.

On the political scene, the Zionists had been lobbying since 1945 in the United States, whose new world responsibilities made it the most important actor on the international scene. In Palestine, the Jews were the toughest enemy of the British, as expressed in a multiplicity of underground and terrorist actions. Britain's economic weakness in these postwar years, its failure to totally stop illegal immigration and to destroy Jewish underground organizations, and the growing support of the Jews by the Americans (and, somehow, by the Soviets as well) all led to the British submission of the Palestinian question to the United Nations in 1947. On November 29, 1947, this body decided on a partition plan, which was quickly accepted by the Zionists and immediately rejected by the Arabs. Again, the Arabs united, and terror broke out.[11]

On February 7, 1948, the Cairo Arab League Conference reached the decision to fight the Jewish state in the making by employing the regular Arab armies. It refused, however, the demand of the Arab Executive Committee, representing the Palestinians, to concede any piece of "liberated" Palestinian land to its jurisdiction.

The British withdrawal from the country in May 1948 and the subsequent Israeli Declaration of Independence were followed immediately by the first Israeli-Arab war, which began with an all-Arab invasion of the new state. Hundreds of thousands of Arab inhabitants of what was now Israel fled the new state, becoming refugees. Cease-fire arrangements ended heavy fighting only after eighteen months. At the end of the war, Israel had gained more territory than had been allotted to it by the UN partition plans. It had not, however, achieved peaceful relations with its neighbors.

D. THE PALESTINIANS AMONG THE ARABS

According to Israeli sources, the number of Palestinian refugees in 1948 was about 500,000. More realistic figures would securingly put the number about fifty percent higher. Residents of the north (Haifa, Acre, Safed) fled to Lebanon or Syria; those from the central area (Ramla, Jerusalem) went to the West Bank or the East Bank (500,000); southerners from Jaffa or Beersheba reached the Gaza Strip (200,000). Other groups settled in Iraq (5,000), Egypt (6,000), Saudi Arabia, and Kuwait.[12] Only 160,000 Arabs remained in Israel.

The social structure of Palestinian society outside Israel exhibited a traditional break between urban educated notables and the mass of peasants. Those refugees who were of the former background were usually assimilated into the large cities, but those who were of peasant origin created the refugee camps and became a proletariat employed in town or on the land.[13]

The United Nations Refugee Welfare Agency (UNRWA) was the major institution in charge of the Palestinian refugee camps, supervising their educational system, health services, and welfare allocations. Although it extended numerous essential services, the UNRWA's action also created a psychological dependence on external factors.

In general, there was a sharp segregation between Palestinian refugees and the indigenous population. This estrangement was particularly severe among the local peasants, who, having been totally involved with their own land, were less able than others to integrate newcomers. In this sense those who fled Israel in 1948 became a homeless people wherever they went.[14]

To the extent, however, that "to feel at home" is also a function of political and formal rights, the most comprehensive attempt was made by the Jordanian regime to integrate the Palestinians, including the refugees. As early as 1949 a well-prepared assembly of Palestinian notables in Jericho called by King Abdallah demanded the annexation by Transjordan of the West Bank, which was actually occupied by Amman's Arab Legion. This annexation (except for Jerusalem) in fact represented the implementation of an understanding achieved by the Jews and Abdallah before the war. The change of the country's name to Jordan symbolized the new reality. All Palestinians on Hashemite land now became citizens of a sovereign state, in which they constituted a wide majority of the population. Notables on the West Bank were given important functions in the king's administration, though at the same time, severe means of control (mainly in the refugee camps) were created.[15]

Amman aspired first to strengthen the East Bank because of the annexation of the more populated and prosperous West Bank (460,000 local residents and 280,000 refugees). As a result of this policy, about 130,000 refugees who had originally been settled in the West Bank moved to the East Bank between 1952 and 1961; by 1967, 60,000 others had followed.

At the political level, the Hussainis were now in the opposition, while the Nashashibis and their allies, who had been the oppositionists of the

Mandate period, became the supporters of the new regime. What served most to keep Jordanian rule alive, enduring, and undefeated in all these years (1948–67), however, was the powerful idea of Arab unity. This idea, which was recognized and accepted by both the Palestinians and the Jordanians, reflected their flexible definition of their respective national identities. This flexibility is mainly derived from the distinction between two concepts. One is that of *aqawmiyyah*, meaning people, group, or tribe, and is used to express the idea of ethnic nationalism, that is, a political allegiance and commitment of individuals and groups in the Arab world to the realization through a grand unity. The second is that of *mataniyyah*, which can be defined as a political allegiance and commitment stressing patriotic attachment to a single country.

The absence among the Palestinians of clear criteria for the definition of their national boundaries was similar to Amman's political approach, which was crystallized by Abdallah. . . . In this respect he saw the realization of his political dream in a "Greater Syria" which would include Syria, Lebanon, Palestine and Transjordan. This political resemblance between the two parties (the Palestinian nationalists also wanting expansion) in defining the collective boundaries even made it possible for the Jordanian regime to share, in some measure, in a common ideology with the Palestinians and on occasion even to cooperate with the most extremist of their Palestinian rivals.[16]

In 1960, the Jordanian rulers even decided to grant citizenship to any Palestinian interested, no matter where he lived. This was intended to strengthen Jordan's legitimacy as the Palestinian homeland. It was aimed at both Palestinian inhabitants and the other Arab governments, which, under Gamal Abdel Nasser's leadership, were raising the Palestinian national issue against Israel as well as against pro-Western Jordan itself. These tensions with the radical Arab states related to the public discussion of that period on the issue of the "Palestinization of Jordan versus the Jordanization of the Palestinians."[17]

The situation was quite different in the Egypt-dominated Gaza Strip. In 1948, there were about 285,000 inhabitants in the strip, more than half of them refugees. Egypt kept this population isolated. The government encouraged Palestinian nationalism and supported political bodies that expressed the inhabitants' national identity. Any political factor beyond its control (such as the Arab Executive Committee, which fled to Gaza in 1948) was eliminated. At the same time, Egypt tolerated the creation of paramilitary groups for terrorist action within Israel, which released feelings of frustration among the inhabitants.[18]

In Syria, in contrast to Egypt, the Palestinians could become Syrians, serve in the army, and hold public office. The small number of Palestinians were not a threat, and their allegiance to the Syrian state served its aspirations to lead the Arab world in the Palestinian struggle.

The worst conditions for the Palestinians were certainly those they found in Lebanon. Here, in the context of the sharp divisions that already separated the country's religious-ethnic communities, they were clearly not wanted. The Christian rulers confined the Palestinians to their camps, refused them access to citizenship, and controlled their moves within the territory.[19]

E. PLO AND FEDAYEEN MOVEMENTS

After the mid-1950s, however, Pan-Arabism was again widely dominant in the area. Nasser's modernist, secular Pan-Arabism in Egypt, soon imitated by Baathism in Syria and Iraq and later by revolutions in Yemen and Libya, totally transformed the Middle East. The Palestinian cause was again a public matter linked by the Arab leaders to the issue of the unity of the Arab nation.[20] Hence, Palestinians were attracted by Pan-Arabic organizations.[21]

The enthusiasm of the 1950s, however, soon gave place, in the 1960s, to more realistic outlooks. The United Arab Republic, which unified Egypt and Syria, had failed, as had the revolutionary movement in Lebanon, while endless civil wars were taking place in Yemen and Iraq. As a sign of the times, those in power in the local bodies of the Gaza Strip were moderate notables. Disillusion was deep among the younger generation of Palestinians while Egypt, Syria, and Iraq were fighting each other for leadership and all three of them turned against Jordan and Saudi Arabia, the pro-West conservative bloc.[22]

This divided Arab world was unable to react to Israel's challenge to their refusal to cooperate in the use of common water, the Jordan River (the Israeli-Jordanian-Syrian border), and operation of its own water pipe to the Negev Desert. The only response the Arab states were able to muster at the time was the reawakening of the Palestinian issue. Accepting an Iraqi proposal, Egypt called for a meeting of the Arab League to decide upon practical steps to be implemented in this respect.[23]

In February 1964, an Arab summit in Cairo proclaimed the creation of a Palestinian Liberation Organization (PLO), with Ahmed Shuqairy at its head. The Hashemite Kingdom, of course, was the main victim of the move, which was a covert attack against the union of the two banks of the Jordan. Its reluctance notwithstanding, however, Amman allowed "symbolic" elections to be held in the areas of Palestinian concentration in order to form a National Palestinian Council, scheduled to meet in Jerusalem in May 1964.

At the same time, six other Palestinian movements of recent creation were establishing a competing umbrella organization, the Political Bureau of the Palestinian Liberation Movement. One group, the Fatah, participated in both structures but the latter was soon to disappear.

The PLO was explicitly recognized and financed by a second Arab summit in September 1964. This meeting also confirmed the formation of a Palestinian Army of Liberation (PLA), to be constituted by regular regiments. Because of the sharp divergencies dividing its sponsors, the new movement could not define its ideology with clarity. The general formulas elaborated by the Palestinian Covenant—adopted by the NPC first in May 1964 in Jerusalem and later, with corrections, in July 1968 in Cairo—depicted the Palestinian people as refugees with a right to their homeland (see exhibit 2.2). Israel was to be eradicated, and a restored Palestine was to find its place within the frame of the Arab nation. The Palestinians themselves, it was said, were to forward their interest, as well as those of the Arab world as a whole.[24] The issue of the Palestinian state as such was carefully eluded. Shuqairy soon expounded the new organization's networks in the fields of education, welfare, and health services. A theoretical right was given to every Palestinian eighteen or older to participate in future national elections.

King Hussein of Jordan agreed only to a limited scope of activities for the PLO in Jordan. Yet in 1966, two years after its creation, its military arm, the PLA, already numbered four to six thousand fighters. More specifically, there were the Hittin Brigade located in Syria; the Qadisiya Brigade, which was divided into several parts (Iraq, Jordan, and, mainly, Lebanon); and the Ayn Jalut Brigade, in Egypt.[25] These forces certainly were an asset even though they were totally controlled by, and subject to, the various Arab governments.

However, other groups were able to escape these constraints. The Fatah was (and still is) the strongest among them.[26] Created in 1959 in Cairo around the *Filistina* review, its leaders were originally very close to the Muslim Brothers. In 1964 it developed a paramilitary structure, the Asifa, and it was supported by Syria. From the very beginning the Fatah was highly pragmatic in outlook and ready to cooperate with any factor that could be of assistance in creating a Palestinian state. The leadership was also quite cohesive in its allegiance to Yasser Arafat, even though there were other strongmen as well, such as Khalil al-Wazir, Faruq Qaddumi, and Salah Khalaf.[27]

From another horizon altogether came other groups of nationalist Palestinians. A key example is the story of George Habash, a Christian physician of Marxist conviction. Habash participated in the (Pan-) Arab National Movement (ANM) during the 1950s and gradually became involved in Palestinian nationalism. In 1967, he created the Popular Front for the Liberation of Palestine (PFLP), which was to remain faithful to an all-Arab revolutionary vision of the Palestinian struggle. The "Palestinian masses' popular war against Zionism" was but the "spearhead" of the socialist combat in the Arab world as a whole.

One of Habash's early followers, associated with him as early as the

Exhibit 2.2
The Palestinian National Covenant (Excerpts)

art. 1 - Palestine is the homeland of the Palestinian Arab people and an integral part of the Great Arab Homeland, and the People of Palestine is a part of the Arab Nation.

art. 2 - Palestine with its boundaries that existed at the time of the British Mandate is an integral regional unit.

art. 3 - The Palestinian Arab People possesses the legal right to its homeland and when the liberation of its homeland is completed it will exercise self-determination solely according to its own will and choice.

. . . .

art. 5 - Whoever is born to a Palestian Arab father afer this date [1947] within Palestine or outside it, is a Palestinian.

art. 6 - Jews who were living permanently in Palestine until the beginning of the Zionist invasion will be considered Palestinians.

. . . .

art. 9 - Armed struggle is the only way to liberate Palestine and is therefore a strategy and not tactics ...

art. 10- Fedayeen action forms the nucleus of the popular Palestinian war of liberation.

. . . .

art. 15- The liberation of Palestine, from an Arab viewpoint is a national duty to repulse the Zionist, imperialist invasion from the Great Arab Homeland and to purge the Zionist presence from Palestine...

. . . .

Source: Y. Harkabi, "The Palestinian National Covenant," in *The Arab-Israel Conflict*, ed. J. N. Moore (Princeton, N.J.: Princeton University Press, 1977), 103–20.

days of the ANM, was Naief Hawatmeh, from the East Bank. In the footsteps of Habash, Hawatmeh left the ANM and participated in the creation of the PFLP. Two years later, however, in 1969, Hawatmeh adopted a perspective on the struggle that emphasized the class issue more than the national problem and, consequently, redefined the revolution in terms of a combat against "all reactionaries," whether Arabs or Jews. On this new ideological basis, Hawatmeh split from Habash's group and set up his own movement, which was later called the Democratic Front for the Liberation of Palestine (DFLP).

The PFLP faced other splits as well. In 1968, a pro-Syrian militant and former captain in the Syrian army, Ahmed Jibril, left Habash to create the PFLP General Command, which was to cooperate mainly with Syria.

Several other groups were sponsored directly by various states, mainly Syria, Iraq, and Libya. The Syrian-Palestinian movement al-Saiqa (Vanguards of the Popular Liberation War) was established in 1968. It was headed by Zuhir Muhsin, an old-time Baathist until his death in 1979; most of the officers are Syrian, and the headquarters are situated in Damascus. The Saiqa's competitor is the Arab Liberation Front (ALF), which was launched by Iraq in 1969. This group is led by Abd al-Rahim Ahmed, and most of its members are Iraqi, Lebanese, or Jordanian. Unlike most other movements, and under the inspiration of Iraqi Baathism, the ALF is opposed to a Palestinian state, striving instead for the political unification of the entire Arab world.

Among the smaller groups, the most active is Black June, a splinter of the Fatah formed in 1976. It is headed by Abu Nidal (or Sabri al-Banna), the Fatah's former representative in Iraq. Considering itself the watchdog of the Palestinian revolution, it often turns against "mild" elements or "traitors" within the Palestinian camp. This group is not to be confused with Black September, which was created by the Fatah in 1971 in response to Jordan's repression of the PLO in 1970. It was headed by Salah Khalaf (Abu Iyad) and constituted a kind of "special force" for particularly difficult and dangerous tasks. This list is by no means exclusive; exhibit 2.3 is more complete. By 1970 a general estimate of the number of members of the major fedayeen organizations gave 10,000 members to the Fatah, 7,000 to the Saiqa, 3,000 each to the PFLP and the ALF, 1,000 to the DFLP and 500 to the PFLP-GC. The total number of fedayeen was about 25,000. This figure included those involved in all kinds of activity and the combatants themselves numbered but 5000 to 6000.[28]

In the meantime (December 1967), Shuqairy was dismissed from the PNC chairmanship. His successor, Yahya Hamuda, remained in power only until 1969, when several movements, headed by the Fatah, managed to take over the leadership of the PLO. Almost all fedayeen organizations now made up a federation structured as a classic national liberation movement (see exhibit 2.4). The sociopolitical context too was now different: the Six-Day war had created the very circumstances of a guerrilla conflict.

F. THE SIX-DAY WAR

The period from Autumn 1966 to Spring 1967 was one of agitation.[29] In November 1966 Syria and the United Arab Republic (Egypt) concluded a "defense agreement" which created a unified Arab Command in Cairo. Fedayeen incursions to Israel from Syria and Jordan now multiplied— fourteen incidents occurred in the month of April 1967 alone. Israel's responses were sometimes of wide amplitude: at Al-Samu in Jordan (November 13, 1966) eighteen were killed and fifty-four wounded; in the outskirts of Damascus (April 7, 1967), six Syrian planes were shot down by the Israeli Air Force.

From May 13, 1967 on, the events unfolded rapidly. On this day, and with the full support of the Soviet government, the Syrian authorities warned the members of the Security Council of the United Nations that "imperialist and Zionist quarters" were plotting against Syria. On May 16, Cairo radio reported that a state of emergency had been declared. The same day, and under the order of President Gamal Abdul Nasser, the Egyptian chief of staff demanded that the Commander of the United Nations Emergency Force in Sinai (UNEF) "withdraw all troops immediately." These UNEF soldiers were in the area to control the demilitarization of the Sinai Peninsula and the Gaza Strip, and to ensure free Israeli navigation on the Red Sea and through the Tiran Straits. They were originally stationed there in 1957 with the evacuation of the Sinai by the Israelis at the conclusion of the Sinai operation. This operation had been conducted (in concert with the Anglo-French Suez attack) by the Israelis in order to eliminate the Egyptian bases in Gaza (from which acts of infiltration were perpetrated), and to break the maritime blockade against Eilat, Israel's port on the Red Sea.

Secretary-General U Thant complied with the Egyptian request to remove the UNEF soldiers, and on May 17, 1967, Cairo's army started moving. Five days were enough to reach Gaza and the international border, thereby destroying the formal status quo and the security balance which had been the rule for a decade. On May 22, Nasser finally announced the reinstitution of the blockade against Israel in the Straits of Tiran.

An overwhelming enthusiasm inflamed the entire Arab world and Nasser was now hailed by all as the undeniable leader of the Arab nation. King Hussein came to Cairo on May 30 and signed a military treaty with the United Arab Republic; this was extended to Iraq during the following days. As Charles W. Yost commented, "The armed forces of Egypt,

Exhibit 2.3
The Fedayeen Organizations[1]

Movements	Structural Characteristics[2]	Ideological Orientations[3]
Palestine Liberation Army (PLA)	regular brigades in Syria, Iraq, Lebanon, Jordan, Egypt; all under the local national army's command	each brigade or company, according to local political regime
Palestine National Liberation Movement (Fatah)	politico-military structures; El-Assifa is the military arm, Black September the "special force"	nationalistic ideology; symbols reminiscent of Islamic Arabism
Popular Front for the Liberation of Palestine (PFLP)	politico-military structures; symbiosis between military and political functions	Marxist-revolutionary orientation; Palestine as a first step toward an all-Arab revolution
Democratic Front for the Liberation of Palestine	same as PFLP	Marxist-revolutionary orientation; the Palestinian revolution should take place simultaneously to the all-Arab revolution
Popular Front for the Liberation of Palestine - General Command (PFLP-GC)	mainly paramilitary structure	Syrian Baathism
Palestine Liberation Front (PLF)	terroristic network	Iraqi Baathism
Palestine Arab Organization (PAO)	terroristic network	Nasserism
As-Saiqa	mainly paramilitary structures	Syrian Baathism
Popular Liberation Forces	terroristic network	undefined
Arab Liberation Front (ALF)	terroristic network	Iraqi Baathism
Action Group for the Liberation of Palestine (AGLP) (existed until 1971)	mainly political structure	Nasserism
Popular Struggle Front (PSF)	terroristic network	undefined

Exhibit 2.3
(continued)

Movements	Structural Characteristics[2]	Ideological Orientations[3]
Arm of Arab Revolution (AAR)	terroristic network	pro-Khadafi orientation
Black June	terroristic network	pro-Iraq
Popular Organization for the Liberation of Palestine (POLP)	militia in refugee camps in Syria	pro-Syria
Popular Revolutionary Front for the Liberation of Palestine (PRFLP)	terroristic network	revolutionary Marxism
Ansar	mainly political structure	Communist Party
Arab Sinai Organization (ASO)	mainly paramilitary structure	Nasserism
Arab Nationalist Youth for Liberation of Palestine (ANYLP)	terroristic network	pro-Libya and Iran Islamic fundamentalism
Front for Participation in the Palestinian Revolution (FPPR)	political-terroristic structure	fringes of Communist parties
Arab Communist Organization (ACO)	like FPPR	like FPPR

Source: IDF spokesman material, unpublished.

[1] the organizations listed here are those which are known sufficiently to be characterized, at least in very broad lines. These organizations were in existence by the early 1970s.

[2] By "political structures" we mean organizational units in charge of ideological issues, propaganda or organization work at the level of party-like activity. By "paramilitary structures" we mean military units characterized by some size, military training, and practical capabilities but which do not belong to a regular army. By "terroristic network" we mean interconnected cells numbering a handful of members who, from the underground, specialize in small scale expressive violence.

[3] The ideological orientations are labels which are most often very vague but which are indicative of political tempers and which, in any case, are those employed by the fedayeen themselves.

Exhibit 2.4
The Palestinian Liberation Organization

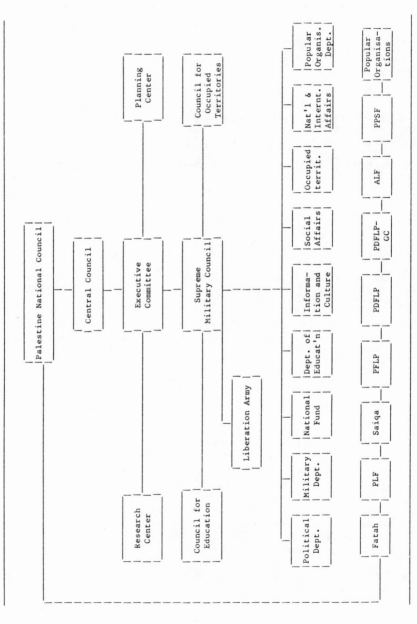

Source: IDF Spokesman material, mimeograph (July 31, 1977).

Jordan and Syria were [now] more and more concentrated around Israel's frontiers and there seemed every likelihood that they would soon be reinforced by other Arab states."[30]

Israel's Foreign Minister, Abba Eban, was on an emergency mission to Europe, the United States, and the United Nations in an attempt to raise an international reaction to Nasser's unilateral moves. This effort was fruitless and three weeks after the beginning of the crisis—on June 5, 1967—Israel attacked on three fronts; six days later, a ceasefire, imposed by the Security Council, found a Middle East transformed.

The Israelis were in control of the Gaza Strip and the entire Sinai down to the Suez Canal on the Egyptian front; the Golan Heights, including the city of Kuneitra, on the Syrian front; the West Bank of the Jordan River, including Samaria, Judea, and East Jerusalem, on the Jordanian front. As for the Golan, where the population is Druze, it was partially restituted to Syria with the disengagement agreements following the 1973 Yom Kippur War; the rest was annexed by Israel. The Sinai, inhabited by Beduin tribes, was given back to Egypt within the framework of the disengagement agreements and Camp David. East Jerusalem was annexed by Israel soon after the Six Day War and unified with Israel's capital. The inhabitants, however, remained Jordanian citizens. With those of Samaria, Judea and the Gaza Strip, they made up the core of the Palestinian population, a population which then knew political effervescence as well as demographic expansion.

In 1982, it was estimated by American sources[31] that besides the Arab Israeli citizens (500,000), there were about 700,000 Palestinians on the West Bank (including East Jerusalem), and 450,000 in the Gaza Strip. Outside Israeli control, there were still one million Palestinians on the East Bank (where they constituted about two-thirds of the population), 400,000 in Lebanon, 320,000 in Kuwait, 250,000 in Syria, 120,000 in Iraq, and smaller groups in a great many other countries. The total number of Palestinians was about 3,800,000, not including the Israeli citizens. More than one million (1,150,000) had no Israeli citizenship but were subject to Israeli authorities. They exemplified for these authorities a most acute case of inflation of power. The pre-1948 direct Zionist-Palestinian confrontation was renewed with the Israelis now in the role of occupier. This occupier, moreover, had achieved its present position of power as the result of interstate belligerence and was not concerned with, nor ready to pay attention to, the political claims of the population. In practice, it adhered to the spirit, if not the wording, of Resolution 242 of the Security Council of November 22, 1967, which defined the United Nations' view of the Middle East crisis. This resolution aspired to a withdrawal of Israeli armed forces from territories occupied in the recent conflict, without specifying what is meant by "territories"; it also recommended the termination of all claims, the acknowledgment of the sovereignty and territorial integrity of every state, and the right of every state to live in peace within secure and recognized boundaries. Finally, it affirmed the necessity for achieving a just settlement of the refugee problem. This was the only mention of the Palestinian problem in this resolution.

The Israeli-Palestinian conflict, however, was soon to become the major aspect of the Middle East reality.

NOTES

1. J. Shimoni, *The Arab National Movement in the Land of Israel* (Tel Aviv: Am Oved [Hebrew], 1947), 269–428.

2. A. M. Lesch, *Arab Politics in Palestine 1917–1930* (London: Cornell University Press, 1979).

3. Y. Bernard, *British Rule in Palestine* (Washington D.C.: Public Affairs Press, 1948).

4. S. Hadawi, *Bitter Harvest: Palestine 1914–1967* (New York: New World Press, 1967), 48. See also J. Nevo, "The Palestinian Arabs' Attitudes toward the Jewish Settlement and the Zionist Movement," *Zionism and the Jewish Question* (Jerusalem: Zalman Shazar Institute, 1976 [Hebrew]).

5. Y. Porat, *The Emergence of Arab Palestinian Nationalism, 1919–1929*, (Tel Aviv: Am Oved, 1978 [Hebrew]), 39.

6. *Ibid.*, 41–42.

7. *Ibid.*, 184.

8. S. Dotan, *The Combat Struggle over the Land of Israel* (Tel Aviv: Ministry of Defense, 1981 [Hebrew]), 29.

9. Y. Porat, *From Riots to Revolt: The National Palestinian Arab Movement 1929–1939* (Tel Aviv: Am Oved, 1978 [Hebrew]).

10. J. Teguer, "The 1936 Arab Revolt in the Perspective of the Jewish-Arab Confrontation in Palestine," Zalman Shazar Institute.

11. Dotan, 373.

12. Y. Amos, *Palestinian Resistance: Organization of a Nationalist Movement* (New York: Pergamon, 1980), 7–8.

13. R. Sayigh, *Palestinians: From Peasants to Revolutionaries* (London: Zed Press, 1979), 100.

14. *Ibid.*, 113.

15. Y. Harkabi, *The Palestinians: From Quiescence to Awakening* (Jerusalem: Magnes, 1979 [Hebrew]), 145.

16. S. Mishal, "Jordanian and Israeli Policy in the West Bank," in *The Hashemite Kingdom of Jordan and the West Bank*, eds. A. Sinai and A. Pollack (New York: American Academic Association for Peace in the Middle East, 1977), 214.

17. Y. Harkabi, *The Arabs' Plan of action against Israel* (Jerusalem: Academon, 1975 [Hebrew]), 44. See also C. Bailey, *The Participation of the Palestinians in the Politics of Jordan*, Ph.D. dissertation, Columbia University, 1966.

18. Harkabi, *The Palestinians*, 27.

19. See also M. Efrat, *The Palestinian Refugees: Economic and Social Research*,

1949–1974 (Tel Aviv: David Horowitz Institute, Tel Aviv University, 1976 [Hebrew]).

20. Amos, 14; E. Said, *The Palestinian Question* (New York: Times Books, 1979), 131.

21. S. Avineri, *Israel and the Palestinians* (New York: St. Martin's Press, 1971), 8.

22. Amos, 19.

23. A. Sinai, and A. Pollack, (eds.) *The Hashemite Kingdom of Jordan and the West Bank* (New York: American Academic Association for Peace in the Middle East, 1977), 31.

24. Y. Harkabi, *The Arabs' Position in the Israeli-Arab Conflict* (Tel Aviv: Dabir, 1971 [Hebrew]), 69.

25. IDF Spokesman material (mimeograph), July 31, 1977 (Hebrew).

26. Y. Harkabi, *The Fatah in the Arab Strategy* (Tel Aviv: Maarakhot, 1969 [Hebrew]).

27. E. Yaari, *The Fatah* (Tel Aviv: Levin-Epstein, 1970 [Hebrew]), 66–85.

28. S. Mishal, *The PLO Under Arafat: Between Gun and Olive Branch* (New Haven: Yale University Press, 1986), 12.

29. C. W. Yost, "The Arab-Israeli War: How It Began," *The Arab-Israeli Conflict: Readings and Documents*, ed. John Norton Moore (Princeton: Princeton University Press, 1977), 293–309.

30. *Ibid.*, 306.

31. S. Mishal, 59.

Part II In the Field

3 Israeli Policy toward the Territories and Their Inhabitants

A. A NEW ADMINISTRATION

As a result of the Six-Day War, hundreds of thousands of persons suddenly became subjects of the IDF. The Israeli government instituted and staffed dozens of new offices to endorse official responsibility for this new population. The Palestinian areas belonged to two different juridical systems—the Jordanian system in Judea and Samaria and the old mandatory system in the Gaza Strip. There were also sharp demographic contrasts between these areas. Of those living on the West Bank, 50 percent were agriculturalists and villagers. The Gaza Strip was composed of only 30 percent agricultural laborers; most of the population were employed as construction, factory, or service workers. While 1948 refugees represented now only 10 to 15 percent of the population of Judea and Samaria, they constituted more than 50 percent in the Gaza Strip.

This disparity was taken into consideration by the flexible administrative structures set up by the Israelis. Each area was headed by its own military governor, responsible to the general coordinator of operations in the administered territories. Each governor was assisted by counselors, who represented the various relevant ministries of the Israeli government—agriculture, industry, education, and welfare.

Soon the regional administration was divided into military and civilian departments. The former was in charge of security matters, from police to intelligence, and the latter of regular municipal or regional administrative problems. A further decentralization subdivided several regional functions into smaller units. Each of these was governed by a local military commander with two assistants, one for security issues and the other for civilian matters. The direct hierarchical superior of the general coordinator, and therefore the head of the whole structure, was the defense minister, who, from 1967 to 1973, was Moshe Dayan. The coordinator's formal bond to the IDF headquarters and the chief of staff was less important; virtually all decisions were made by the defense minister.

Israel in effect abided by the provisions of international law.[1] The 1907 Convention of The Hague (art. 43) stipulates, indeed, that the conqueror of a territory is to hold to the existing local legislation and that the military authority should be invested with the status of legislator and executive power. Accordingly, in agreement with the coordinator, the military governors published a series of decrees establishing the legal basis of Israel's rule over the administered territories. The first of these was issued on June 6, 1967, just one day after the outbreak of the Six-Day War. It stated, "the IDF has taken over the control of security and public order." A few days later, a second decree stated that the existing law in each territory would be maintained until superseded by further decrees.

On June 28, however, Israel implemented a drastic change by annexing East Jerusalem, again by decree. Although the 1949 Fourth Geneva Convention forbids annexation of conquered land, Israel contended that Jordan's former annexation of the same territory had also resulted from a military conquest (the 1948 war). Israel's stand was further strengthened by the wide consensus on the defensive character of the 1967 war; the convention does allow for annexation under such circumstances.

Fifteen years later, the Golan Heights were annexed, while at the same time the Sinai was returned to Egypt in the framework of the Camp David Agreements. Yet, for the wide majority of the territories' inhabitants—those of Judea, Samaria, and the Gaza Strip—these changes were of minimal legal impact. Some tax laws were affected, as were some other minor municipal arrangements. Wider juridical realms such as labor, social, and penal codes have remained almost unchanged for nearly two decades.

The very process of lawmaking in the territories is extremely cautious and complex. It is generally at the level of the regional governor that a new legal disposition is first suggested and formulated. The proposal is then sent to the International Law Department of the IDF chief attorney, where it is carefully considered. Next, it must be accepted by the juridical counselor of the Ministry of Defense, after which it is submitted to the coordinator for confirmation. It is finally proposed to the minister of defense, who may well involve the prime minister in his decision if the matter is of wide importance. This was the process, for instance, for the decree that endowed women in the administered territories with equal voting rights in municipal elections.[2]

The major institutional innovation, however, was the formation of military courts to stand alongside the existing civilian courts. These new juridical bodies were set up in Gaza, Nablus, and Ramallah to deal with all security-related matters.

The assignment of cases to either court is the ultimate responsibility of the juridical counselor of the governor, who makes the decision personally in cases that are unclear. These military courts (numbering one or three judges) employ military officers who are professional lawyers. A defendant may appoint a lawyer of his choice or have one appointed by the court. On the other hand, the civilian courts employ local attorneys and jurists, nominated by the regional governor. The civilian courts hear penal and civil cases. Cases involving Israeli defendants are not tried here but are referred to a court in Israel, while complaints against the authorities must first be handled in the local military court before any appeal can be made to the Israeli Supreme Court.[3]

B. DEFINING A POLICY

The definition of an Israeli policy toward the Palestinian population and territories has been the object of numerous, often acute debates. For instance, many hold that the administered territories are indispensable to Israel's security and to its defense against terrorism. As Dayan put it, "[Thanks to the territories] we are able to reach every place, to search and liquidate [terrorists] in Nablus, Jenin, Hebron . . . to fight terror everywhere."[4] The underlying assumption is that the Palestinian problem is only one aspect of the more basic Israeli-Arab conflict over the very existence of the Jewish state. This stand is supported by the fact that the creation of the PLO, the activity of the fedayeen, and the wars in the Middle East themselves all took place before Israel's occupation of these territories and, in fact, led to the outbreak that caused this occupation.[5] According to this position, security considerations exclude any return to the pre-1967 Israel-Jordan international border, which would leave the Jewish state with a fourteen-kilometer width in the central area of Netanya. In contrast, the Jordan River, at the other end of the West Bank, is a natural obstacle and the safest guarantee of a peaceful border. This argument is reminiscent of the Germans' annexation of the Sudetenland in Czechoslovakia, which granted them a secure mountainous borderline.

Security and strategic concerns, however, are not the only ones that preoccupy the Israelis with respect to the role of the administered territories. There are also the symbolic national and religious meanings of the land and its sites. "Jew," after all, is "Judean"; Hebron, Nablus, Bethlehem, and, mainly, Jerusalem are the very pillars of biblical history. All these are "homeland earth," and it follows that: "We have to enhance the settling of Jews in this country; villages, factories, farms, towns and cities should multiply [as well as] national and private cooperation with the Arabs in Judea and Samaria."[6]

Above all these, however, stands the unequivocal rejection of the prospect of an independent Palestinian state. Even if the Palestinians are ready to make do with a small Palestine alongside Israel, how will such a tiny political entity be able to sustain itself without turning against the regional status quo? And in this case, without calling in the present allies of the PLO, the radical Arab states and the Soviets? In such a perspective, how is it possible to envisage that Israel would voluntarily concede assets it now holds, which would unavoidably be turned against it?

The possibility of returning the administered territories to Jordan would seem to counter this contention, for they would then belong to an entity large enough to accept the status quo—one that, moreover, would be interested in its maintenance by virtue of the newly gained land. It is then argued, however, that the Jordanian government never acquired any legal sovereignty over Judea and Samaria (which was also annexed by conquest). Hence, Israel's own rights over these areas are no less than those of Jordan.[7] In brief, the total or at least partial annexation of the administered territories is demanded.

On the other hand, however, these territories are not an empty desert. The population, as emphasized by doves like the left-wing Laborist Itzhak Ben-Aharon, is not willing, and will never be willing, to live under Israeli rule.[8] Similarly, Israel is by no means about to give up its Jewish character and become a "binational" state. Israel, then, has nothing to offer the inhabitants in terms of national identity and collective identification or of integration into a "homeland."

Whatever the divergences among Israelis with respect to the land in question, there is much wider and unambiguous agreement as far as the inhabitants of the territories are concerned. In this regard, minimalist aspirations are consensual: any solution of the Middle East crisis or the Palestinian conflict should exclude a common national framework for both the Israelis and the inhabitants of Gaza or the West Bank. Some right-wing leaders (see Begin quotation in exhibit 3.1) see no alternative to offering Israeli citizenship to the Arab inhabitants of the administered territories, but they expect that this offer will be turned down by the wide majority, who will thereby remain "foreigners" in a "Greater Israel."

Consequently, on November 15, 1967, the government decided that the authorities in the administered territories should minimize their presence among the population. The bridges over the Jordan River would remain open so that the link between the inhabitants of these territories and the Arab world could be maintained. The aim of the Israelis was to encourage "normalization" of life under occupation; in no way did they aspire to social legitimization.[9]

Exhibit 3.1
Israeli Attitudes

Yitzhak Rabin (Labor Party, former Prime Minister, Defense Minister in 1985)

"I believe that we cannot ignore the fact that the Palestinians exist and that a Palestinian problem exists. But we are still far from re-cognizing what is called, without any further specification, a Pales-tinian entity. We must solve the problem ... only within the framework of a Jordanian-Palestinian State."

Yigal Allon (Labor Party, former Foreign Minister)

"According to the compromise formula I personally advocate, Israel — within the context of a peace settlement — could give up the large majority of the areas which fell into its hands in the 1967 war. Israel would do so not because of any lack of historical affinity be-tween the Jewish people and many of these areas.... Both to preserve its Jewish character and to contribute toward a solution of the Palestinian issue, Israel should not annex an additional and significant Arab population."

Shimon Peres (Labor Party, former Defense Minister, Prime Minister in 1985)

"[My concept constitutes] a program for an Israeli Federation which will give autonomy to the inhabitants of Judea, Samaria and the Gaza Strip who can define themselves as Palestinians if they so wish. Such a federation could constitute the first step toward the estab-lishment of a future confederation with Jordan, but that should be viewed as an additional option and not as a condition for the estab-lishment of the [proposed] Federation or for the creation of rela-tions between it and Jordan."

Menachem Begin (Herut-Likud, former Prime Minister)

"Judea and Samaria are an inseparable part of Israel's sovereignty. It must be clear that whoever is prepared to surrender Judea and Samaria to foreign rule, inevitably prepares the ground for a Pales-tinian state.... Members of the Arab nationality ... will be given a free choice between adopting Israeli citizenship and retaining their previous citizenship. If they opt for naturalization, they will have full rights ... like Jewish citizens."

Source: M. Curtis, J. Meyer, C. I. Waxman, and A. Pollack, eds., *The Palestinians: People, History, Politics* (New Brunswick, N.J.: Transaction Books, 1975), 256, 260, 262–63, 266.

As a corollary, no dialogue of political significance was to be developed with local bodies referring in any manner whatsoever to a Palestinian entity that could be even remotely linked to any kind of Palestinian sovereignty. Accordingly, numerous attempts by Palestinian personalities from Jerusalem, Nablus, or Hebron to initiate talks with the Israelis on the establishment of a Palestinian state on the West Bank and the Gaza Strip remained unanswered; instead, between 1967 and 1970 no less than one hundred political associations were dissolved.[10]

In these circumstances, the municipalities became the main frameworks expressing some degree of popular representation. As such they undertook new responsibilities in realms like education, welfare, and trading, thereby replacing the central Jordanian agencies. This was generally endorsed by the occupation authorities. Thus, the mayors became the leading political figures in the administered territories.[11] They were in constant contact with the governors and even with the minister of defense. Many practical problems found solution through these direct contacts.

The first minister of defense in charge of the administered territories, Moshe Dayan, founded the general policy; his personality was not a minor factor in its formation. As an Israeli-born deeply aware of the Arab environment (he knew the language), he was able—and liked—to maintain face-to-face relationships with public, scholarly, and literary Arab figures. Moreover, as a former chief of staff, he was acquainted with every senior IDF officer posted in the administered territories. This assured him both direct information about any event, and their best performance on the job. "His wish was to live with the Arabs and not against them. The West Bank Arabs appreciated the man of Nahalal [the agricultural settlement where Dayan grew up] and respected him. Other Israeli leaders found it difficult to communicate with Arabs. Dayan succeeded."[12]

C. NEW DIRECTIONS

Finally, the small size and immediate proximity of Israel and the territories account for the speed with which decisions were made and implemented.[13] The outcome of Israel's policy is, however, quite debatable. The elections for the municipalities held in 1972 and in 1976 illustrate the ambiguity of this policy's results. The authorities had to exert heavy pressures on the Arab public, who were faced with the PLO's opposition to these elections. In sharp contrast to elections in Arab lands, opposing lists of candidates competed with each other in most towns and cities, and, even more spectacular, women were granted the right to vote and to run for office. In these ways, the elections were a success for the Israeli administration.

Yet, as was already discernible in 1972 and was affirmed in 1976, it was the PLO that actually won this democratic game.[14] This fact came as a shock to the Israelis. In the meantime, Dayan had left the Ministry of Defense in 1973 to be replaced by Shimon Peres (up to 1977), Ezer Weizman (1977–1980), and others. Israel's policy in the administered territories became more confused. A case in point is that of the expulsion to Jordan of Basam Shaqa, the mayor of Nablus, because of virulent anti-Israeli speeches. Under the subsequent international pressure, Defense Minister Weizman eventually accepted Shaqa's return home and even to office.

By the mid-1970s, it was clear that Israel had failed to develop solid bonds with moderate elements in the territories. This was also the period following the Yom Kippur War (1973) and the aftermath of the Rabat summit (1974), which recognized the PLO as the sole legitimate representative of the Palestinians. Thus, after the 1976 local elections in the West Bank, every Palestinian in the administered territories "seemed PLO." It was clear, too, that the pro-Jordanian traditional notables were powerless in the face of the growing influence of Palestinian militancy. The Israelis understood that they themselves had contributed to the weakening of moderate elements by abolishing all political prerogatives and means of political manipulations that had been the privilege of the notables until 1967.

The Camp David Agreements, signed by Israel, Egypt, and the United States in 1978, recognized the "legitimate rights of the Palestinian people" (see exhibit 3.2). A five-year autonomy period was to be instituted for the inhabitants of Judea, Samaria, and the Gaza Strip before a definite settlement was concluded. For the Israeli government, such innovations required finding appropriate partners within the Palestinian population. It thus prepared a political offensive against the PLO strongholds in the West Bank and in the Gaza Strip—primarily the municipalities elected in 1976.

The authorities in charge of the territories were restructured and formally divided into a civilian administration and a military authority. The declared aim of this change was to implement the Israeli-Egyptian treaty by finding "someone with whom to speak."[15] Israel's role in the administered territories responded now to a legitimate and fundamental principle, the fulfillment of Palestinian rights as envisaged by Camp David. Seeing the opposition of Jordan, the PLO, and most Arab countries to the Israeli-Egyptian treaty, most of the pro-PLO municipalities were antagonized by this new attitude; only a few organizations and leaders showed some readiness to cooperate. One by one, every uncooperative mayor was dismissed and replaced by an Israeli officer. Within a few weeks, the PLO had lost all grip on municipal services and resources. The pro-Jordanians, as well, were prevented from cooperating

Exhibit 3.2
Camp David Agreements (September 17, 1978) about the West Bank and the Gaza Strip

---

art.1.   Egypt, Israel, Jordan and the representatives of the Palestinian people should participate in negotiations on the resolution of
the Palestinian problem in all its aspects...

(a)   Egypt and Israel agree that ... there should be transitional
arrangements for the West Bank and Gaza for a period not exceeding
five years. In order to provide full autonomy to the inhabitants ...
the Israeli military government and its civilian administration will
be withdrawn as soon as a self-governing authority has been freely
elected by the inhabitants ...

(b)   Egypt, Israel and Jordan will agree on the modalities for esta-
blishing the elected self-governing authority in the West Bank and
Gaza... A strong local force will be established, which may include
Jordanian citizens ...

(c)   As soon as possible but not later than the third year after the
beginning of the transitional period, negotiations will take place to
determine the final status of the West Bank and Gaza ... and to
conclude a peace treaty between Israel and Jordan ...

. . . .

art.4.   Egypt and Israel will work with each other and with other
interested parties to establish agreed procedures for a prompt, just
and permanent implementation of the resolution of the refugee problem.

Source: U.S. Department of State Publication 8954, Near East and South Asian Series
88, September 1978, pp. 7–8 (excerpt).

with the new civilian authority, both because of their weakness facing the pro-PLO elements in the population and because of their allegiance to King Hussein, who also opposed Camp David.

Only in the very margins of society could Menachem Milson, the first head of the civilian administration (appointed in September 1981), find partners. These were the so-called Associations of Villagers. The first such association was officially registered in 1978 in Hebron. Soon endowed with substantial budgets for development projects (water, roads, technical assistance), this model of association had some success among the rural inhabitants of the West Bank. Several scores of such associations were set up during 1981–82, and their organizational roof was headed by a former minister in the Jordanian government, Mustafa Dudeen. Officially anti-PLO but "loyal to the Palestinian interest," most of these new groups were led by nonpolitical and unknown figures.

For the PLO as well as for Amman, however, membership in such associations was tantamount to treason. Hence, the head of a Ramallah association of villagers, Yussuf al-Khatib, was killed by a PLO squad, and others were threatened; the IDF distributed arms to the members of these groups. Jordan announced that any collaborator with these associations would be sentenced to death and his property confiscated. Many resignations were registered in the weeks that followed.[16] Similarly, nuclei of academics and professionals in Bethlehem and East Jerusalem who were ready to start a dialogue with Israel were soon paralyzed. They received some financial aid from the authorities to publish a newspaper, but this publication was boycotted by the population at large. These attempts led to nothing substantial.[17]

D. JEWISH SETTLEMENT

The efforts of the civilian authority were certainly not helped by the impetus given to Jewish settlement by the same government that had signed the Camp David Agreements and appointed Milson. Israel indeed gradually achieved control over a large part of the land that was the ground for a powerful movement of settlers. It was now one of the principal factors in the alienation of the Palestinians from the incumbents. In spite of the limitation by international law on seizure of land, by 1984 about one-third of the West Bank (1,500,000 dunams), concentrated around Jerusalem, the Jordan Valley, and West Samaria, had become the property of the Israeli government.[18]

For a large part, this land represents plots left behind by those who had fled the IDF in 1967 and had not returned. In addition, land registered as the property of the king of Jordan or of his administration is by law the Israeli government's, as is land defined as "vital for security needs." There are also plots that belonged to Jews before 1948 (Jewish communities existed in several places that were annexed by Jordan in 1948); these have now been returned to their families. Some Arabs have sold their land to Jewish individuals and institutions.

Private Arab land is not generally expropriated for settling purposes; a 1979 Supreme Court decision related to the Alon Moreh settlement ruled out this possibility. Nevertheless, including uncultivated land, which as such is automatically defined under Israeli rule as "state land," the space controlled by the authorities under one form or another amounts to no less than two-thirds of the territory in the West Bank (see exhibit 3.3.).

Following this trend, a 1966 Jordanian law of urban and rural planning has been reformulated. It places all bodies in charge of physical planning under the supervision of a Supreme Council for Planning, which is exclusively staffed by Israeli officials. This is an additional tool for encouraging the settlement of Jews in the area.

There were about 80 Jewish settlements in the West Bank in 1983; 79

Exhibit 3.3
Jewish Settlers in the West Bank

Year	Jewish Population on the West Bank	% of Jewish-Israeli Settlers in Total Population
1972	800	0.0
1976	3200	0.1
1977	4400	0.2
1978	7400	0.3
1979	10000	0.4
1980	12500	0.5
1981	16200	0.6
1982	(22000) estimate	

Source: G. Shafir, "Changing Nationalism and Israel's Open Frontier," Tel-Aviv
    University, mimeograph, 1984.
Data are compiled from the Statistical Yearbook of Israel, (1977: 23, 1978: 35, 1979: 35,
1982: 34)

more are planned.[19] The wide majority of these settlements are of a rural
nature (up to 300 families), but the urban concentrations will constitute
the majority of the population (from 1,000 to 10,000 each) in places like
Ariel, Elkana, and Maaleh Adumim. Until 1984, generous aid was offered for the acquisition of apartments (80 percent of the price on long-
term government loans).

The present Jewish population of the West Bank (1986) numbers about
25,000. These people have become objectively interested in the annexation of the territories by Israel, by virtue of their place of residence.
Their worst anxiety is a duplication of the withdrawal from Sinai dictated
by the Camp David accords, which involved evacuation of all the Jewish
settlements in that area. More particularly, the members of Gush Emunim ("the Bloc of the Faithful") are incessantly active on the public scene
against any expression of "defeatism." The movement is guided by a
mystic version of Zionist pioneerism that refers the tie with the land to
the biblical covenant between Israel and God. By no means is it ready
to compromise with the Palestinian national movement or any other
advocate of a withdrawal from Samaria, Judea, or Gaza.

For these people, "the struggle concerns the genuine dimensions of
Zionism . . . the process of redemption in its real meaning—the redemption of the people and the redemption of the land, and in its divine
meaning—the redemption of the Godhead, the redemption of the
world."[20]

The Arabs resent this presence of Jewish settlers, which indicates an
ambition toward irrevocable annexation of the area by Israel; their re-

lations with the Jews in Hebron and Nablus are fraught with incidents. The stoning of Jewish cars by Arabs is frequent, and the settlers respond with vigilantist actions that in some cases even include beatings and armed vandalism.[21]

In May 1984, an underground Jewish network was revealed that numbered about thirty people, among them active members of Gush Emunim, sons of rabbis, and IDF reserve officers. Almost all inhabitants of West Bank settlements,[22] they were accused of placing bombs in buses in East Jerusalem, of sabotaging the cars of several city mayors (Basam Shaqa of Nablus lost both legs in this action), and of attacking the Hebron Islamic College, where several students were killed.

Jewish-Arab relations have not been eased either by the daily subordination of Arabs to Israeli soldiers and policemen. A 1983 report prepared by the assistant to the legal adviser to the government, Yehudit Karp, showed that discrimination was quite frequent in the way policemen handled the problems of Arabs in events involving Jewish settlers. It was found that damages caused to Jews by Arabs were immediately taken care of but that the contrary was rarely the case. The latter type of complaint is most often ignored. Soldiers are also frequently tempted to "overdo it" when arresting Arabs for demonstrating or stoning. Some officers take a blatantly antagonistic attitude toward Arab civilians and are seldom removed from their functions even after their behavior is well known to their superiors.[23] Only on rare occasions are soldiers and officers put on trial for offenses of this kind.

E. REPRESSION

Repression itself is a matter of routine. Censorship of newspapers and books is a good example. The daily *al-Fajer*, the major Palestinian newspaper, represents the PLO line. Its distribution is not prohibited by the authorities, but it is banned whenever it attacks the Israeli government too bluntly or praises fedayeen activity with too much enthusiasm.[24] The journal responds by appealing to the Israeli Supreme Court of Justice, which often overrules the decision of the authorities. These, in turn, of course are also able to enter the legal labyrinth. In 1983, *al-Fajer* was sued on the grounds that it failed to comply with the legal requirement that every journal publish the name and address of its chief editor. Since, however, editor Jo Nasser had been kidnapped several years earlier, his actual "address" was unknown. In the meantime, as a result of a tacit "gentleman's agreement," *al-Fajer* was allowed to continue publication.

A particularly difficult problem for the censor is the control of the enormous literary production—poetry, novels, and essays—characterized by virulent nationalistic overtones. Paradoxically, the works of Israeli Arab poets and writers such as Samih al-Qasem, which are published in Israel, are officially forbidden distribution in Samaria or Judea. Even the Arabic translation of one of the books of Zeev Schiff, a Jewish moderate journalist and specialist on military matters, has been banned in the administered territories because of a foreword judged too anti-Israeli. The censor, then, must define guidelines beyond the mere banning of anti-Semitic pamphlets. These are among the major difficulties faced by any repressive military regime of occupation.[25]

Another example concerns the employment of foreign scholars at colleges and universities in the administered territories. These scholars, as a rule, are sympathetic to the Palestinian cause and on several occasions have expressed positive feelings for the PLO. Such statements are soon reported to the authorities, who demand the restriction of these scholars' freedom of movement. All foreign scholars were required to formally acknowledge the illegality of participating in anti-Israeli activities and organizations. The new regulation awoke a harsh debate, first in the territories and later in Israel, focusing on its repressive character.[26]

Israel also uses other, more unpleasant coercive means, the most radical of which is expulsion. Statistics, supplied by Israeli and Arab sources, differ widely on this matter, but the number of exiled persons to Jordan and Lebanon from 1967 to 1970, for example, seems to vary between twenty-five and thirty per year.[27] Neither can economic forms of manipulation be ignored. Well-known figures, for instance, may be subjected to various sanctions. Mustafa Natsha in Hebron was forced to close down his factory, and Muhammad Milhim in Halhul, his drugstore. Gamal Treifi of al-Bireh had to reduce the production of his quarry because he could not be supplied with dynamite.

House arrest is another sanction frequently utilized by the Israeli authorities against people accused of fomenting trouble. For many years Bashir Barqoti, a leading leftist, has been forbidden to leave his home village; this is also the case with Ibrahim Dakak, the head of the Engineers Union, and Samiha Halil, the president of the Association for the Family.

Other means of repression may be called "collective sanctions." Thus, in Hebron, the response to the killing of six Jewish settlers by a PLO squad included the destruction of the entire commercial block surrounding the settlers' house. The houses of fedayeen (sometimes even those who "just riot") are often blown up by official order. A case of special severity was that of a seventeen-year-old boy who stoned the car of Bethlehem's military governor. The youngster was caught on the spot and beaten up. His sister was soon fired from her position as a schoolteacher, and a few days later his parents were sent to Jericho on the Jordanian border.

Deterrence is the main motive for the use of coercion. It is hoped that such measures may keep direct involvement in PLO activities at its lowest possible level. It is expected that individuals and prominent figures will be less eager to actively support the Palestinian nationalist organizations if they know that the Israelis are prepared to impose significant sanctions in return. Similarly, environmental or collective punishments are meant to dissuade the many who are willing to close their eyes or even to offer aid to acts of sabotage, anti-Israeli rioting, or any other form of dissent. It is hoped that families will strengthen their control over their members who might engage in a course of action that would carry an unbearable price for all relatives. The intensification of such constraints, according to some, such as Arik Sharon, the defense minister in the early 1980s, should bring the day when "even one stone on an Israeli car will no longer be allowed."[28]

F. SOCIAL AND ECONOMIC TRANSFORMATIONS

Along with the vicissitudes of the occupation, however, a rapid growth of resources and a substantial improvement in the standard of living have characterized the administered territories and their populations since 1967. From a situation of very high unemployment before June 1967 (43 percent in the Gaza Strip, 13 percent in the whole area) and of frequent reliance on welfare money (70 percent in the Gaza Strip received such money, and for more than half of them, this was the only income), the annual average rate of increase reached 13 percent for the GNP between 1968 and 1979, 11 percent for the per capita income, 9 percent for the level of private consumption—all these in real terms.[29]

A few examples may illustrate the impact on the population. In 1974 electric or gas stoves were owned by 8.3 percent of the families in the Gaza Strip and the West Bank, while in 1979 the figure was 17 percent. In 1967, refrigerators were owned by 5 percent and televisions by 2 percent; by 1979 the figures were 42 percent and 47 percent, respectively. In 1968, there were 7,500 motor vehicles; in 1979, 33,000. Telephone ownership increased from 6,300 (1967) to 19,000 (1980). At the same time, unemployment was almost eradicated largely due to job opportunities in Israel: there were already 50,000 residents of the territories working in Israel in 1968; there were 73,000 in 1979.

Today as in the past, however, the major economic activity is still agriculture (37 percent of the GNP in 1980 on the West Bank).[30] Most of the peasants have small lots (48 percent of the agricultural units measure less than 20 dunams). Nevertheless, they have been able to increase their crops greatly with a minimum of professional Israeli guidance. At the same time, the number of workers employed in the fields has decreased from 44 percent of the local West Bank labor force in 1968 to 28 percent in 1979. One clear indication of this economic progress is that the Gaza Strip and the West Bank now represent the largest export market for Israel itself (consuming 25 percent of all Israel's exports).[31]

Yet these developments are by no means the expression of a particular Israeli concern: the civilian budget for administering the territories was a mere 1.7 percent of Israel's national budget in 1980; of this sum only one-tenth concerned development projects. The proximity of the territories to Israel and the related possibilities of employment of Arabs in the Jewish state are undoubtedly the major factors in the economic boom. Furthermore, the Israeli occupation of the West Bank and the Gaza Strip did also result in an influx of money from the PLO, Jordan, and the Arab world designed to sustain the *tsumud*, the "firm resistance" to the occupation.

Concomitantly, deep social changes have appeared. The educational system particularly underwent a genuine revolution. Vocational secondary education, for instance, witnessed from 1967 to 1981 the creation of twenty-six workshops in nineteen cities in fields such as carpentry, draftmanship and accountancy for boys and sewing, embroidery, and cosmetics, for girls. From 1967 to 1980 some 33,500 graduated from these schools.[32] The total number of children in any kind of school grew by 83 percent, of girls by no less than 95 percent. While in 1967, 57 percent of the children between ages five and eighteen attended class, the figure in 1980 was 87 percent.[33]

Finally, while in 1967 no institution for higher learning existed in the territories, in 1980 there were already five academic colleges, with 6,176 students and 311 lecturers (see exhibit 3.4).

Moreover, several other colleges are on their way to academic recognition. In 1983, a new college opened its doors in al-Bireh to join the Abu Dis College, which was established in the same town two years earlier. Similarly, three new colleges were established in Old Jerusalem. In a general manner, Jordan and the PLO provide the financial basis for these institutions of higher learning which are allowed to open their doors by the Israeli authorities. About 20,000 youngsters had completed high school education in 1983, 70 percent of them passing nationwide matriculation exams.[34] According to estimates, 98 percent of these youngsters remain in the country, and the most successful of these attend the local colleges and universities. Those who leave the country to study usually return afterward. Thus a new social stratum has appeared, strikingly distinct to the observer. On the campus, particularly, "[one] can see veiled female students 'à la Khomeini' while others, nice girls, are in jeans. Male students come and go. Some have a kefiah, others a tie and hold a James Bond case. The new mixes with the old, the conservative with the innovative."[35]

Exhibit 3.4
Universities in the Administered Territories (1980)

University	Founded	Recognition	Students	Lecturers*	Sponsors	Fields
Bir Zeit	1924	1973	1,367	124	Christian institut.	literature, natural sciences, education (BA & MA)
Freres University Bethlehem	1973	1973	811	85	Catholic institut.	Lit., nat. sc., soc. sc., hum., bus. admin., nursing
El-Najah Nablus	1918	1975	1,982	100		nat. sc., soc. sc., psy., educ., architecture, English
Islamic College Hebron	1971		473	25	local notables	Islamic studies (BA)
Al-Azhar Seminar Gaza	1954		200	40	Al-Azhar of Cairo	Islamic studies (2-year college level)

Source: The General Coordinator of Operations in the Territories, Thirteen-Year Survey, 1967–1980, Israel: Ministry of Defense, 1981: 22.

* 81 out of the 311 lecturers are nonresidents, most of them in Bir Zeyt.

G. A FORM OF THE WATCHING-OVER MODEL

In terms of the two basic strategies of incumbents toward the population that were described earlier, Israel's approach to the West Bank and Gaza may be characterized as a "watching-over" model. It is true that as far as the land itself is concerned, the Israeli political class is divided by many varied opinions. Regarding the Palestinian population, however, a wide consensus among the incumbents opposes any integration, and by no means do they seek local loyalties among the residents of the administered territories. Here, the keyword is deterrence, translated into the means employed to prevent inhabitants from cooperating too closely with insurgents. The role of repression is reflected in the attitude toward local media, the behavior of the IDF and the police during periods of unrest and otherwise, and the settlement of Jews in the administered territories.

Milson's attempt to find partners for talks while simultaneously attacking PLO political strongholds is a break in this picture. This attempt, however, has never been very systematic, nor has it been sustained by adequate resources. The only wide-scale investment of economic means here has been directed at Jewish newcomers. Thus, in the last analysis, even after 1980, the basic Israeli model has been closer to the watching-over model than to the penetration one. Few sacrifices were made, then, by the Israelis in favor of the population of the territories. The proximity of the *metropole* and the influx of resources from Jordan and the PLO caused impressive progress in terms of standard of living, education, and economic development. However, these improvements were not conditional upon the demonstration of allegiance to the incumbents, and they in no way moderated the repressive character of the regime.

The lack of interest in building the loyalty of the local occupied population is based upon the Israelis' own dedication to the Jewish character of their state, which could be threatened by too large an Arab minority. On the other hand, there is fear in Israel of a Palestinian state, too small, too poor, and too burdened with acute social problems to be satisfied with an enduring status quo.

In fact, the occupation of the West Bank and Gaza is understood as only one aspect of Israel's own struggle for official recognition by the Arab world. It provides an asset to sell, or a trump card to play, in the long-standing confrontation or "game" over the Middle East's acceptance of the presence of the Zionist state. Whatever the fate of these territories, it should be decided in relation to Israel's interests in the conflict with her neighbors.

In this sense, the Palestinian issue has long been neglected by the incumbents as a problem in itself. Having nothing substantial to offer to the Palestinians as such, Israel maintains a regime in the administered territories that does not aspire to be a focus of identification and legitimization but rather an instrument of domination—a watching-over model—until events turn a new page in the history of the region.

NOTES

1. M. Nissan, *Israel and the Territories: A Study in Control* (Ramat Gan: Turtledove, 1978); J. Soker, "Eight Years of Israeli Administration in the Territories," *Skira Hodshit* 7 (1975):7–9 (Hebrew).

2. General Coordinator of Operations in the Territories, *A Thirteen-Year Survey, 1967–1980* (Israel: Ministry of Defense, 1981); IDF, Principal Education Officer, *Israel: Two Years after the War*, Israel: IDF, 1969); R. Israeli, ed., *Ten Years of Israeli Rule in Judea and Samaria* (Jerusalem: Magnes, 1980).

3. M. Negbi, "The Supreme Court of Justice and Press Freedom," *Davar*, June 12, 1980, 9 (Hebrew); A. Hadad, "Five Years of Rule," *Haaretz*, June 5, 1972, 15 (Hebrew).

4. I. Alon, ed., *Ministers about the Territories* (Tel Aviv, published by the Israeli Labor party, 1973 [Hebrew]), 66.

5. A. Shalev, *Lines of Defense in Judea and Samaria* (Tel Aviv: Center for Strategic Studies, 1983 [Hebrew]), 21–95.

6. Alon, 68.

7. I. Landers, "Three Theses about the Status of the Territories," *Davar*, November 28, 1979, 7.

8. Alon, 74.

9. S. Gazit, "About the Civilian Administration," *Davar*, March 19, 1982, 13.

10. Nissan, 85; R. Halabi, *There Is a Limit: The Story of the West Bank* (Jerusalem: Keter, 1983 [Hebrew]).

11. J. Habakuk, "Who Is Who in the Territories," *Haaretz*, December 7, 1980, 20–21.

12. Halabi, 27.

13. S. Gazit, "Five Years in the Occupied Territories," in *The Arab-Israeli Conflict*, (Jerusalem: Ministry of Education, 1975 [Hebrew]).

14. J. Litani, "Encouraging Moderates or Encouraging Illusions?" *Haaretz*, December 31, 1978, 9; Z. Barel, "The West Bank without Mayors," *Haaretz*, June 19, 1983, 8.

15. M. Milson, "How to Do Peace?" *Davar*, January 8, 1982, 8, 13, 24.

16. Z. Barel, "Autonomy of Associations," *Haaretz*, September 2, 1982, 9.

17. J. Litani, "Leaders in the Past," *Haaretz*, November 30, 1981, 9; R. Podhatsur, "Autonomy of Failure," *Haaretz*, May 13, 1983, 12–13; Z. Schiff, "New Rules," *Haaretz*, December 12, 1980, 13.

18. J. M. Benvenisti, *Preliminary Report, No. 1: The West Bank Data Base Project* (mimeograph), n.d.: 14–17.

19. Ibid., 27.

20. G. Shafir, "Changing Nationalism and Israel's 'Open Frontier' in the West Bank," Tel Aviv University, Department of Sociology, 1984 (mimeograph), 20.

21. Ibid., 22.

22. *Koteret Rashit*, February 5, 1984.

23. A. Eilon, "The People of the Book," *Haaretz*, March 12, 1982, 13.

24. M. Negbi, "The Supreme Court of Justice and Press Freedom in the Territories," *Davar*, June 12, 1980, 9.

25. El-Peleg, *Davar*, October 20, 1980, 16; Y. Beilin, "With Silk Gloves," *Davar*, December 3, 1976, 16–17.

26. A. Levav, *Maariv*, December 3, 1982.

27. B. E. O'Neil, *Armed Struggle in Palestine: A Political and Military Analysis* (Boulder, Colo.: Westview Press, 1978), 67.

28. *Haaretz*, November 17, 1981.

29. General Coordinator, 3.

30. Benvenisti, 7.

31. Ibid., 9.

32. Ibid., 5.

33. Ibid., 19.

34. *Haaretz*, October 3, 1983.

35. D. Rubinstein, *Davar*, September 2, 1980, 5.

4 The Antiguerrilla Military Alignment

A. THE DEFENSIVE ALIGNMENT

Israel's policy against the PLO's paramilitary activity is much more comprehensive than its attitude vis-à-vis the civilian population. The IDF alignment is concerned primarily with the security within the administered territories and in Israel. In reality, however, it cannot confine itself to these areas, because the PLO also fights from outside of them. Thus, the IDF has had to reach the borders and cross them. After the Six-Day War, the IDF's first move was to deploy troops throughout the newly occupied territories.[1] Garrisons were settled in former Jordanian camps, and paratrooper or selected infantry ("Golani") units built training bases. These troops carried out motorized patrols between villages and in the cities. They were in charge of the security in public buildings and of identity checks on the road. In every district, a unit of Border Police under the local military command was charged with responsibility for current security while the men of the Shabak, the General Security Service, were weaving their intelligence networks within the population.

This alignment has become increasingly sophisticated in response to the problems that have confronted it over time. Infiltrations of PLO squads from Jordan or Lebanon were answered by a complex system of defense along Israel's borders. This included a road for motorized patrols, watch towers, electronic detection devices, and a two-meter-high illuminated barbed wire wall. If all these fail, a dust path between the wire and the road will show footprints revealing the direction and number of infiltrators. This system is manned by thousands of soldiers constantly, day and night.[2]

Gradually, the military control of the population has become more and more severe. A decision was made that inhabitants of the West Bank and the Gaza Strip who worked in Israel would not be allowed to stay overnight. Cars from Nablus and Ramallah were frequently stopped and searched by the military or the Border Police; those who crossed the bridges to Jordan were carefully interrogated and checked.

Jewish settlements along the borders, both new ones in the Jordan Valley and the Golan Heights and older ones along the Lebanese border, were strengthened by small contingents of soldiers, while the inhabitants themselves were given weapons and were mobilized to participate in guard duties. According to Israeli strategic thinking, these settlements situated on major arteries should constitute a force able to slow down a major sudden attack from the border, providing the IDF time to operate its reserves.[3] Therefore, it was important to supply a variety of weapons to those settlements, to build fortifications, and to assure the regular military training of the inhabitants. Such arrangements were deemed essential, both for the eventual contribution of the settlements to an Israeli-Arab conventional conflict and for an efficient self-defense against unconventional small-scale Palestinian actions.

The passive defense system of Israel, which covers the whole country, consists primarily of rescue units, which must be rapid, professional, and well trained.[4] In case of emergency, they must reach civilian victims as soon as possible and administer first aid before transporting them to the hospital. This network also includes regular reserve military units, which are generally composed of older men. These soldiers are in charge of security on public sites (roads, cinemas, or shopping centers) in normal times, and in case of emergency, they can quickly be sent with their own weapons, vehicles, and communication equipment to any point where military manpower is necessary.

Passive defense is not to be confused with the civilian guard, a vast body of tens of thousands of civilians who voluntarily carry out guard duties in schools or hospitals and patrol residential neighborhoods at night. This civilian guard constitutes the backbone of a disciplined organization of nonmilitary population.

If a terrorist incident takes place, however, the special antiterror unit is called first. This unit arrives at the site of action, by car or by helicopter, while regular soldiers and policemen close the area to the public and block any possibility of escape for the attackers. Within the area itself, the antiterror unit is joined by elite sharpshooters, headquarters officers, and government officials, usually from the Ministry of Defense. When the terrorists hold hostages, the civilian authorities start negotiating, although this is generally done only to facilitate the military action.

The antiterror operation does not always end with success. In Maalot, a Galilean town, a Palestinian squad killed more than twenty children. Similarly, several civilians lost their lives in a fedayeen attack against a Tel Aviv hotel. When such actions take place in the administered territories, a curfew is immediately ordered in the area, houses are searched, inhabitants are eventually checked for identification and questioned, and dozens of suspects are apprehended.

In 1978, a PLO squad that arrived by sea hijacked a Tel Aviv-bound bus; the incident resulted in dozens of deaths. Since then the shores have also been watched regularly by key forces.[5] These consist primarily of the rapid and well-armed Dabur gunboats, radar stations, and motorized shore patrols. They also use Israeli-made Westwind planes to discover boats and submarines.

The defensive Israeli alignment, however, extends beyond the sea, as well; it involves numerous types of activity abroad.[6] It responds to actions such as the PLO's diversion of an El Al plane to Algiers in 1969, the shooting at El Al passengers in Munich Airport in February 1970, the Swissair disaster a few weeks later, the unsuccessful attack on an El Al flight in September 1970, and the Japanese Red Army massacre in Lod in May 1972. To such agressiveness, the Israelis do respond with original solutions.

Every airport with plane connections to or from Israel has to take special security measures, implemented jointly by local and Israeli personnel. Every El Al flight is accompanied by armed guards. Local troops protect the landing and the takeoff of Israel-bound flights. Special procedures for checking luggage are defined.[7] Over time, Israeli land and air personnel are given special antihijacking training in weapons, first aid, and basic psychology.

Similarly, Israeli institutions, embassies, consulates, and other agencies are protected by cooperation between Israeli and local security services. In several countries, for instance, local policemen guard the Israeli premises from the outside and Israeli security men guard from the inside. Armored doors are the rule for many institutions.

B. THE OFFENSIVE ALIGNMENT

Israel's main antiguerrilla efforts, however, concern its offensive alignment, which is principally based on the intelligence services.[8] Israeli intelligence places great importance on the study of its enemy's ideological and political perspectives and attempts to gather the widest information about the different tendencies, characters, orientations, and "specializations" of the various Palestinian movements. The structures of the organizations are another target for intelligence, as are their patterns of recruitment, the motivations of their members, and their political links. The more firmly anchored the sources of information within the PLO itself, the more crucial the knowledge they may eventually yield, possibly even including long-range plans and future operations. Since fedayeen squads in operation are given a wide margin of freedom, to be used according to field circumstances, the antiguerrillas' interest is to infiltrate both the circles of decision makers and the operational units. This latter case involves a number of particular difficulties. First, the operation of transmitting information is extremely complex. Second, in their use of this information, the incumbents must take special precautions so as not to injure their informers and their own people.

Within the guerrilla movement, the structures that are most easily infiltrated are of two kinds: the nonfighting services, linking the paramilitary forces and the political bodies; and the organizational frameworks, which bind the latter to the civilian population. These weaker links, according to the Israeli approach, should be exploited to penetrate the guerrilla movement with undercover agents, assuming an ideological commitment. Such agents may thus be able to climb the military hierarchy, particularly in light of the high rate of turnover of operational leaders in this type of struggle.

Another precious source of information is found in the prisoners. This source must be exploited immediately; once the insurgents' headquarters learn about the capture of their men, they are liable to take precautions that render the information useless. For this reason, incumbents are reluctant to announce the arrest of terrorists before getting all their information. Consequently, members of the intelligence service often accompany antiguerrilla operations, in order to start the investigation of prisoners "on the spot." This may lead to immediate continuation of the operation (to catch people in their hideouts, locate weapons, and the like).

In some cases—and they are apparently quite frequent—intelligence discovers information that cannot be used in regular, open military operations but only by specialists, taking action in the shadows like the guerrilla himself. Examples of such cases might include the pursuit of key members of the guerrilla movement outside of their bases or fighting the guerrillas' intelligence networks. Such actions compel the insurgents to strengthen their defensive apparatus and, sometimes, to perpetually shuttle from place to place.

Another important aspect of antiguerrilla tactics is the operation of psychological warfare. By propagating stories about prisoners, for instance, false information is transmitted about plans, equipment, or knowledge of the incumbents in order to mislead the insurgents. The main goal of psychological warfare, however, is to influence the motivation of the individual guerrilla fighter. This involves the diffusion of rumors that may shake the guerrilla leaders' authority, give a positive image to those who have "understood their past errors," and influence quarrels between rival organizations.

These tactics seem to be widely applied by the Shabak (the General Security Service). Since 1967, it has stood several paces ahead of its enemy in this respect. No less than 85 percent of sabotage cases in Israel and in the administered territories are solved every year; most operators are captured or eliminated. Most cells of the PLO in the territories are "neutralized" before any action—in 1979, out of 138, 114 cells were dismantled before they had acted, only 29 of which were already fully equipped; the figures are respectively 146, 103, and 26 for 1978; 109, 77, and 37, for 1977. To obtain such results, the Shabak had to infiltrate the PLO networks deeply and recruit hundreds of informants among the population.[9]

The collaboration of inhabitants, obviously, is more frequent when the PLO is weaker within the population of the neighborhood, refugee camp, or village in question. On the other hand, the PLO has learned to isolate its cells from one another, even when they have to cooperate in some operations. In such cases, only one person knows the whole scheme of the operation, and this individual transmits the specific orders directly to each group regarding the supply of the weapons or vehicles or operation of the explosives.

Such an arrangment requires that the Shabak, in turn, be more imaginative. According to a rumor, for instance, in the early 1980s a head of the Fatah in the Gaza Strip was made to tell all he knew in a most unconventional way. His hideout had been located after several months of searching; it was an orange plantation in the southern part of the strip, at the Egyptian border. The place was surrounded by Israeli soldiers, and the man fired back until he was wounded and lost consciousness. Several hours later he woke up in an "Egyptian" hospital. Nurses and doctors speaking Arabic with Egyptian accents surrounded him until a high-ranking "Egyptian" intelligence officer entered the room. Explaining to the man that he had been saved by Egyptian forces from within the plantation, he questioned him in detail. Totally confident, the Fatah leader delivered everything he knew to the Shabak.

Intelligence abroad is left to the Mossad (the Institute, in Hebrew). Because the Mossad operates in foreign countries, its actions receive more media coverage. Thus, it has been said that Mossad men killed Hassan Salama, one of the chief military commanders of the PLO, in January 1979 in Beirut. Six years earlier, supposedly, a Mossad-guided mission killed three prominent figures of the Fatah in the same city. In October 1979, Hainal Hindi, a writer by profession and the PLO's representative in Cyprus, was dangerously wounded by the explosion of his car in Limasol. One year earlier, two other members of the PLO Cyprus office had been killed in the street and on October 19, 1981, the head of the propaganda department of the PLO was also killed in his Roman hotel. All these events were ascribed to the Mossad.[10]

The late 1970s and the early 1980s witnessed an intense secret war between the Israelis and the Palestinians in numerous countries. The latter hit embassies or Jewish institutions, the former key PLO men.

Such actions require special task forces in addition to the intelligence networks.[11] Antiterror units operating abroad obviously exist, but very little information, if any, has been discovered.

In Israel, two antiterror units exist. One is a section of the Border Police, under the authority of the national police, and the other belongs to the army. These units are very selective and are trained and equipped for all forms of face-to-face combat. Quite often, they operate in civilian clothes. When necessary, these units are assisted by sharpshooters and other specialists. They are highly mobile, employing special vehicles and helicopters. On emergency duty twenty-four hours a day, they are able to reach any point of the country in minimal time. Their physical training includes shooting from moving cars, jumping from vehicles, attacking ground targets from helicopters, and landing on house roofs. They are also expected to know Arabic and geography, including in-the-field orientation.

C. KINDS OF ACTIVITY AND FORCES

The Israeli military antiguerrilla capacity includes a variety of patterns and types of forces, appropriate to both the defensive and offensive alignments. In accordance with the evolution of the conflict's forms, at any given point in time, some forces are emphasized more while others are drawn to the back of the stage. Some forces—such as the Shabak, the Mossad, and the antiterror units—are always active but as far from publicity as possible.

In the early 1970s there were frequent infiltrations of PLO squads from Lebanon against schools, buses, and private homes. Israel reacted by building the defensive border system, while attacks in Lebanon (e.g., the destruction of Middle East Air planes by commandos in Beirut) served as retaliation. It was expected that Lebanon, if held responsible for the PLO activities from its soil, would react by limiting the Palestinians' freedom of maneuvers. Commando units were then most instrumental.

The political equilibrium in Lebanon, however, was vacillating while the Palestinians' coalition with the anti-Christians (the Druzes, the Shiites, and the Sunnites) was gaining power. Israel's reaction gradually changed accordingly; air raids and sea attacks were used against the PLO bases more frequently. Paratroopers and selective infantry (Golani) units were used for ambushes within Lebanon and for the occupation of villages in nightly search operations against Palestinian squads. During the late 1970s, Israel took advantage of the divisions between Lebanese militia; its closest ties were with the Phalangists the major paramilitary force of the Maronite party, whom it armed. It also actively supported a southern Lebanese Christian force. The territory controlled

by this force was substantially widened in 1978 with the Litani operation, whereby Israel occupied a strip of land between its border and the Litani River for several weeks. This operation cleared this area of PLO bases and preceded the vast 1982 invasion of Lebanon by the IDF. All the various branches of the IDF participated in these episodes. In 1982, especially sophisticated antiguerrilla tactics such as encirclement were used, compelling the guerrilla commandos to engage in conventional combat and to succumb to the superior forces. Despite the repeated use of the same tactics as the troops advanced northward, the surprise effect was maintained by the use of sea forces for landing soldiers at unexpected spots.

On the other hand, the demonstrations in the administered territories were another challenge that required its own tactics. Ever since 1967— whether in response to the appeal of Jordan, of the PLO, or both— shopkeepers' strikes, boycotts of schools, riots, and car stonings periodically disturbed daily life in the territories. Curfews were imposed, and armored vehicles and numerous troops were often called in. A particularly instrumental force in this respect has been the Border Police, who since the 1970s have been undergoing special training for handling civil unrest. Its men usually patrol by car; they carry light equipment including gas masks and tear grenades.[12]

Many of the Border Policemen who serve in the administered territories are Israeli Druzes or Arabs. Their presence is expected to ease the relations with the inhabitants. The intensity of the problem of public disorder in these territories, however, has unavoidably raised the question of the individual soldier's reactions to incidents. Every soldier serving here receives a written statement from the Higher Command that prescribes in detail the appropriate behavior toward the population in any situation. With respect to the use of firearms, it is specified that shooting is justified only if it is necessary for saving human life. Even then a verbal warning must be given and the first shot must be fired 80 degrees in the air. If shooting at people is nevertheless necessitated, the fire should be directed toward the feet and used only on the order of the highest-ranking officer on the site. Furthermore, firearms may be legitimately operated only after water, tear gas, sticks, rubber bullets, and any other means at the soldier's disposal have been tried and shown ineffective.[13]

Yet, and as shown in Chapter 3, the situations that cause confrontation between soldiers and inhabitants in the administered territories are so varied and frustrating that young officers and soldiers often have to make decisions under the impulses of the moment. Behaviors that contrast with regular Israeli norms are therefore frequent. Beating civilians on unjustified grounds and unnecessary firing on rioters often occur.[14]

D. THE MILITARY MODEL: A DEFINITION

The above description indicates that Israel's military response to guerrilla violence combines both defensive and offensive alignments. The context of this deployment includes the emphasis in the Israeli consensus upon the vital character of any matter related to national security. This ethos requires an unconditional readiness to invest any means in whatever issue is defined as imperative for the security of the Jewish state. Israel possesses the necessary resources: a very large army, a developed war industry, and advanced technology. It is true that the guerrilla side feels at ease in the desert and in caves, in the populated casbah of Nablus or Ramallah, and in the refugee camps. Nevertheless, the West Bank and the Gaza Strip are restricted territories, and the IDF shows a high capacity of adjustment to most varied situations. It is against a well-greased and far-reaching war machine that the PLO aspires to emerge according to Mao's teaching as "a fish swimming in the sea."

NOTES

1. S. Gazit, "Five Years to the Administered Territories," in *The Israeli-Arab Conflict*, ed. E. Gilboa and M. Naor (Tel Aviv: Matkal Ed., 1981 [Hebrew]), 225–55.

2. *Maariv*, April 1, 1980.

3. A. Shalev, *Lines of Defense in Judea and Samaria* (Tel Aviv: Center for Strategic Studies, 1983 [Hebrew]).

4. I. Zayad, "Territorial Defense and Civilian Defense in Anti-Terror War," *Maarakhot*, 1979, 270–71 (Hebrew).

5. Colonel Moshe, "The Defense of Shores against Infiltrations," *Maarakhot* 283 (1980), 51–60 (Hebrew).

6. "Arab Terror and the Fight against It," *Daf Lamasbir* (Jerusalem: Merkaz Hahasbarah, (1972) [Hebrew]), 17.

7. *Dapei Meda* (1970) no. 11.

8. S. Gazit and M. Hendel, "Intelligence against Terror Organizations," *Maarakhot* 278 (1981), 10–15.

9. Z. Schiff, *Haaretz*, June 9, 1980.

10. *Davar*, October 10, 1980; *Haaretz*, January 24, 1979.

11. Unofficial sources.

12. Interview with Moshe K., a captain on duty in the West Bank.

14. Z. Schiff, *Haaretz*, May 10, 1982.

5 Palestinian Politics under Israeli Occupation

A. 1967: EVENTS AND CONJUNCTURE

The Six-Day War ended with an Israeli presence in the West Bank, the Gaza Strip, the Sinai Peninsula, and the Golan Heights. The events were rapid and had an astounding effect on the Palestinian population. Caught by panic, thousands of families left everything behind and sought refuge on the other side of the Jordan River. Soon after June, however, the cautious Israeli attitude calmed the newly occupied population. In addition, throngs of tourists visited the historical and religious sites, bringing to the restaurants, hotels, and open markets an unprecedented boom.

This was also the time, however, that Yasser Arafat and the Palestinian underground were trying to expand their influence, while from Amman, King Hussein launched campaigns of protest in order to maintain his own authority. Thus, a few months after the end of the Six-Day War the first shock wave of terrorist actions hit, amplified by shop strikes and school boycotts. Terrorism, however, was unable to weaken the Israeli presence, which destroyed the PLO's hope of escalating the conflict into a "revolutionary war."

As a result, Arafat and his lieutenants left Jerusalem for the East Bank. Amman's expectations of a civil revolt, too, proved unrealistic, as the strikes and boycotts were less of a nuisance to the Israelis than to the Palestinians themselves. A relatively calm situation was restored in the West Bank until 1969, and until 1972 in the Gaza Strip.

Within the politicized strata, among the political "families," however, new processes that would be of great importance in the following years were already in motion.[1] The strongest faction in 1967 was made up of pro-Jordan leaders who had been a part of the Hashemite establishment. They included people like Muhammad al-Jaabari of Hebron; Anwar Nusayba and Anwar al-Khatib of Jerusalem; and Hichmat al-Masri and Mazuz al-Masri of Nablus. Their counterparts in Gaza were Rashid al-Shawa and his friends. These people had been members of Parliament in Amman and members of the Gaza Assembly; they had been ministers and diplomats, mayors, and heads of central agencies. Committed generally to the status quo ante (except for the attachment of the Gaza Strip to Jordan, which they supported) this "family" was not reluctant to reach practical arrangements with Israel. Associated with this faction, though constituting a new generation within its ranks, was a group of less aristocratic origin, made up of upwardly mobile professionals and businessmen. Most had studied in foreign universities and had been employed in the civil service. Moved by pragmatic considerations, like the former group, they, however, were somewhat more conscious of the Palestinian question.

Another group was more popular among the urban middle and lower middle class, peasants, and residents of the refugee camps. This school had always been in direct opposition to the former; it comprised anti-Hashemite movements.[2] Among these were the Muslim Brothers, religious fundamentalists who opposed any differentiation between state and religion and who aspired to a renewal of Arab unity grounded in Islam. Similarly unitarian but based on a nonreligious nationalist outlook, Nasserism was well alive in the political life of the Palestinian society. It was close to—though in competition with—the more socialist-oriented all-Arab Baathist nationalism.

Finally, there was the Communist party. It was small and tightly structured within a complex web of cells that were actively involved in a wide variety of sociopolitical organizations. They had outstanding leaders in Bethlehem (George Hisbon) and Beit Sahur (Atalla Rishmawi) and strong networks in Nablus, Jerusalem, and Gaza. In contrast to all other factions, the Communists openly recognized Israel's right to exist. This attitude, however, reflected that the bond to Soviet policy was not necessarily related to practical stands vis-à-vis Israel; Soviet interests in the Middle East conflicts were frequently ambiguous.

Palestinian nationalism was the third political family in the 1967 occupied territories. Encompassing many new middle-class elements and refugees, it was basically anti-Hashemite like the second school but was obviously more localist, emphasizing the Palestinian issue. Different groups variously related the "Palestinian revolution" to the "Arab revolution" and "Palestinian nationalism" to "Arab socialism." All of them, however, primarily referred to the "liberation of Palestine," and this reference was most virulently and determinedly anti-Israeli. In the course of time, the Fatah, PFLF, DFLP, al-Saiqa, and the other groups created new forms of coalitions and injected new dynamics into their

PLO roof organization, which was emerging as the principal political factor in the administered territories.

Yet, in the late 1960s, the calm situation in the territories hardly announced the troubled future. Jaabari himself welcomed the first Jewish settlers in Hebron in 1968. For several weeks they were lodged in a hotel belonging to the family of Fahd Qawasmeh, the future successor to Jaabari as mayor of the city. The same Qawasmeh was later expelled by the Israelis. The settlers established a definitive Jewish neighborhood, Kiryat Arba, on Jaabari's land with his consent.

The calm situation in the territories during this period was not unrelated to the events that took place in Jordan in September 1970, following the PLO's strengthening on the East Bank. Hussein's army launched fierce attacks on PLO bases and liquidated the fedayeen presence in his country. Shortly after this campaign, a diplomatic campaign was initiated by Amman in favor of the creation of a federation between the two banks. Israel exploited this move, as well as the influence of September's events, in order to organize elections of the municipalities, which, under the circumstances, were in effect the major local Palestinian bodies.[3]

The elections in the West Bank, held in 1972, drew 84 percent participation. (No elections were held in the Gaza Strip, since under the Egyptian code such elections were not stipulated.) This turnout was an extraordinary success, especially since the PLO had called for a boycott. In almost every municipality the pro-Jordanian candidates overcame the other parties. In particular in Nablus, 73 percent participation was registered, despite numerous threats made to candidates and several acts of sabotage against their property.[4]

The results show a 50 percent average rate of turnover of council members. Politically and socially, however, the change was minimal; the same forces and the same types of leaders were elected.[5] One exception forecast future developments and reflected new processes: the election of a new mayor in Ramallah, Karim Khalaf, who was pro-DFLP.

The following elections for the various commercial offices—in Jenin in October 1972, in Nablus in January 1973, and later in all other cities—confirmed the solid hold of the pro-Hashemite notables. In this climate, the Israelis accepted the founding of universities and colleges, often sponsored by the traditional leadership.[6] At the same time, the occurrence of terrorist acts decreased sharply—from 339 acts with 105 victims in 1971 to 34 acts with 7 victims in 1972.[7]

In October 1973, the Yom Kippur War broke out. An all-Arab solidarity was exhibited by an oil embargo on "friends" of Israel such as Holland. The Arab League did not hesitate to issue threats of precipitating a general world oil crisis. On the battlefield, Israel's military superiority was shaken by the surprise effect of a well-coordinated Egyptian-Syrian offensive. In 1974, in Rabat, an enthusiastic Arab summit crowned the PLO the sole legitimate representative of the Palestinian people, thereby neutralizing Jordanian activity in the administered territories. These events expanded the scope of processes that were already in motion. The new universities appeared dominated by PLO influence, as did the new newspapers that were licensed to publish.

In parallel, terrorist actions gradually grew as the Lebanese bases that replaced those lost in Jordan became operational. On April 11, 1974, a squad of the PFLP General Command killed sixteen civilians and two soldiers; one month later (May 15) a DFLP group attacked a school in a Galilean town (Maalot), which resulted in twenty deaths and seventy wounded, mostly children. The streets in the administered territories were less peaceful; the PLO became more popular and many understood the Rabat decisions as commanding an irrevocable struggle for the destruction of Israel. For others, these decisions meant that the PLO could be Israel's only partner in any future settlement of the conflict.[8] The PLO's growing influence and support were further strengthened by the United Nations' decision (October 1974) to invite the PLO to the General Assembly debate on the Palestinian problem, and a few weeks later to give Arafat himself the floor (November 1974). This climate was not unrelated to the failure of the secret negotiations between Jordan and Israel (August 29 and October 19, 1974).

B. PROTEST AND ENROLLMENT

The first territories-wide protest wave after 1968 broke out in February 1976. The direct pretext was a public prayer held by a small number of Jews on the Temple Mount, near the Omar and al-Aqsa mosques. The first day of demonstration attracted only five hundred persons; but in the following days and weeks, thousands crowded in the centers of all major cities in the West Bank. The Border Police and paratroopers were called in to restore order.[9] Several children were killed in the violent dispersion of these gatherings. However, the hour of peaceful cooperation still seemed within reach. Once the immediate situation was calm, the incumbents still believed that cooperation could be renewed. Thus, in 1976, new municipal elections were held as scheduled. However, the Baathist, Basam Shaqa, won the elections in Nablus; a pro-PFLP, Muhammad Milhim, won in Halhul; and the pro-DFLP Ibrahim al-Tawil, in Al-Bireh, and Bshara Daud, in Beit Jalla, were elected. Qawasmeh won for the Fatah in Hebron. The only pro-Jordanian to be reelected in a big city was Bethlehem's Elias Frej. The growing popularity of the PLO in the world, in the context of the Yom Kippur War and the strengthened all-Arab solidarity, only partly accounts for these results.

While Arafat, more than anyone else, represented the Palestinian cause in the world, many voted in Nablus, Ramallah, and Al-Bireh for George Habash and Naief Hawatmeh. This reflected the systematic organizational work of factions that were a minority in the PLO as a whole and therefore were highly motivated to develop and strengthen their constituency in the field.

The Left's anchorage in the population of the administered territories had been well prepared by a Palestinian National Front, which was created in 1973, during the days of calm before the Yom Kippur War.[10] Initiated in the underground by the Communists, the PNF drew strong participation from the PFLP and the DFLP. The Communists sponsored this framework with the purpose of joining the Palestinian revolutionary movement with the help of the PLO's left wing. They collaborated enthusiastically with the most radical elements, leaving the door open to only a few Fatah representatives.[11]

The PNF was soon hit hard by the expulsion of several of its leaders from the territories. Yet its two years of the only official existence (it was definitively outlawed only in October 1979) marked a turn in the organizational-political process in the Palestinian movement. The model of political structure and the techniques of political articulation illustrated by the Communists were quickly adopted by the major nationalist movements in close contact with them within the PNF. Numerous specialized networks addressing themselves to different social categories were established and activated by people who did not always declare their membership in the mother movement.

There was, for instance, the unofficially Communist Working Women's Organization, which had branches in several towns and cities. It organized courses and lectures and was a convenient channel for the party's propaganda. Another organization established in collaboration with the Israeli Communist party was the Committee for the Prisoner and His Family. This group was aimed at aiding the relatives of Palestinians imprisoned in Israeli jails, and it eventually sponsored interventions with the authorities in their favor. More instrumental for civil unrest campaigns, a high school student movement and voluntary working committees were committed to what is euphemistically called "community action," which deals mainly with the organization of political demonstrations and distribution of written propaganda. However, the major stronghold of the Communist party was the Trade Union Confederation, in which it dominated about half of the professional branches (twenty out of forty).

By following this model, the PFLP, the DFLP, and even the Fatah tried to anchor themselves within the population. In the process, however, they got involved in numerous conflicts among themselves and with the Communists. One example was the opposition of those branches of the Trade Union Confederation led by the Communists and the leftists against those sectors dominated by the Fatah. New conflicts and splits also arose between the leftists and the Communists within this same confederation and within unions. Similarly, by gradually rejecting both the Fatah and the Communists, the leftists also increased their influence among the Association of Palestinian Writers, which has been active enough to organize yearly public conventions.

The leftists, like the Fatah, have their own voluntary working committees and high school movements. The DFLP is particularly influential in the Jerusalem Club of Civil Servants, which numbers several hundred members, and in Samiha Halil's Association for the Family. Created in 1965, this latter movement declared itself at its onset as intended to aid underprivileged families but became a major institution on its own, involved in a great variety of domains.[12] It organized a Committee for Research on the Palestinian Legacy; it publishes a "Monthly of Society and Legacy"; it has opened a study center for girls and a library. It also grants scholarships and subventions for higher education, as well as assistance for the education of small children. It runs a network of souvenir and folklore shops, employing numerous women at weaving and knitting work. It established a folklore museum in 1972. This immense activity requires about 400,000 dinars per year in the early 1980s; the municipalities have been the organization's major official source of funding. Israel is not required to contribute, since, as Samiha Halil says, "we won't beg anything from those who fight against the goals of our nation."[13] The leftists seem to have surpassed the Communists on this level of political organization, while the Fatah remains somewhat behind.

As for the pro-Jordan notables, who were the strongest party only a few years before, though weakened and silenced temporarily, they remained in control of important assets. The Israeli occupation, it is true, removed them from the positions they held in the Jordanian establishment, without granting them any compensatory advantage. No longer were they ministers, MPs, or high-ranking officials, and they lost much of their former power over wide segments of the population. However, they still dominated institutions such as the Supreme Islamic Council and the Office for Muslim Affairs (the Waqf). The first body was reorganized in July 1967 as the Islamic leadership in Jerusalem. It is the major authority over Muslim holy sites, and it founded the Jerusalem Fund, officially recognized by the World Muslim Conference. The Waqf was reestablished by Jordan in 1966 in order to be in charge of all Muslim religious matters. It was headed then by the mufti of Jerusalem, Sheikh Sad al-Alami. Although these organizations were of limited importance in the public life of the Palestinian population, the wide resources channeled through them reached numerous related interest groups.

In another area, the Association of Commercial Offices, which has existed since 1969, is led by rich businessmen, generally of pro-Jordanian allegiance. This association is a roof for local offices (Nablus, Bethlehem, Ramallah, Al-Bireh, Hebron, Jenin, Tulkarem, Jericho, Kelkilyah, Jerusalem); its headquarters are located in Jerusalem. These offices are linked to branch-based agencies, such as the numerous associations for the marketing of agricultural products. This sector, as a whole, is deeply interested in solid ties with the Hashemites, because the largest part of the territories' external trade with the Arab Middle East depends on the bridges over the Jordan River. Finally, the pro-Jordanian party is also in control of a veteran women's organization run by women of traditional families.

This general picture shows both high organizational density and a political and social diversity. Trade unions, women's organizations, youth movements, university clubs, and charity associations all serve as meeting places for politicized people under the guise of social or cultural interests. Some frameworks—mostly unions—exist on paper only for the purpose of obtaining financial support from the outside. On the other hand, the groups that are active are eventually forced by the incumbents to go underground. The incumbents, however, hesitate to outlaw such clubs or unions, which are generally more efficiently controlled when regulated by an official license. These circumstances, in fact, also imply competition and rivalry among these groups and organizations. Under a regime of occupation, however, cooperation is essential. It is well known in the field that the House of the Trade Unions in Beit Haninah, near Jerusalem, is a site of frequent coordination meetings. This building was originally the home of various professional associations; in the late 1970s it became the informal "Parliament of Occupied Palestine."

Another Parliament is the Council for Higher Education, in existence since 1977, which was created in response to the multiplication of universities and colleges. The proclaimed goal of this body concerns the technical and academic problems of the institutions it supervises. In fact, its members include not only representatives of universities but also heads of cities, social organizations, and trade unions—in 1980, there were fifty-five members in all, thirty-eight West Bankers and seventeen Gazeans. These people are also representative of movements and, unofficially, constitute a kind of national political body.

Yet the disagreements cannot be hidden from anyone. Internal discussions at Beit Haninah and at the Council for Higher Education are revealed in public. Since the early 1970s dailies, weeklies, and monthlies of all allegiances have regularly published their respective parties' propaganda—about the common enemy, Israel, and about themselves and their rivals.

Al-Quds, for instance, founded in 1968, represents the pro-Jordan line under the management of its owner, Mahmud Abu Zuluf. Hence, this journal is the object of especially heavy pressures from the nationalists (in 1975, Abu Zuluf's car was bombed).[14] *Al-Shab* began publication in 1972; its sympathy goes to the PFLP and the DFLP. It is owned by Mahmud Ali Yaish, who is a devoted pro-Syrian. The editor, Ali al-Khatib, was expelled to Lebanon in 1975. *Al-Fajer* has been published since 1972, daily since 1974. It represents the Fatah and is its main medium in the administered territories. Bulus Azay al-Ajluni, its owner, lives in the United States and for a time was the official adviser to the PLO's delegation at the United Nations. In 1974, Jo Nasser, the editor, was kidnapped; he has not reappeared. Besides these dailies, there are a number of less frequent publications, including *Al-Teyah,* a Communist weekly; *Al-Udah,* a pro-Fatah weekly headed by Raymonda al-Tawil (who has also headed a press agency since 1978); and *Al-Shraa,* a leftist bimonthly.

These complex and far-reaching frameworks and organizational means constituted the tools of the revolt of the late 1970s.

C. REVOLT AND REPRESSION

The tensions that had been building up for nearly a decade erupted during the late winter and spring of 1976. On May 1, one man was killed during a demonstration in Nablus, which was harshly suppressed by the IDF. On May 15, when Jenin was shaken by riots, one boy met his death. On the sixteenth, a girl met the same fate, again in Nablus. On the seventeenth, in Kalkilyah, soldiers shot at rioters and one youngster was killed. On the eighteenth, an outburst of violence in Jerusalem had a similar result. The government's strong-arm tactics quelled the wave of riots for a while, but it soon rose again. Beneath the surface, the organizations felt strong enough to confront the incumbents.

In June, the Ministry of Finance announced that it was going to impose an 8 percent value-added tax (VAT) in the administered territories, as in Israel. The justification was the growing interdependence of the economies of the territories and Israel. The tax was to be collected from July 1 on, but negotiations and pressures delayed the application for one month. Civil protest and riots were again set in motion all over the territories. Pupils and students attacked strike breakers, and on August 17, the students invaded the Chamber of Commerce of Jerusalem to prevent a decision against the strike. A few days later, Jewish biblical scrolls were destroyed at the synagogue of the Tomb of the Fathers in Hebron. In retaliation, the governor widened the Jews' rights to the site, which is sacred to the Muslims as well. Calm was restored in Hebron, but the VAT protest was taken up in other towns.

On December 7, shops were closed all over the West Bank. Riots and repression expanded to the Gaza Strip, and it was a whole restless week before some calm returned. This was only temporary, however; in summer 1977, a renewal of terrorism was noticeable. Nine Jews were wounded by a bomb placed in a bus station in the northern Jezreel Valley on August 16. Six people were wounded in Nablus by an explosion one day later. During the same week, similar incidents occurred in Netanya, Jerusalem, and Gaza. On September 19, a soldier was killed in Gaza. Three more civilians were wounded in October by an explosion at the central bus station of Tel Aviv. Two bombs were discovered before explosion in Jerusalem, but one more exploded and shook Petah Tikva.

Israeli reactions were not slow in coming. A plan for the settlement of Jews in the West Bank was announced; several new settlements were soon inaugurated. Other repressive measures were planned, and the army was given strict instructions to follow a hard line. However, both sides, the Arabs and the Jews, were taken by surprise by Anwar Sadat's initiative, his visit to Jerusalem, and the beginning of peace negotiations. Palestinians and Israelis waited for the events to develop and left the confrontation at a standstill.

Sadat's initiative rapidly raised divergences. The Arab radical regimes criticized it unhesitantly and in the sharpest terms. The leftists in the PLO followed them a few hours later. The Fatah-PLO leadership waited one whole day to finally condemn irrevocably the visit of an Egyptian president to Jerusalem. King Hussein was more cautious and for some time remained ambivalent. On December 2, 1977, a summit including Syria, Iraq, Libya, Algeria, South Yemen, and the PLO—including the 1974 Rejection Front groups around the PFLP—created the "Steadfastness Front" to conduct a merciless struggle against the Egypt-Israel peace process.

Of all the Palestinian parties, the notables, understandably, reacted in the least negative way. In fact, they were almost frankly positive. Elias Frej, the mayor of Bethlehem, Anwar al-Khatib of Jerusalem, Hichmat al-Masri from Nablus, and others even met with Sadat in Jerusalem and welcomed him. Numerous leaders were invited by the Egyptian president to Cairo. Most of them accepted, and they formed four delegations, which made the trip during the next few months. During this period the population anticipated new developments; organized nationalism stood aside, waiting until it could control the people again. This happened only when it was confirmed that the Egypt-Israel peace process did not hold any drastic change for the Palestinian condition— owing, inter alia, to the PLO's and Hussein's refusal to join in.

Extremists on both sides contributed to the renewal of tensions. The Jewish annexationist movement, Gush Emunim, demonstrated more vigorously than ever before against any territorial concession to Egypt.

They attacked the Peace Now movement, which had just appeared and had already attracted tens of thousands to demonstrations in favor of maximal Israeli concessions for the sake of a peace agreement.

On the other hand, terrorist acts initiated outside of Israel and the territories were instrumental in exacerbating the crisis. The bloodiest event took place on the Haifa-Tel Aviv road when a gang landed on the Mediterranean shore, hijacked a tourist bus, and compelled it to drive to Tel Aviv. The bus was stopped by security forces at the entrance to the city, but the liberation of the passengers cost dozens of victims. In retaliation, on March 14, 1978, the IDF launched the Litani operation, an invasion of southern Lebanon. The operation achieved the elimination of PLO operational bases up to the Litani River and widened the area controlled by the pro-Israeli Christian militia of Haddad. A buffer strip was designated for supervision by UN troops. Within the territories, the operation immediately reopened an era of civil unrest, with huge demonstrations of solidarity with the PLO in Lebanon.

The Camp David Agreements recognized the existence of a Palestinian problem and proposed a five-year interim period of home rule for the inhabitants of the territories. This interim was to be followed by a definitive settlement decided upon by consensus of all parties. Reservations were voiced among the local leaders, and only a few endorsed the propositions. The outcry of rejection was even more general outside the territories. A Council for National Guidance (CNG) was constituted in order to prevent any collaboration of Palestinians with the incumbents in the framework of the peace agreements.

This new body divided the administered territories, including the Gaza Strip, into four areas, and its members were organized accordingly.[15] There were three representatives of the North, four of the center, two of the South, and two from the Gaza Strip. Other members represented sociopolitical organizations (unions, women, and students) and newspapers. The inner committee of the CNG included the three main leaders, Basam Shaqa of Nablus, Karim Khalaf of Ramallah, and Fahd Qawasmeh of Hebron. More than two-thirds were leftists, a few of whom were Communists; the Fatah constituted a small minority, as did the pro-Jordanians (see exhibit 5.1).

Civil protest rose with unprecedented tensions. The universities were the strongholds of the revolt; most extremist articles found their way into the Palestinian newspapers despite the censor's vigilance; huge meetings took place in every city; leaders met daily with foreign journalists. On May 2, 1979, a vast demonstration encircled Bir Zeyt, closing the town to vehicles and ending with street combat with soldiers (sixty-four people were arrested, most of them students). After similar outbursts in Bethlehem and Hebron, in early June a demonstration of tens of thousands was held in Nablus, with the participation of the leadership of the CNG.

In parallel, terrorism approached a new peak. A PFLP cell was discovered in Bir Zeyt University; in December 1978, a new group (the Progressive Movement), which included a number of Israeli Arabs, was arrested in the West Bank; in May 1979, a Fatah network of several cells was dismantled; seventy persons were arrested in Gaza in early September for membership in various PLO cells. Explosions wounded three persons in Jerusalem on July 6, another twelve in Netanya on July 25, and three others in Jerusalem during August.

At this point, the authorities expelled Basam Shaqa, provoking the immediate resignation of twenty-five mayors throughout the territories and a new wave of demonstrations. Some calm was restored with the cancellation of the expulsion order. Tension soon rose again with the murder of a young Jew in a street in Hebron (January 31, 1980), which was countered by the imposition of a prolonged curfew in the city. In Gaza, at the same time, a grenade killed four Israelis.

On January 25, Israel pulled back from a major portion of Sinai, in accordance with the peace treaty. This was another opportunity for a general strike of protest against Camp David followed unanimously in East Jerusalem, the West Bank, and the Gaza Strip. On both sides, hasty provocative and retaliative actions were taken. The Israeli government confirmed the right of Jewish private persons to buy land from Arabs in the West Bank. On February 10, the government decided to allow Jews to settle in Hebron. On March 23, a decision was made to create a new Jewish neighborhood in that city, and on April 3, it was agreed to resettle the old Jewish quarter. During this period, on February 27, Jewish settlers began to stone private houses in Halhul in retaliation for the inhabitants' stoning of Jewish cars. Similar events occurred in Ramallah and Al-Bireh, where pamphlets were distributed by the extremist Kakh movement led by Meir Kahane calling for the emigration of Arabs.

In reaction, the CNG leaders crystallized their own tactics. Karim Khalaf wrote in *Al-Fajer* that the Palestinian population had to defend itself according to the following six-point plan: (1) mass demonstrations all over the territories; (2) a total transportation strike of several days; (3) a general economic boycott of Israeli products and institutions, including stopping work in Israel and isolating the Jewish settlements in the territories; (4) a motorized parade in Jerusalem; (5) establishment of a civilian passive defense in Arab neighborhoods and villages; and (6) vigorous reactions to any Israeli "provocation."[16]

The Israeli authorities at this time were weak, for unrelated reasons. Ezer Weizman, then a member of the right-wing Likud but among the more "dovish" members of this party, resigned from his position as

Exhibit 5.1

The Committee for National Guidance: Figures, Institutions, Allegiances

Allegiances	Figures	Institutions
DFLP	Karim Khalaf^(*) Samiha Halil^(*) Ibrahim al-Tawil^(*) Bshara Daud^(*)	Mayor, Ramallah; board, Al-Fajer President, Association for the Family Mayor, Al-Bireh Mayor, Beit Jalla
PFLP	Muhammad Milhim Ali Yaish Akram Henin Khidad Abd al-Shafi	Mayor, Halhul Board, Al-Shab Board, Al-Shab President, Red Crescent, Gaza
Communists	Bashir Baruti Ibrahim al-Dekak^(*) Audel Aanam	Board, Al-Tlia President, Association of Engineers President, Workers' Unions
Baathists	Basam Shaqa^(*) Walid Hamdalla	Mayor, Nablus Mayor, Anbata
Fatah	Fahd Qawasmeh^(*) Amin al-Khatib Halmi Hanun Mamon Al-Sid Zuhir al-Reis Samir Katba	Mayor, Hebron President, Union of Charity Associations Mayor, Tulkarem Board, Al-Fajer President, Association of Lawyers President, Association of Medical Doctors
Jordan	Abd al-Aziz al-Switi Sad al-din^(*) Shia Ali al-Taziz Girsi al-Khura	Mayor, Jericho Mufti of Jerusalem Commercial Affairs Association of Lawyers
Neutral	Samikh Tazia Akrama Tsabri	Association of Pharmacists Supreme Muslim Council

Source: Israeli officials.

(*) Also members of the Council for Higher Education and/or of a board of one of the universities or colleges in the administered territories

minister of defense. Menachem Begin, then prime minister, took charge temporarily. The responsibility of the territories then fell to his deputy minister of defense, Mordechai Zippori, who had difficulties developing a personal approach in his confrontation with General Rafael Eytan, the chief of staff, and General Danny Mat, the general coordinator of activities in the administered territories.

Growing protest brought the population of the administered territories close to upheaval. Khalaf was quoted by Radio Damascus as saying, "We see ourselves totally involved in the *tsumud*, the firm resistance to the occupier; the only way to solve our conflict is the gun." In a letter to a Kuwaitian daily he declared, "The stone of the conquered and Sacred Land is stronger than airplanes."[17] Armed struggle was loudly praised and openly relied upon.

Again in a parallel trend, or in reaction, on June 2, 1980, several cars of West Bank mayors were dynamited in the first incident revealing the existence of a Jewish underground (the members of which were caught only in 1984). Basam Shaqa and Khalaf were seriously wounded; Shaqa lost his two legs. An Israeli explosives expert lost his sight while disarming a bomb in the car of Ibrahim al-Tawil, the mayor of Al-Bireh.

Thousands of demonstrators took to the streets again, burned tires, stoned Jewish vehicles, and came in conflict with the IDF. The difficult position of moderate leaders caused men like Rashid al-Shawa (Gaza) and Elias Frej (Bethlehem) to consider resignation from mayorship; the chambers of commerce ordered their members to join the demonstrations and the strike. Bir Zeyt University organized a Palestine Week (in November), with the collaboration of al-Najah students, the Bir Zeyt municipality, the Ramallah Scouts, and many other organizations. Palestinian flags, signs, and badges were worn by every participant; enflamed speeches, poems, and essays competed in extremism. A couple of days later the university was closed by the authorities for one week. Then a group of students declared a lockout for ten more days.

Nervousness was perceptible in governmental circles. Decisions were hasty and were intended to provoke an escalation. The creation of ten settlements was announced, as was the confirmation of a project for an intersea channel (from the Mediterranean to the Dead Sea crosscutting the Gaza Strip and Judea). The prime minister's office officially announced that it would move its quarters from West to East Jerusalem. Most spectacular, a new bill confirming the annexation of East Jerusalem was passed by the Knesset, the Israeli Parliament. In the administered territories, soldiers began to force shopkeepers to open their shops.

At the same time, Qawasmeh and Milhim were expelled to Jordan, despite huge street demonstrations. Following the expulsion, the Israeli Supreme Court decided that the two men should be present at the juridical debate about their case. Thus, a special meeting of the military court took place in Jericho (December 5) on the border; the expulsion was confirmed. In January 1981, the government further decided to nationalize the Arab-owned Jerusalem Electricity Company; this decision, however, was soon overruled by the Supreme Court on the grounds of international law stipulations and illegal proceedings.

The government's policy in the administered territories was sharply criticized from many sides in Israel itself. Thus, for instance, before he was set at the head of the civilian administration, Menachem Milson himself, the orientalist scholar who had been an official adviser to Dayan's administration, was one of the sharpest critics of Israel's policy. According to him, all Israeli defense ministers—beginning with Dayan— had neglected the pro-Jordanian party and had left the door open, without any appropriate reaction, to the penetration of the PLO and its most radical elements.[18] Milson recommended a radical change, namely, the demonstration of firm support for the pro-Jordanians.

During the same period, a crisis broke out over aircraft missiles that Syria had introduced into Lebanon. Israel threatened to take preventive action: to destroy the missiles by a unilateral military attack. A U.S. envoy, Philip Habib, was quickly sent to the area. Although he was unsuccessful in achieving the withdrawal of the missiles, Habib was able to prevent the Israelis from taking a drastic step. Moreover, he concluded the first Israeli-PLO cease-fire agreement at the peak of Israeli bombings of Palestinian bases in the vicinity of Beirut. These bombings were a reaction to the shelling of Galilean settlements from PLO strongholds in eastern Lebanon.

After Habib left the Middle East, the situation in the territories regained priority. Arik Sharon, then the defense minister, defined his policy within the new framework of the Camp David Agreements, which assigned the Israelis the task of encouraging the population toward an interim stage of home rule. Israel wished now to find cooperative local leaders; in view of this goal, Menachem Milson was appointed to top responsibility over the newly created civilian administration. Sharon had just separated this civilian administration from the military government, because Israeli rule was to be considered in a new light. From a plain occupation, which resulted in the existence of a military government, the incumbent wanted to be looked at as also having a legitimate mission vis-à-vis the inhabitants, that is, preparing them for autonomy. In this context, the establishment of a civilian administration was essential.

However, because these steps were bound to Camp David, they were firmly rejected by the Arab League, as well as by all PLO factions. Only a few organizations and personalities in the territories differed from this stand. The generalized boycott of the new administration and the renewed public protest were answered by fierce counterattacks and countermeasures. Bir Zeyt University, for instance, was closed after its first

demonstration against the new arrangements, and its president was arrested. The daily *Al-Fajer* was forbidden, and an emergency meeting of the CNG was followed by the arrest of four of its members. Leaders of unions and other associations, twelve persons in all, were put under house arrest, including the chairman of the Medical Association, a notorious Communist of Nablus. Endless demonstrations shook the streets, but repression went on. A Hebron school for girls was siezed because it was situated in the ancient Jewish neighborhood of the city. Appeals for moderation from middle-of-the-road leaders like Elias Frej and Rashid al-Shawa, were resolutely dismissed by the incumbents. A general strike on February 2, 1982, was followed on March 11 by the outlawing of the CNG itself on the ground of 1945 defense regulations (art. 84/1–6).

Next, the mayors and municipal councils were assaulted because of their refusal to recognize the civilian administration. As a test case, Milson invited al-Tawil of Al-Bireh to his office. The invitation was ignored, causing an immediate dismissal of both the mayor and the town council. An Israeli officer was immediately appointed to fill the post temporarily. The mass protest to these actions, which was held in the town on March 20, resulted in the death of a seventeen-year-old pupil. This in turn provoked another wave of protests all over the administered territories. As Milson said on Israeli TV, "This [was] the most important battle against the PLO, comparable in importance to the 1948 War of Independence." Most of the mayors were dismissed the same way. Shaqa of Nablus and Khalaf of Ramallah soon followed al-Tawil, as did al-Shawa of Gaza and several others. Walid Hamdalla of Anbata was brought to court. The civilian administration was now in control of one of the major mechanisms of political articulation—the municipal budget and organization.

In parallel, non-PLO Palestinians were actively searched and counted. The notables were by no means eager to transgress Amman's ban on Arab-Israeli cooperation, but Milson was able to find partners in the Associations of Villagers. Mustafa Dudeen, an experienced political broker, was a convenient ally who succeeded in enrolling dozens of villages in such associations, the roof-framework of which he headed himself. All allocations for agricultural development in the territories were channeled through these associations, which multiplied and expanded. These new developments were set back, however, by Amman's firm opposition. The announcement of the death penalty and confiscation of property for anyone who collaborated with these associations impeded further expansion.

The annual day of Arab protest against Israeli rule, the "Day of the Land," is usually very bloody. In 1982, it was much quieter than usual. The attack by Alan Goodman, a Jewish fanatic, on Muslims at the Temple

Mount reawakened passions, as did the trial that followed. Yet, at the time that Israel started its invasion of Lebanon (June 1982), there was a state of relative calm in the administered territories.

D. THE UNDERLYING POLITICS

The assets, competition, and rivalries of the Palestinian organizations that led the struggle against the incumbents are behind these events. At the same time, the Hashemite party became weaker. It was against this background that the municipal elections of 1972 and 1976 were successfully held despite the PLO's opposition. Pro-PLO Helena Cobban recalls that in 1972, the PLO argued for a boycott, for ideological reasons, of the elections organized by the Israelis. It was only "when it became clear that many West Bankers would exercise their vote [that] the PLO had quietly argued for returning the existing local councils, as a bloc, so as not to introduce any changes under Israeli sponsorship." In 1976, Cobban continues, the pro-PLO community leaders in the West Bank again argued strongly for participation on their terms and were able to persuade the PLO leaders outside of the value of this course. On the other hand, West Bank sociologist Salim Tamari comments that the PLO wanted to participate in the elections in order to create solid loci of political power which would back the political demands of the PLO for independence and also act as barriers against compromises with an autonomy which would maintain the West Bank and Gaza under Israeli sovereignty.[19]

Tension between outside PLO leaders and local figures around the issue of the municipal elections may also be explained in an additional way. The Fatah, as the leading force in the PLO on the external—and principal—scene of the conflict, was in fact reluctant to encourage the development of a powerful local leadership that it could not control. Such a leadership might challenge its status in the nationalist movement. The basic weakness of the Fatah in this respect was the physical remoteness of its leadership from the "field," that is, the territories themselves. Conversely, because of their own weakness within the PLO the radical fronts were eager to strengthen their assets in the field and to take advantage of the Fatah's hesitancy. This generalization does not include the Communists, who tried everything to gain acceptance in the PLO. For the fronts, however, the municipal elections of 1976 were proof of the profitability of their efforts: leftists, mainly of the PFLP and the DFLP, ousted many of the notables from office and from their positions on municipal councils. Similarly, these elections reflected the weakness of the Fatah.

Thus, new, powerful men, mostly radicals, appeared on the local scene. Because these individuals were identified with the PNF, many commentators saw this as the victory of the PLO and the defeat of Israel; in fact it was a defeat for both. The Baathist Shaqa, George Habash's close ally, soon achieved the status of the major leader of the administered territories. The battle against the VAT gave him the opportunity to expand his influence far beyond Nablus. He established a territories-wide committee, grouping unions, commercial associations, youth organizations, and other movements, and opened a relentless public combat against the authorities. While both the Fatah and the pro-Jordan notables sought to overcome this development, the importance of a solid front against the incumbents required that these internal divergencies remain covered. Thus, on behalf of the common cause, a Fatah-pro-Jordan coalition crystallized and challenged the radical leadership by sponsoring new initiatives. VAT demonstrations were called for by Shaqa, and other demonstrations were called for by al-Shawa, Frej, and Qawasmeh.

Yet the dominance of the Left in the CNG permitted it to appoint its men to related bodies such as the Council for Higher Education. Against the background of the "near revolt" in the territories in the late 1970s and early 1980s, the Left's capitalization of its position in the CNG created a situation quite close to a "revolution within the revolution." People and movements who were still linked to the Fatah or the notables were pressured to change their orientation. This pressure was most often channeled under the cover of the requirement of allegiance to the CNG as the leading local PLO body.

One of the many expressions of these antagonisms was found at the first mass meeting called by the CNG, which took place at the University of Bethlehem. The participants "spontaneously" stood up and compelled Frej, the mayor of the host city, to leave the grounds because he had sympathized earlier with Sadat's peace initiative. In response, the Fatah–pro-Jordan coalition called for another meeting in Gaza twenty days later. The radicals were not invited, and those who tried to attend were stopped on their way by Israeli soldiers or were neutralized by Gazean youngsters at the meeting place. In another such case, the mayor of Hebron, Qawasmeh, responded to a governmental decision to settle Jews in his city by calling for a mass gathering there of Palestinians from all over the territories. Fearing Qawasmeh's potential political gain from such a demonstration, Shaqa launched an appeal to demonstrate on Hebron's behalf at every public place in the territories. This enhanced the leadership status of the CNG. Qawasmeh's demonstration took place on March 24 but was of lesser impact.

The political reality strengthened the link between the Fatah and the pro-Jordanians beyond purely tactical considerations. This was expressed in pro-Jordan Frej's meeting with Arafat in 1979. Moreover, this bloc also joined forces with the Islamic fundamentalist groups which were becoming increasingly effective. On January 11, 1980, for instance, a CNG demonstration in Jerusalem was countered by a group of Muslims shouting, "No to a Communist state."

More important was the Fatah–pro-Jordanian coalition's success in mobilizing international assets for the purpose of competition with the radicals. At the 1978 Baghdad Conference of the Arab League, the bloc was able to bring about the creation of a fund, financed by oil states, to be jointly controlled by the Fatah-led PLO and Jordan. This fund aimed at the strengthening of the *tsumud* in the administered territories served to strengthen the coalition of Arafat and Hussein.

Moreover, every opportunity was seized by the Fatah-led PLO to call for the resignation of the mostly leftist mayors in the territories. This was said to be intended to demonstrate the illegitimacy of Israeli rule, but the mayors themselves, who always refused the suggestion, knew what such a move would mean for them in terms of power assets. Thus, for instance, after the Jewish underground gang sabotaged the four mayors' cars, the PLO called from Beirut for an immediate resignation of all heads of municipalities. This appeal was promptly rejected by Shaqa himself, who had just lost his legs. From the hospital, he issued a resolute directive to all Palestinian officials "not to give up to the Zionist occupier" and to remain in office. Three such scenarios were played out until the uncooperative mayors were finally dismissed by Milson.

In neither camp, however, was there total harmony between the diverse components. The Fatah's interest, for instance, was not always identical to the Hashemites'. Quarrels and divergences about the distribution of Baghdad allocations were frequent. Hussein finally created a special Ministry for the Occupied Land, which backed Jordan's autonomous policy and maneuvers in the West Bank (all Baghdad Fund sums were conveyed through banks accredited by the ministry).

Among the leftists, the divisions were no less blatant. A basic lack of confidence existed between the fronts and the Communists, who, in principle, were the most moderate because they recognized Israel. Moreover, most "popular" or "democratic" fronts were actually of the same origin, the PFLP, from which they had split at various times. This did not ease the mistrust among them. Here, too, many of the quarrels focused on the allocation of resources, which, in this camp, came primarily from Syria, Libya, Algeria, and the Soviet bloc.[20]

Money permits the creation and activation of clubs, youth organizations, and charity funds, which are the backbone of political activity. It should be noted that after 1967, civil servants, including teachers and officials at all levels, continued to receive their salaries from the Amman government. Similarly, the Hashemite regime's financial support of the Islamic establishment never ceased. Less conspicuous, but no less important, a substantial part of the budgets of all Palestinian organizations went to widows and orphans of those who had fallen for the Palestinian cause as well as to the relatives of those who were in prison. Legal aid for any person brought to trial and compensation for fines incurred through participation in street demonstrations were provided. Scholarships for study abroad and at local universities and welfare money were all advantages that supporters of the revolution could obtain.

The open bridges, the international bank relations, and summer visits of relatives greatly facilitated the transfer of money, which could never be totally controlled by the Israeli authorities. Even if one channel was cut off, many others were still available.

E. THE TURN TO THE RIGHT AND THE IMPACT OF "PEACE FOR GALILEE"

It would be a mistake, however, to deduce from the political strength of the left that Hussein and Arafat were unpopular in the streets of Nablus, Ramallah, and East Jerusalem or even that they were less popular than Habash, Hawatmeh, or Assad. The wide majority of the people did not belong actively to any organization, and though they identified with Palestinian nationalism and could be moved by revolutionary slogans, for the most part they took a very pragmatic view of their condition. They aspired, above all, to liberation from the Israeli presence even if this aspiration meant accepting a Jewish state "outside."

The heavy ideological jargon of the PFLP or the DFLP was alien to this popular mind. Moderate plans seemed more possible, because they could bring about positive results in a short time. In this context one understands, for instance, the separation that occurred during the first weeks of Sadat's initiative between political figures and the "people in the streets." As emphasized by W. F. Abboushi, a political scientist at Bir Zeyt University,

In terms of the population, the mayors represent the majority of the people of the West Bank. On the issue of Sadat's visit, however, the mayors did not represent the majority. The general sentiment of their own cities and towns, as well as of the rural population, was for Sadat's peace initiative.[21]

The Camp David Agreements, as well as the weakness of mass protest in the late 1970s, led to some disillusion with the radical slogans. Thus where Shaqa and the extremists had failed, al-Shawa could succeed. Indeed, on December 2, 1981, he headed the principal anti-VAT demonstration, which began in Gaza. The mayor of Nablus was then neutralized in his own city by al-Masri's pro-Jordan local commercial office. Even Mustafa Dudeen's Associations of Villagers were able to achieve some success when they channeled budgets for electricity, roads, and water pipes. Thus they made headway with slogans that referred to a future non-PLO Palestinian state, links between such a Palestinian entity and Jordan, and even a Camp David-inspired autonomy.

The incumbents themselves contributed to the gradual strengthening of the rightist coalition among the Palestinians when they outlawed the CNG (1981) and dismissed the mayors who had boycotted the civilian administration (March 1982). Thus, even though a police station was invested in Kfar Abba, a military post stoned in Deheishe, and the Jewish settlement Migdal Oz assaulted—in a six-week period when more persons were killed in demonstrations than during the previous fifteen years of Israeli occupation—during this same period the moderate camp was definitely achieving supremacy over its radical rivals. In March 1983, a party in Nablus organized openly against Shaqa. At the same time, the Associations of Villagers sought for reconciliation with Amman and asked the IDF to end its military protection of their leaders.

The Israeli army invaded Lebanon in June 1982; the ensuing purge resulted in the eradication of the PLO's major bases and politicomilitary centers. As a consequence, the wave of unrest that had been shaking the administered territories since the late 1970s ceased almost totally. It was now obvious that the radical Rejection Front which refused any solution that was less than the destruction of Israel, was unrealistic. Limited and pragmatic goals appeared now clearly to many as the only ones to have a chance. The possibility of any effective action on the part of the Arab nations was again precluded by their endless divisions. Besides the rift between the Arab League and Egypt, quarrels put Jordan, Saudi Arabia, and Iraq at odds with Syria and Libya. Echoing these conflicts, armed struggles broke out within the PLO among the various movements, and even within the leading force of Palestinian nationalism, the Fatah. In the administered territories themselves, anti-Israel demonstrations were being replaced by protests of Syria's campaign against Arafat. The popularity of the Palestinian leader increased as he drew closer to Hussein, an official process that reached its peak with the 1984 session of the Palestinian National Council in Amman. The strongest spokesmen of the left were silenced in Samaria and Judea and, under the pressure of the population at large, had to express reservations vis-à-vis Damascus.[22] Shaqa himself openly sympathized with the PLO leader, while the leftist Jerusalem daily *Al-Shab* wrote: "Syria may overcome Arafat militarily but she will not politically because he is the one who has the overwhelming support of the Palestinian people."[23]

It was understandable, then, albeit unprecedented, that a terrorist action on a Jerusalem bus in December 1983 raised a public protest by several well-known Palestinian notables, who voiced their reactions in the Israeli media as well as in Arab newspapers.[24] A joint statement was released: "We believe that it is essential to point out that attacks against civilians bring harm to any form of understanding that could be reached between Palestinians and Israelis. . . . Such actions are to be condemned wherever they occur, in Jerusalem, Al-Hilweh or Nablus. . . . Violence will not solve the Palestinian problem. It stands in opposition to the official position of the PLO's lawful leadership."[25] It was signed by Karim Khalaf, Anwar Nusayba, Mustafa Natsha, Paul Adjlumi, and Hanna Seniora. Natsha further elaborated for the Israeli daily *Haaretz,* and Raymonda al-Tawil did the same for Israeli radio. In Gaza, too, the action was condemned by figures such as the mayors of Dir-Al-Balah and Khan Yunis.

Hussein was even able to call a session of the Jordanian Parliament, of which dozens of West Bankers are members. Al-Masri of Nablus was officially appointed by the king as the representative of the administered territories in the Jordanian Senate; many others were chosen for the lower house. The weekly *Al-Biader Al-Syasi* published the results of an opinion survey, according to which 94 percent of those interviewed supported Arafat, 89 percent were in favor of a PLO-Jordan dialogue, and 40 percent wanted to widen such a dialogue to include Egypt.[26] On the other hand, 58 percent wished for the strengthening of PLO ties with the Israeli Left.

A moderate figure was elected to the chairmanship of the Council for Higher Education in the territories. Anton Mansur was made deputy president of Bethlehem University. In Tulkarem, Pithi Dadu, a rich merchant who had been opposed to the leftist mayor, Hanon, was elected to the important position of head of the town's Agricultural Marketing Association. Other moderates were chosen as the new heads of the chambers of commerce of Kelkilya and Jenin. These men were also local representatives of Israeli firms and thereby directly interested in gainful relations between the Jewish state and Jordan. These relations have made possible such recent projects as a juice factory in northern Samaria and a wide-scale exportation of Israeli watermelons to Arab countries.

F. THE MAKING OF A POLITICAL POWER

In accordance with our theoretical expectations, the PLO became, during Israeli rule, the determinant political force of the mid-1980s in Judea, Samaria, and Gaza. Israel, because of its own ideological codes, was never able to develop an antiguerrilla policy vis-à-vis the population other than the watching-over model. Its aspiration to remain a Jewish state excludes the integration and assimilation of the Palestinians. In fact, Israel wants to negotiate the plight of the territories in the framework of the resolution of its conflict with the Arab states, excluding any independent political Palestinian entity. Israel thus makes do with an attitude toward the Palestinians that takes for granted their fundamental hostility to the Jewish state; its only ambition in this respect is to deter the inhabitants from supporting the PLO in the most threatening aspect of this movement's activity, terrorism.

The Israelis themselves have never tried to create local movements, organizations, or institutional positions that could advance Palestinians' identification with their state. In the period when Milson was in charge of the civilian authority, the support given to political nuclei in the city or to Associations of Villagers indicated a possible new direction; however, these moves were widely counterbalanced by a heavier use of coercion against local bodies and unprecedented encouragement of Jewish settlement in the area.

The incumbents, in fact, never really intended to become a focus of allegiance or identification for the population. The limited nature of these ambitions created a political vacuum that was further aggravated by the early removal by the Israelis of the pro-Jordanians from office and positions of power. Not ready to fill this vacuum themselves, the incumbents offered the Palestinian nationalists the opportunity of systematically infiltrating the population and also, actually, to compete with each other.

This infiltration took the form of a multiplication of organizations of the greatest diversity. New leaders emerged at the local level—mainly in the municipalities—which were the grounds for all territories' legal and semi-legal frameworks. Because it acted mainly from the outside, however, the Fatah-led PLO was loath to encourage the growth of a powerful local leadership which would be able to challenge the status of the central direction. Thus, for many years the mainstream of Palestinian nationalism was cautious enough not to sustain here the creation of structures of coordination, aspiring mainly at the strengthening of the population's allegiance to its cause. The radical factions (often with the help of the communists) were weaker in the PLO's central institutions, and were more eager to develop new foci of power in the territories that could improve their position in the movement.

However, once successful, the radicals could not leave the Fatah-led PLO without reaction. This reaction led first to a coalition with the pro-Jordan elements who still had hold of important institutional assets. The competition turned, finally, to the advantage of this coalition, thanks to favorable circumstances such as the dismissal of radical mayors by the incumbents and the weakening of the external PLO position following the Peace for Galilee Operation. These events bluntly demonstrated the utopian character of the extremist anti-Israeli stand, and strengthened the remarkably pragmatic attitude of the inhabitants themselves who were, more than ever, interested in a practical solution which would force the occupier to pull out as quickly as possible. Thus, a few years of intense activity—with the backing of the Baghdad Fund—changed the intra-Palestinian power relations, allowing the Fatah-led PLO, together with the pro-Hashemite party, to accede to a dominant status in the mid-1980s.

NOTES

1. D. Pirhi, "Political Positions in Judea and Samaria 1972–1973," in *Ten Years of Israeli Rule in Judea and Samaria*, ed. R. Israeli (Jerusalem: Magnes, 1981 [Hebrew]); P. Inbari, *A Triangle in Jordan: Secret Talks between the U.S., Jordan and the PLO* (Jerusalem: Keter, 1982), 34–35 (Hebrew).

2. A. Cohen, *Political Parties in the West Bank under Hashemite Rule* (Jerusalem: Magnes, 1980 [Hebrew]); A. Cohen, "Does a Jordanian Option Still Exist?" *Jerusalem Quarterly* 16 (1980):111–20.

3. Y. Levita, "Another Step toward the Creation of Normal Interactions," *Skira Khodshit* 1 (1972):30–31 (Hebrew).

4. S. Stempler, "The Significance of the Success of the Elections in Samaria," *Skira Khodshit* 4 (1976):32–33.

5. S. Shamir, et al. *The Professional Elite in Samaria* (Tel Aviv: Shiloah Institute, Tel Aviv University, 1975), 130 (Hebrew); S. Mishal, "The Anatomy of Municipal Elections," *Hamizrakh Hakhadash* 4 (1974):63–67 (Hebrew); M. Izhar, "Elections to Municipalities in Judea and Samaria—Political Aspects," *Medina, Memshal Veyakhasim Beinleumiim* 5 (1974):119–26 (Hebrew).

6. M. Vinter, "The Educational System in the Administrated Territories," in Israeli, 107–15.

7. Israel Information Center, *Facts about the Administered Areas*, 1974.

8. R. Halabi, *There Is a Limit: the Story of the West Bank* (Jerusalem: Keter, 1983 [Hebrew]).

9. M. Golan, *Peres* (Tel Aviv: Schocken, 1982 [Hebrew]), 187.

10. G. Golan, *The Soviet Union and the PLO*, Adelphi Papers, 131, 1976.

11. Inbari, 25.

12. Well-informed sources.

13. *Monitin*, January 1982 (Hebrew).

14. D. Rubinstein, *The Book of Journalists* (Tel Aviv: Israeli Association of Journalists, 1975), 181–88.

15. See Appendix.

16. *Al-Fajer*, April 25, 1980.

17. *Al-Rai-Elam*, June 6, 1980.

18. *Al-Hamishmar*, May 23, 1980.

19. H. Cobban, *The Palestinian Liberation Organization: People, Power and Politics* (Cambridge: Cambridge University Press, 1984).

20. See chapter 7 and 8.

21. Quoted by Cobban, 176; from E. Nakhleh, ed., *A Palestinian Agenda for the West Bank and Gaza*, (Washington D.C.: American Enterprise Institute), 7–8.

22. *Al-Fajer*, November 24, 1980; G. Ben-Dor, "The PLO and the Palestinians," CSS Memorandum, *The War in Lebanon*, Tel Aviv University, No. 8, 1983, 24–42.

23. *Al-Shab,* November 21, 1983.
24. *Al-Kuds,* November 18, 1983.
25. *Al-Fajer,* December 8, 1983.
26. *Al-Biader Al-Syasi,* December 3, 1983.

6 Direct Action

A. THE FEDAYEEN: THE GENERAL PICTURE

Turning to the military aspect of the confrontation within the administered territories, it is important to note that since 1948, the Gaza Strip has always been the main source of trouble for Israel. The numerous refugees in this area constitute a frustrated population for which hostile action against Israel has been a major outlet of pressures and tensions. Up to 1955, actions within Israeli territory involved theft and personal damage; these were mostly individual affairs, independent from any organized movement.[1]

However, toward the mid-1950s, the Egyptian government introduced a commando group called the fedayeen, which initially numbered some 700 men. Sabotage against Israel was encouraged and was carried out under the authority of the Egyptian intelligence. The model consisted of small three- to four-man squads infiltrating into Israel and causing material damage, then returning to their base or crossing over to Jordan. In the latter case, other operations could be launched on the way back home to the Gaza Strip. The pre-1967 Jordanian border was particularly appropriate for infiltration because of its length and sinuosity. At some points, the border was only twelve to fifteen kilometers from Israel's central cities of Tel Aviv, Netanya, and Petah Tikva; as for Jerusalem, the border divided the city itself.

At first, the Israeli response was essentially defensive. More soldiers—mainly from the Border Police (Mishmar Hagvul), established in 1950—were sent to man a detection and ambush system along the borders. With the recrudescence of fedayeen terrorism, small units carried out retaliation operations beyond the border against villages that served as bases for the infiltrators. Quite frequently a neighborhood was encircled, its inhabitants moved away, and some houses and buildings blown up.

Sometimes herds of sheep were confiscated and brought to Israel. It also happened that inhabitants were killed by mistake. The worst such case was in Kibiah in mid-October 1953, when several tens of civilians were slain and wounded. In 1955, the Israeli government officially adopted the position that the neighboring countries would be held responsible for infiltration from within their borders. The chief of staff, Moshe Dayan, declared, "We are not able to prevent every action against any water pipe or tree . . . but we are strong enough to take a price for each action that will be too heavy for the Arab villages, the Arab armies, the Arab governments."[2] Retaliations against Egyptian and Jordanian public and military targets multiplied over time, in keeping with the Arab infiltrations. Unit 101, commanded by Arik Sharon, was particularly instrumental in operations of this kind.

The Sinai campaign, orchestrated with France and Britain in October 1956, ended this episode. Following Nasser's nationalization of the Suez Canal from the British and his provision of aid to Algerian rebels against France, the Israeli leader, David Ben-Gurion, interested these two Western powers in a common action against the Egyptian regime. In the framework of a secret agreement, Israel invaded the Gaza Strip, destroyed the fedayeen bases, occupied the Sinai Peninsula, and opened the Tiran Straits to Israeli ships. Yet the French and the British soon interrupted their own action on the Suez Canal and withdrew, under the combined pressure of the United States and the USSR. Israel's own withdrawal was obtained only after the United Nations took over the occupation of the Sinai and the Gaza Strip and guaranteed freedom of navigation in the Gulf of Aqaba. As a consequence, fedayeen activities stopped in Jordan, as well.

In the mid-1960s, however, infiltrations began again, this time at the initiative of the new nationalist movements. The first Fatah action was in January 1965 against Israel's major national water pipe. The attack itself caused little damage, and the commander of the squad was killed on his way back by a Jordanian patrol. However, the incidence of such infiltrations from the Hashemite Kingdom and Lebanon multiplied. Water pipes, electric plants, and fueling stations were regular targets of commando operations. Israel renewed its systematic retaliation campaigns. The largest action took place in Samoah during November 1966, where many buildings were blown up.

War broke out following Nasser's expulsion of the UN troops in the Sinai, his military reoccupation of the territory up to Gaza, and his blockade of the Tiran Straits. The new offensive treaty concluded between Egypt, Syria, and Jordan notwithstanding, the Six-Day War of June 1967 ended with the Israeli conquest of the Sinai, the Gaza Strip, the Golan Heights, and the West Bank.

Again the military circumstances were transformed. One million former enemies were now under Israeli military occupation. Moreover, Jerusalem was united, and tens of thousands of its Arab inhabitants were considered an integral part of a city populated by a Jewish majority. Over time, job opportunities in Israel for the inhabitants of these territories multiplied, while direct contact with the Arab world was also maintained through the open bridges over the Jordan River. These circumstances were obviously ideal for a determined guerrilla movement.

Effectively, 1967–68 was a period of intense paramilitary activity. Yasser Arafat himself was hiding in Jerusalem; he and his lieutenants strove to weave a network expanding to the city, the Judean Mountains, and the desert. Hopes that relied on the "armed popular struggle" were soon disappointed as the Israelis achieved greater control over rural areas, protecting sites, institutions, public transportation, and public centers, and tightening their grip on the underground. A few months later, Arafat moved his headquarters to Jordan, while the battle in the field was getting more and more difficult.

From Jordan, the PLO, now under fedayeen leadership, progressively formulated a new strategy. This program emphasized the Palestinian ethnic unity of the two banks of the Jordan; the one, the East Bank, was free and should provide the necessary effort to assure a solid linkage with the second, the occupied West Bank. This strategy, needless to say, represented a fundamental threat to the Hashemite regime.[3]

The IDF, however, was able to adapt itself to the new circumstances. This was the period of the pursuit-and-purge operations in the Jordan and Beit Shean valleys. Paratroopers and commandos firmly drew the distinction between the banks by cutting off the eastern side. Almost any attempt at infiltration was doomed to failure, while Israeli control was sharply intensified within the villages of the occupied bank, as well as at the bridges. Direct attacks were also made on nearby PLO bases on the other side of the river, even though such actions were risky. In March 1968, for instance, a wide-scope campaign on the village of Karameh, on the eastern shore of the Jordan, ended with heavy Israeli losses because of the intervention of Jordanian artillery.

In general, the IDF's continuous efforts brought a gradual eastward retreat of the PLO bases. Indirectly, this retreat was to a large degree responsible for the clash that followed between the Palestinians and Amman: with the Palestinians nearing the capital, acute tension soon arose between the fedayeen and the Jordanian army. The aspirations of the PLO for an independent base of action were more than the Hashemites could tolerate without jeopardizing their rule.

The Zarka affair precipitated the crisis. Three international planes were intercepted in the air and were forced to land at Zarka, a Jordanian airport, where the hijackers and their chiefs behaved as though they were on their own land. This constituted the halfway mark of Amman's loss of authority over its own territory. A few weeks later, King Hussein reacted by fighting the PLO. The clash ended with the total withdrawal of the PLO from the kingdom's boundaries in an episode known as Black September.

The PLO's evacuation from Jordan could not be stopped by Syria or Iraq, which vehemently opposed it. With American encouragement, Israel issued an ultimatum that it would not allow any foreign army on the soil of Jordan. This evacuation brought an end to the "battle of the two banks." Terrorist actions continued mainly in the Gaza Strip, where the various Palestinian movements had been more successful than anywhere else in anchoring themselves in the populated refugee camps since 1967. Recruiting fighters from among the inhabitants of these camps was not difficult, and shooting at Israeli soldiers, throwing grenades at buses, and liquidating "collaborators" became daily occurrences.

At the beginning of 1971, however, a cease-fire was called on the Suez Canal, where for an entire year Israelis and Egyptians had sustained bloody hits in a static war over the presence of Israel on the northern shore of the canal. General Arik Sharon received the High Command of the Gaza Strip. His troops, most of them experienced, were now organized according to the requirements of antiguerrilla warfare. The whole strip was divided and subdivided, down to the smallest neighborhood. A restricted and highly mobile unit was in charge of each geographical square, searching incessantly for combat contact with PLO fighters and liquidating them, mostly during action. Within the refugee camp, roads were built, houses destroyed, and inhabitants resettled in "secure" areas. By the end of 1971, almost all the PLO paramilitary networks had been dismantled.[4] Accordingly, the rate of terrorist activity dropped sharply, and it has remained at a low level ever since.

As on the West Bank, however, terrorist acts will never totally stop. Those directed at the Israelis will not always outnumber the liquidation of Arab "traitors." The most famous case in Gaza was the killing of the imam of the city in 1977; but, as shown by exhibit 6.1, this was by no means the only instance.

B. THE GUERRILLA CREDO

The PLO, like the FLN, the EOKA, and the Vietminh, is determined to use guerrilla means to achieve political aims. This is expressed in a 1980 essay found with a prisoner, written by a member of the Front of the Popular Struggle. Although this group is small, it is quite representative of the Palestinian guerrilla movement as a whole. This credo thus throws light on the ideological, tactical and strategic outlooks of the Fedayeen

Exhibit 6.1
Internal Terror: Selected Instances

Year	Place	The Story
1969–71	Gaza	Several figures were liquidated for collaboration with Israel: priest Nimri, head of the A-Shati camp committee; a Baptist nun; a taxi driver who refused to drive a wounded fedayeen; an elderly woman in Nutzeirat; two young Arab women. In April 1971, a masked man infiltrated into the Ma-Shipa hospital and killed an intern who had refused to care for a wounded fedayeen of the PFLP.
1972	Gaza	Mayor A-Shawa was attacked by a grenade when driving his car; the grenade did not explode and the fedayeen also missed when shooting at him with a gun.
1977	Ramallah	An El-Bireh inhabitant, an official of the Ministry of Education, was shot because of his positive attitude toward Sadat's initiative.
1977	Gaza	For the same reason, the Imam was killed after he condemned the radicals publicly.
1978	Ramallah	Three notables were killed in the main street, among them Abdel Nur Genkhi, rich merchant.
1980	Gaza	Four men were liquidated as "collaborators," two of them were in the delegation to Cairo in support of Sadat's initiative; another one was Deputy Mayor of Gebelya.
1981	Ramallah	A leader of the Association of Villagers and his son were killed while driving to their village.
1983	Bethlehem	Molotov cocktails were thrown at the house of Dr. Nimer Aiad, in the refugee camp of Deheishe.
1983	Nablus	A group of youngsters assaulted the local leader of the Communist Party and injured him.

Source: Miscellaneous sources (Israeli officials, IDF information, dailies).

in general, as well as on the problems and hardships they confront in their struggle.

The writer acknowledges, "Our Palestinian reality is hard and requires us to learn with seriousness from our experience during the last thirteen years." He recognizes that "military action has not evolved favorably, up to now, in the conquered land despite all our efforts. . . . [Only] if we learn about the possibilities available to us in a scientific manner will we be able to improve our action, to widen our responsibility and to push forward the Revolution."[5] The piece goes on:

We have to set up organizational structures of the greatest efficiency which should be under a supreme command able to act independently from any external authority. . . .

[Our error] since 1967 [was that] the revolution aspired at the creation of structures controlled from the outside with respect to all aspects of our action and activity. Such structures cannot be called a secret organization; they are not even an organization. Most members are incompetent in clandestine work or in secret fighting; they have no guidance either. None of the existing cells is able to plan an action beyond its own dimensions.

Thus, we are convinced of the possibility [and of the imperative character] of the creation in the territories of an organization grounded in local elements and headed by its own leadership. This organization should have the control of . . . all revolutionary resources. . . .

The best structure for secret action is the pyramidal model with a centralist-democratic command. Because of the objective difficulties, each cell should number no more than three men. Only one of them should be in command [and he would be the contact with the headquarters]. There would be local headquarters, regional headquarters, and so on. This organization would be able to assess the members, to gather information, to carry out actions according to directives from above. The whole territory should be divided into limited areas and each one should be related to the Supreme Command. . . . This structure would help us to continue the fight even if one of the cells is caught and destroyed. . . .

Our action needs strong cadres with a clear and crystallized consciousness and a high readiness to sacrifice. . . . Among the Palestinian youth who live under the conquest, there are elements who are able to shoulder these roles and this burden. The only thing to do is to develop a revolutionary consciousness. . . .

The organization must [therefore] draft new members and select them. A new member should be thoroughly examined so his qualities can be rightly evaluated. . . . In [too] many cases we have seen people caught because they did not have a precise view of their action, they did not have the necessary toughness, they misunderstood the very essence of a secret organizational activity.

Recruiting abroad our new members, by the means of short meetings with an official of the revolution—even if he is a senior figure—is not satisfactory and it has revealed itself a failure. The new member is then unable to stand up to the threatening Israeli intelligence. . . . Many have been arrested and put in prison before they could carry out the simplest action.

Recruiting abroad is [also] exploited by the enemy who sends youngsters and has succeeded in 'buying,' in order to come in contact [with the revolution] and to obtain information about our organization, our training and about those who have already been recruited. . . . Every youngster who goes abroad is suspect in the eyes of the enemy, who arrests him and questions him. . . . This pattern [of recruitment] also attracts opportunists interested in money and adventure . . . and when they come back, they do not want to work or are not able to. Though not all of them are a failure. . . .

Our worst enemy is the Israeli intelligence. This intelligence already has vast experience in warfare against organized cells. . . . This service has succeeded because of its means and its experience and has bypassed the defensive phase for the offensive phase. . . . It has bases in every village and neighborhood . . . [and only] a strong local secret organization is powerful enough to challenge [it]. . . .

Israeli domination is the primary target we have to strike at by any means . . . with all the toughness and violence we are able [to show]. . . . At this stage we have no choice but to turn against civilians. Action against the army only according to the noble concept of "soldiers against soldiers" does not fit the concrete situation we face. The enemy controls the best military technology in the world, its forces alone outbalance all Arab armies together.

The structure this text suggests is typical of any politicoparamilitary underground movement. What is revealing is the absolute absence of any mention of a political hierarchy distinct from the military command structure. This indicates that, according to the writer, such a crystallization is not in the reach of the PLO in the administered territories. The reasons are actually given in the text itself: the particular efficiency of Israeli intelligence, which gives shape to the offensive posture of the incumbents' alignment. More telling than the recommendations, the criticisms reveal the type of guerrilla movement existing in the 1980s in the administered territories. They speak of people frequently recruited abroad, who are not a very selective cohort; these make for groups that are directed from the outside, and that usually do not endure for long; the main outlet of action open to these groups is blind terror.

C. FROM HIJZI TO TAMRI: TWENTY YEARS

Many Israelis have accumulated a wide in-the-field experience of the Palestinians. They are also reliable witnesses. In an illuminating radio interview, a senior intelligence officer, Avraham, remembered:

Last week, we "celebrated" the nineteenth anniversary of Fatah. On the same day, nineteen years ago, a mine was set, very primitively, on our national water carrier; nothing happened. . . . One week later we caught Mahmud Bakr Hijzi— with a few youngsters, he had tried to set a mine near the water reservoir of Lakhish. He was the very first Fatah fighter we ever caught. He was just a small criminal without any education nor motivation. . . . Nineteen years later, during the Peace for Galilee Operation, we caught Tsalah Tamri. He was a totally different man; he had an academic background and was highly motivated.

The various movements within the PLO do differ from each other in this respect. Those of a more radical orientation are also more selective in their recruitment; in comparison to the PFLP or the DFLP, the Fatah is still characterized by a lower educational and motivational average. However, in all major organizations the more senior ranks are filled by individuals of a higher level. Moreover, says Avraham, "today one cannot find illiterate people among the fedayeen anymore." This is due to the transformation of Palestinian society where, in absence of a motherland, "education is viewed as of the highest value because [Palestinians] are able to take [it] with them to any place and [it] cannot be taken away from them."

Avraham emphasizes that PLO fighters are frequently ready to fight to the death and to carry out the most courageous actions, even though, from a strictly professional viewpoint, their military capacity is often very elementary.[6]

Other Israeli officials were ready to supplement Avraham's testimony in the frame of personal interviews. H, for example, the military attorney at one of the military courts in Judea and Samaria, has perused hundreds of files of PLO fighters captured by the Israelis. His conviction is that every major organization affiliated with the PLO has senior representatives on the West Bank and in the Gaza Strip. Most activists here are linked to local headquarters but are not related to each other.

He remembers the case of a twenty-five-man group that acted in the Ramallah area and, among other things, killed two members of an Association of Villagers. The group was under the command of the Beirut PFLP headquarters while, most interestingly, the two dominant figures were a former student back from the United States and a building worker with no formal education. Another group, active in Bethlehem, was of DFLP allegiance. It numbered thirty-five students, mostly Christian, and their task consisted of preparing dynamite devices. This group, too, according to H, was part of a wider organization in which different groups, unknown to each other, specialized in various missions.

On the other hand, there are also groups that constitute independent local initiatives. H recalls the case of a group of hotel waiters who wanted to start sabotage activity and another group of peasants who infiltrated an Association of Villagers in order to get Israeli weapons and use them afterward against "traitors" and Israeli targets. As a rule, according to H, people are recruited to movements by relatives, friends, or acquaintances. Once they are caught, however, they enjoy the legal aid of lawyers—mostly local Arabs, but also Israeli Arabs or Jews—who are paid indirectly by the PLO itself.

J, another military attorney, adds that his own observations lead him to think that not every movement is similarly involved in various guerrilla activity. Basically, he contends, the Fatah mainly invests in military actions, the radical fronts in political activism, and the Communists only in political militancy. Moreover, those dedicated to politics are generally better educated than the fighters. The latter, most often, are recruited in the casbah or in the refugee camp. The students who participate in fedayeen groups are mainly those who have studied abroad and owe their scholarship to the PLO, which obliges them now to "pay back."

G, president of a military court, draws an image emphasizing the "amateur" character of the Palestinian guerrilla. Echoing and confirming other witnesses, he emphasizes that he is by no means impressed by the quality of the people he judges. There are the merchants who travel regularly to Jordan and smuggle weapons and explosives into Israel. These materials are delivered to local cells, organized periodically by underground militants shuttling between the West Bank and Amman.

M, deputy president of another military court, confirms that terrorism mostly attracts people of lower strata, while the wealthier and better educated more often participate in political frameworks, trade unions, clubs, or charity organizations. The universities are the main focus of PLO politics. As for paramilitary action, M adds, there are villages and neighborhoods that are never involved in subversion, while others are incessantly implicated. This suggests that the webs of personal allegiances and territorial entities, so central to Arab society, explain the differential involvement in the insurgency more than the concept of class cleavages.

A, another president of a military court in the West Bank, warns not to draw too sharp a distinction between political activism and paramilitary action. He remembers a dentist who was a leader of the Fatah paramilitary underground in the area and tried to convince a leading figure of an Association of Villagers to leave the anti-PLO organization. Felicia Langer, the number-one Jewish lawyer for PLO people on trial, was the defender of this dentist. A is also cautious about the role of age. The fifteen-to-twenty-five age bracket is the most common among the fighters, but many people standing trial for conveying explosives and setting mines on roads are much older. Moreover, women are still a small minority among the PLO fighters, but A thinks that the percentage of women is increasing.

Stories of intrinsic interest are numerous, such as that of a fifty-five-year-old man who was caught and brought to trial for his affiliation with the PLO. He called for the Jewish mayor of Netanya as a character witness who could tell about the positive attitude toward the Jews that had distinguished his family during the 1930s. Another curious case was that of the son of a very famous Nablus lawyer, who worked at the military court. The boy had been arrested for recruiting youngsters to an underground cell. A similar incident occurred with the Nablus mayor's own son. The fifteen-year-old boy was fined $500 for stoning a military car and was sentenced to fifteen days' imprisonment. The Shaqa family refused to pay the fine, and the jail sentence was prolonged by two months. Apparently, to have a son in an Israeli prison was a kind of honor for the whole family. In Nablus's casbah or in refugee camps like Deheishe or Balata, the PLO seems to be more solidly anchored and more professional.

This heterogeneous picture of the PLO's military activity does not hold for the Gaza Strip as it does for the West Bank. Z, a senior member of the military court of Gaza, emphasizes several differences, some of them related to the past Egyptian—and not Jordanian—presence. More particularly, there is the overall lower economic standard, the higher degree of Islamic religiosity, and the larger proportion of refugees within the population. As a rule, activists are of a lower educational and socioeconomic level than on the West Bank. Among them the religious Altaya Aslamya, a development of the Muslim Brotherhood, is particularly popular in the refugee camp. In terms of political attitudes, the Egyptian past explains the greater enthusiasm among the inhabitants for President Anwar Sadat's 1977 initiative. At the same time, elements of the pre-1967 Egyptian-controlled PLA still constituted the backbone of the Palestinian underground movements.

According to Z, PLO fighting has been more systematic here than on the West Bank from the very beginning. Weapons were smuggled in from Egypt and obtained from the IDF itself by Jewish underworld gangs. These arms were hidden by specialized cells, which handed them over to operational teams when needed. These cells are now activated most often by men who come to stay for short lapses of time. Their best allies are a number of families that are well known for their steady loyalty to PLO organizations, especially the Fatah. From time to time, special task cells were sent from abroad. Best remembered was the case of the liquidation of the imam of Gaza, who supported Sadat's peace policy. He was killed after three unsuccessful attempts that were detected by Israeli security before completion.

The population at large is controlled by anti-Israeli groups by means of terror, money, and political articulation. D, a senior official in charge of a crucial department in the governor's office, reveals that enormous funds reach the strip through local banks, such as the Bank of Palestine, from various places in the world. Even Israeli banks are used from New York or Paris, to transfer funds to "respectable figures who actually deliver the money to the local PLO men." These men act under a multitude of organizational covers, the most important of which, reportedly, is the Red Crescent. Similarly, the chairman of an important professional association is suspected to fill a leading role for the Fatah, in both political and paramilitary unrest. Evidently, warfare and politics are more intimately tied in the Gaza Strip than in the West Bank.

D. IN THE FIELD

The survey discussed in the following passage was carried out during 1983 and 1984. It gathered as much information as possible about the fedayeen from the files kept in court of the trials of 492 subjects.[7] The issues that I and my assistants wanted to investigate were the social characteristics of PLO activists, the organizational schemes and recruitment problems of the various movements, and the type or types of guerrilla activity. The verdicts also permitted an investigation of the working of the juridical system itself as an aspect of Israel's antiguerrilla policy.

The sample is composed of 21 percent subjects from Gaza, 41 percent from Ramallah, and 38 percent from Nablus, all cases chosen randomly from the courts' archives. These were judged between 1978 and 1983, and most (95 percent) concern offenses committed between 1976 and 1983. Not all of the archives were well organized; therefore, we cannot affirm that the geographic distribution in the sample is faithfully representative of the genuine proportions of cases according to areas. We do know, from informants, that Gaza was less restless during these years than the West Bank, in consistency with our data. We also found that military court files are rarely complete and may lack various items of information. Thus, the number of subjects varies from one question to another. These shortcomings notwithstanding, however, the findings seem to indicate a true picture. It is our estimate that the sample represents some 30 percent of all cases relevant to our project, that is, those which took place between 1978 and 1983. This sets the average annual figure at about 3,000 persons brought to trial for this category of offense in Israeli military courts in the administered territories.

The people in our sample are quite young. Their average age was 24.2 years at the time of their trial (SD = 8.673); 7 percent were younger than 18; 80 percent were between 18 and 30; 13 percent were above 30. Almost all of them are men (97 percent); the wide majority are unmarried (72 percent) or at least without children (83 percent).

When looking at the social characteristics of this largely young, unmarried cohort, it appears that most have a solid educational background (exhibit 6.2). A small minority had not received any education at all; the majority had reached a secondary level, and almost half had a higher education. It may be concluded that the underground networks recruit mainly among the educated. In regard to the socioeconomic status (SES) dimension, activists, it seems, are less anchored among the peasants

Exhibit 6.2
Educational Background of Activists (*N* = 492)

Level of Education	%
No school education	7
Elementary school (partial and complete)	11
Secondary school (partial and complete)	36
Post-secondary vocational school	34
University education (B.A. and higher)	12
Total	100%

and other lower social strata than among the middle class. According to the SES standard scale, only 40 percent of our sample consists of people of an occupational status under 30, that is, stable working class; 20 percent belong to lower-middle class (between 30 and 50, which refers to clerks, technicians, and the like); 15 percent to middle and higher status (over 50, which refers to dentists, lawyers, higher administrative positions, and so on); 25 percent are students, that is, of potential middle or higher status.

Moreover, about half of the sample (51 percent) live in a city, 28 percent in a village, 17 percent in a refugee camp, and 4 percent abroad. It clearly appears that the huge peasant population of the territories is sharply underrepresented among the subjects, as opposed to the city dweller. The latter group, it is true, includes many residents of the casbah or the refugee camps situated within the city or in its direct vicinity. Nevertheless, in the context of the data one may deduce that the "normal" activist is a city dweller and mostly of an SES above the lower strata. In contradiction to the impression of some of our informants, most fedayeen are not of lower social extraction.

As for the patterns of recruitment, 8 percent were recruited by a relative, 46 percent by a friend or an acquaintance, 15 percent by a stranger, 19 percent during a stay abroad, 12 percent in other ways (mainly self-recruitment). It thus appears that recruitment is mostly a function of existing relations and not of specialized channels, which undoubtedly expresses an organizational weakness of the underground. The same weakness appears when one considers the kinds of activity and movement affiliations. The subjects, indeed, belong to varied movements, the Fatah, the PFLP, the DFLP, the PFLP General Command, the Saiqa, and the Communists. Moreover, many are affiliated to unknown groups like the Front of the Egyptian Struggle, local versions of the Muslim Brothers, and nameless independent groups. When categorized under the headings of local groups, radicals, and the Fatah, the

Exhibit 6.3
Types and Degrees of Underground Action

Seriousness of the Offense	Degree and Type of Action	% of Cases (n = 492)
1. Less	Lower involvement in organizational activity (contacts with a member of a hostile organization)	37
2.	Higher involvement in organizational activity (participation in secret meetings, distribution of hostile material, attempts to convince others to join in, and the like)	25
3.	Lower involvement in paramilitary activity (hiding a person wanted by the police, not revealing knowledge important to incumbents, driving an activist to some place at his request)	29
4. More	Higher involvement in paramilitary activity (participation in a group of fedayeen planning and/or carrying out a hostile violent action)	9
	Total	100

importance of each is rated as follows: 10 percent, 33 percent, and 57 percent, respectively. The Fatah alone accounts for the majority of underground activism from 1978 to 1983, even though the general picture is one of confusion and internal division.

Exhibit 6.3 shows the types of activities in which the subjects were involved. The thirty-three different offenses we found in the files were categorized according to level of gravity; for each subject, we took into consideration only the gravest offense with which he was charged.[8]

Only a few of the subjects took part in real terrorist activity; most were caught at an early stage of involvement in the underground. The efficiency of the Israeli intelligence explains these findings. On average, the subjects had been in contact with the underground for only thirteen months; 90 percent had been involved for less than three years. The subjects often did not really have the time to commit very serious actions; consequently, the sentences were mostly light: 12 percent were not actually imprisoned; 28 percent were imprisoned for up to six months; 21 percent from six months to one year; 24 percent from one to three years. Only 11 percent received from three to ten years and 4 percent more than ten years. It is no wonder, therefore, that the wide majority of the subjects did confess their guilt and asked for clemency on the ground of former "good behavior" and the light offenses they had committed.

Interesting correlations between the various factors studied were also obtained. As suggested by several informants, the findings show that members of the Fatah are frequently of a lower educational level than those of the radical "fronts" (respectively 4.4 and 4.98 as average scores on a nine-step educational ladder) and also of a lower SES, even when ignoring the relatively large number of students on the Left (respectively 34 and 36 SES average scores). On the other hand, the refugee camps are more widely represented in leftist organizations than in the Fatah (22 percent and 14 percent respectively), while the contrary is true as to villages and cities (78 percent in leftist organizations, 86 percent in the Fatah). The local groups are indicated as the most successful among the refugees, who constituted 27 percent of the membership of this category.

Paradoxically, members of leftist organizations are frequently caught for offenses that are less serious than those committed by members of the Fatah. Considering the continuum of exhibit 6.3 as a four-step scale, the Fatah obtains an average score of 2.85 (SD = .996) and the leftists only 2.09 (SD = .782; t value: 2.79; $p < .01$). Moreover, the Fatah is implicated twice as often as the leftists in the gravest type of activity, although their following in the sample is only 50 percent higher than that of the leftists. Ideological radicalism, if so, does not mean behavioral radicalism. Again, in corroboration with the reports of some of our informants, the radicals are more involved in political militancy—which is less serious from the viewpoint of the law—than in paramilitary activity, and the contrary is true for the Fatah.

Interestingly enough, in many respects, the local independent groups hold a position between the Left and the Fatah. In age, however, they differ significantly. Local groups outside the PLO establishment are particularly attractive to the young. We found 21.4 years as the mean score for these independents, while the figure for the Fatah was 24 and for the Left 24.5 (F ratio: 3.247; $p < .01$).

An additional comparative point is the geographical differentiation. Of the Gazean subjects, 32 percent were refugee camp dwellers; of those from Ramallah and Nablus, 12 percent. This is related to the proportion of refugee camp inhabitants in the general population: while they constitute almost half the population of the Gaza Strip, they represent only 10 percent in the West Bank. Similarly, the SES average score is much lower in the strip (26.00) than in Ramallah (35.56) or Nablus (33.66). Moreover, because Gaza is poorer and contains more refugees, the underground is apparently better organized; actions are less numerous but more serious than in the West Bank (2.4 as against 2.1 in Nablus and 1.8 in Ramallah; F ratio: 12,72; $p < .01$).

Finally, the seriousness of offenses correlates inversely with the occupational prestige of offenders (Pearson correlation: $-.2158$; $p < .01$). This means that people of higher status who are active in the underground are involved mainly in organizational work rather than in direct terrorist action. Similarly, people of higher SES, who were more involved in organizational work, were found to be more veteran than people of lower SES, who were more often involved in terrorism (Pearson correlation between education and veteranship: 2.921; SES and veteranship: .4031; both p's < .01). Evidently, again, Israeli antiterror warfare is more efficient than the means used on the political front.

E. THE MEN BEHIND THE BARS

Viewed from the angle of individual stories, the files of military courts are no less revealing. Typical biographies illustrate who the men in the underground were and what the term *guerrilla* means "in the field."

Ahmed was born in 1947, in a village near Nazareth. In 1948, the village became a part of Israel, and the family fled to Jenin, in northern Samaria. There Ahmed's parents opened a shop, and he himself remained in the town until he completed secondary school. He then went to Beirut to complete his higher education and came back to Jenin, after graduating with a degree in the humanities, to open his own shop of office supplies. In 1976, fulfilling commitment made in return for a study grant, he left for a two-week training course at a Fatah base in Syria. Once back home, he organized a small group of friends; in 1977 they set a mine in a Haifa industrial plant. A few weeks later, a woman came to his shop and handed him explosives to hide for future use. In 1980, at the age of thirty-three, he was sentenced to seventeen years of imprisonment by the Israeli military court at Nablus.

Fatima also belongs to the well-to-do. She never was a refugee; she was born in 1939 in a village near Tulkarem, Samaria, in a settled family. Her elementary education in the village was followed by high school in Nablus and then by university studies in Algeria. She graduated in nursing and remained in Algeria for several years. In 1973, she came back and took a secretarial job at the Nablus Hospital. On a visit to Amman in 1979, Fatima, who had not yet married, met a young man who was staying at the same hotel as she. They became lovers, and the man recruited her for the PFLP-GC. Fatima was to collect information about people of her town and to send it to Amman. In time, Fatima and her friend switched loyalty to the PFLP; several months later she was arrested and sentenced to one year of imprisonment.

Suliman belongs to an even higher social category than Ahmed and Fatima. He is a physician, living in Al-Bireh, Judea, and he owns his own clinic in Ramallah. He is married and the father of two children. A onetime member of several clubs and associations, during his studies in Cairo (1965–75) he became affiliated with the Fatah. He was a dedicated propagandist for the Palestinian cause, writing articles published abroad and recruiting individuals for PLO activity. At the age of thirty-three, he was sentenced to sixteen months in jail.

Abdallah was forty-six when he was arrested. He was a teacher in Halhul and a member of the town council. His brother, a doctor, had completed his studies in Yugoslavia and was living in Jordan. By independent conviction, Abdallah got in touch with the Fatah, through the intermediation of his brother and a cousin, both active members of this organization in Amman. Abdallah proposed that the Fatah start a farm that would be a cover for an operational base within the administered territories. Before long, he was caught by the Israelis and sentenced to six months.

Again, within the same social milieu, Salim was a twenty-two-year-old son of a wealthy family of merchants in Nalt, a village in Judea. From 1975 to 1978, he studied television in Baghdad for three years. During that time, he was recruited by the DFLP, which partially financed his studies. He returned home in 1978; a few weeks later he was arrested and sentenced to four months' imprisonment.

A different type of activist is exemplified by Mahmud. Since the death of his father, Mahmud's family had lived in the casbah of Nablus, in very harsh conditions. Mahmud nevertheless succeeded at school, and after his matriculation he went to India, where he received an academic degree. There he met a member of the PFLP, who recruited him. At the end of his studies he traveled to Damascus to register before joining a training base in Lebanon for two months. Back in Nablus, he became a teacher and, at the same time, got involved in youth organization on behalf of his movement. He was in his early twenties when sentenced to twenty months.

From a similar origin but with a different destiny, Nazmi was of the same age as Mahmud when he was arrested. He was born in Taybeh, Samaria, to a poor family of peasants. His brother was blind, his father in his eighties; he himself had gone to school for only six years and was a building painter. In 1978, he tried to find work in Jordan and went to Zarka, where he was recruited into the Saiqa. After a short stay in Damascus for registration and a three-day training period, he came back to his village, recruited other youngsters, and prepared various acts of sabotage with them. He was arrested just after he succeeded in gathering a few friends. He was sentenced to two years.

Hussein, born in 1951, also originates from a poor peasant family. He was recruited by a relative for the Fatah while on a family visit to Amman. He traveled to Beirut and spent several days in a training camp in Lebanon. Yet when he came back to his village with some money to start "working," he did not demonstrate any initiative. He was arrested only as a formal member of the Fatah in 1979 and sentenced to nine months.

Daud much resembles Hussein and Mahmud. Born in 1965, he lived in a refugee camp next to Jenin. He was an unskilled worker of seventeen when he joined six other youngsters who organized independently. They placed Palestinian flags on public buildings by night, wrote slogans on walls, and prepared Molotov cocktails. On one occasion they threw a Molotov cocktail at a bus driving local workers to Israel; one night they even attacked a police car. The sentence in this case was five years.

Along with such genuinely committed youngsters and adults, the list of PLO members also includes many for whom the revolution simply fits personal needs. Yusuf and Neri are examples of young adults (nineteen and twenty-one) from well-established families, unable to get along with their parents (Yusuf quarreled with his father; Neri was unwilling to enter the family business). Being friends, they decided to leave their village (near Ramallah) together, and to look for a future elsewhere. They worked in Arad, Israel, for three months and then moved to Amman, where they were employed at various jobs. In January 1978, they turned to the Fatah office and expressed their readiness to join the organization in return for higher education scholarships. Yusuf and Neri were sent to Lebanon for training, but unlike others, they remained there for a whole year, because their scholarship arrived late. Despairing of the fedayeen, they decided to escape from the Fatah camp and to return home. Caught by Syrian soldiers, they were imprisoned for several weeks before being released. They finally succeeded in reentering the West Bank but were soon arrested again, this time by the Israelis, who sent them to prison for three months.

F. CONCLUSIONS

From these stories, as well as from the general picture yielded by our quantitative data, several conclusions may be drawn:

1. The Palestinian revolution constitutes a general background of life for the Palestinians and is by no means a matter involving only a small minority of people or confined to restricted interests.
2. Many do share a genuine commitment to the revolution and are ready to sacrifice; others, however, find in the movement solutions for many diverse material or personal problems.
3. This interest in the revolution cuts across all social strata, though, according to origins, status, and aspirations, some groups are more inclined to politically "cleaner" and socially more rewarding activities, while others find their natural outlet in the paramilitary track.
4. A basic paradoxical characteristic of the Palestinian national revolution "in the field" is the contrast between the ability of the revolution to attract competent, dedicated people and its demonstration of endemic organizational weakness, an absence of solid and permanent structures of local underground work and reliance on small-scale independent initiatives.
5. Most astounding is the efficacy of Israeli intelligence, which in most instances gets hold of activists and networks in their very early stages, which, in turn, restricts the severity of sentences.

6. This latter trait, I suggest, perpetually reintegrates people who have been put on trial for pro-PLO activity within the "civilian" society and in effect gives rise to a situation where the commitment to the revolution is quite general but not of great impact.

7. To the extent that activities are carried out, they rarely surpass unsophisticated blind terrorism.

These characteristics can be explained by the Israeli model of military antiguerrilla activity. An offensive alignment sustained by far-reaching intelligence, with a powerful defensive system, this antiguerrilla activity leaves no room for the development of rural guerrillas. At most the insurgents are able to lead a terrorist attack, mostly of a nonselective, blind nature. This terrorism is the only kind of activity that weak underground structures can afford. Similarly, its manpower recruitment is loose and unselective.

Within this context, as in any protracted violent conflict against coercion, the more educated and the more ambitious are the most attracted by insurgency. They are drawn mainly to its radical wing, while within the movement this element also most often prefers the political and organizational roles to tough clandestine warfare.

NOTES

1. M. Greenberg and S. Livius, *BLMS;* IDF Intelligence, History Department (Hebrew), December 1980.

2. Quoted ibid, 3.

3. This analysis was reported by Israeli officials in charge of antiguerrilla warfare.

4. Greenberg and Livius, 8.

5. From a well-documented source; Judea-Samaria Headquarters, IDF *Special Survey,* Research Department (Hebrew), December 1980.

6. Avraham, "Interview," *IDF Station,* January 8, 1984.

7. The Defense Regulations (Emergency, 1945) grant to the chief of staff the power to institute military courts to try civilians in matters pertaining to security. The judges are military officers with legal training. They sit either individually or in groups of three. A court with a single judge is entitled to give sentences of up to three years' imprisonment; a court of three may even give the death sentence, although this has never been done. Appeals are not allowed, but every sentence of a three-judge court has to be approved by the chief of staff. On July 9, 1963, the right of appeal was instituted, but this privilege was not extended later to military courts in the territories (Nablus, Ramallah, and Gaza). The Court of Appeal in Lydda hears those cases which take place within Israel's international borders.

8. Twenty-seven percent of the sample were tried only for one offense; 49 percent for two; 24 percent for three or more.

Part III The International Scene

7 Blessings

A. THE SUPERIMPOSITION OF CONFLICTS

To an extent unprecedented in the history of guerrilla conflict, the local Israeli-Palestinian dispute is also significant on the international scene.

From its inception, modern Zionism, under the leadership of Theodor Herzl, was tied to international reality.[1] In the middle of World War I, a British foreign policy statement, the Balfour Declaration, sanctioned the creation of a Zionist entity in Palestine. A British Mandate, approved by the League of Nations, legitimized it in its earliest stages. Every since, numerous commitments and interests have bound the Zionist enterprise, the Jewish diaspora, and the Western world.[2]

The neighbors, on the other hand, soon became active participants in the Jewish-Palestinian dispute, which reached a peak in the 1948 massive intervention of the Arab League against the Jewish state newly born from a decision made by the United Nations. Western Europe, the United States, and the USSR confronted one another in this area through a merciless war of influence. The anti-Israeli coalition tried to form intimate bonds with Third World nations, mainly the non-Arab Muslim countries.[3]

We have already seen that on the Jewish-Palestinian dispute was superimposed an Israeli-Arab conflict that by no means could be reduced to the former. The presence of a Jewish state in the Middle East was condemned not only because of the Palestinian cause but also as an unacceptable injury to the Arabic-Muslim traditional claim to the territory that spreads from the Persian Gulf to the North African Atlantic shore. Moreover, because an Arab cause was also challenged, this conflict was referred to the Palestinian question, which became thereby a major card in the eternal inter-Arab game for leadership. This contest is rooted in the Islamic view of a united Arab *ummah* (nation), sustained by the community of religion and language, a concept that bluntly contrasts with the contemporary plurality of sovereignties. As a result, the competition of the major powers over influence interferes as well with the game for leadership in the Arab arena, which has gradually become one of rival "conservative" (pro-Western) and "progressive" (pro-Soviet) camps.

At some times, the Jewish-Palestinian antagonism overshadows the Israeli-Arab one; at others, the converse is true. However, each conflict exists on its own, even if it sometimes overlaps, and always intermingles with, the other. The Palestinian issue was dominant in the 1930s, but the all-Arab conflict with Israel accounts, for the most part, for the 1948 war, the Sinai operation in 1956, the Six-Day War of 1967, and the 1973 Yom Kippur War. Again, the Palestinian question has been of primary importance since the Israeli conquest of Samaria, Judea, and the Gaza Strip in 1967. It has thus played an active role in determining the course of the all-Arab conflict and, relatedly, in inter-Arab dynamics. This Palestinian issue developed not only as a local incumbent-insurgent confrontation but also in external arenas, where it was unavoidably linked to the Israeli-Arab conflict.

Because they constitute distinct foci of reference bearing different interests, each cause may eventually exploit the other to its own profit. The creation in 1964 of the PLO, as a direct result of the Palestinian problem, was also dictated by the all-Arab conflict. Palestinian nationalism was an appropriate cause, capable of mobilizing Arab resources and international influence against Israel. Moreover, the creation of the PLO, which was sponsored by pro-Soviet Egypt and Syria, weakened Jordan (and thenceforth the entire pro-West conservative Arab camp) by delegitimizing the annexation of the West Bank by the Hashemite Kingdom. The event was thus a crucial move in the contest over leadership and dominance in the Arab world, and it was also very meaningful for the USSR in its competition with the United States. On the other hand, the 1973 oil crisis was caused by the mobilization of Arab economic power in support of Egypt and Syria's effort in the Yom Kippur War, and it enhanced the status of the Arab states in the world of diplomacy. This was taken advantage of by the PLO, which established diplomatic ties with dozens of states at the time of Israel's greatest international isolation.

The Yom Kippur War constituted a decisive turn in the all-Arab–Israeli issue, which, in the long run, also altered the circumstances of the Jewish-Palestinian confrontation in the international arena. This war demonstrated the limited capabilities of the Arabs in conventional confrontation, even under the best possible conditions (the surprise effect of the simultaneous Egyptian-Syrian attack on the Suez Canal and the Golan Heights on the Jewish Day of Atonement). Hence, the subsequent negotiations between Egypt and Israel over disengagement in the Sinai and, later, over a total Israeli withdrawal from the desert in return for a peace treaty represent the logical lessons of 1973.

Egypt, however, has always been the major, if not the only, Arab protagonist in the Middle Eastern wars. As soon as it withdraws from belligerent actions, the all-Arab–Israeli conflict comes to a standstill, leaving the front arena, again, to the Israeli-Palestinian issue. This, in turn, justifies Anwar Sadat's statement that "this issue is the heart of the Middle East crisis."

The Camp David Agreements redefined the areas of influence of the superpowers. The Soviets lost their influence in Cairo to the benefit of the United States. This Russian setback was, it is true, immediately counterbalanced by Ayatollah Ruholla Khomeini's overthrow of the pro-American regime in Tehran. The Iraq-Iran war, however, gave another advantage to the United States: Iraq gradually retreated from the Soviet area to strengthen its ties with the pro-Western Arab camp.

Even after Egypt concluded a formal peace treaty with Israel, there was no question of its—or any Arab state's—solidarity with the Palestinian cause itself. This consensus of commitment, however, may conceal wide variation in motives. From 1967 to 1973, Syria and Egypt were driven by a need to "save the national honor" after the burning humiliation of the Six-Day War. Since 1979, the Palestinian cause has served Egypt as an excuse to maintain its relations with Israel within a limited frame: for Syria, it is a means to achieve dominance over Lebanon and to justify its own aspirations of leadership in the Arab world.

At any rate, the sympathy for Palestinian nationalism among Arabs throughout the Middle East accounts for the unprecedented amplification of the conflict on the international scene.

B. RESOURCES AND CONNECTIONS

The PLO has been favored by numerous and generous benefactors. It is estimated that this roof organization received $400 million per year from the Baghdad Fund (created in 1978 by the Arab governments).[4] Of this sum, a $150 million budget has been allocated each year under the supervision of a PLO-Jordanian commission for the *tsumud* within the territories. The remaining dollars support diplomatic activity abroad, as well as (until 1982) the politicomilitary structure of the Lebanese mini-Palestine. Individual states, such as Syria, Libya, and Saudi Arabia, and institutions, such as universities, unions, and municipalities in the Arab world, also grant money to specific PLO groups on a regular basis. Moreover, donations are assessed for a National Palestinian Fund all over the Palestinian diaspora.

Furthermore, the profits derived from such PLO activities as mediation in oil negotiations and investment in financial holdings, travel agencies, hotels, and even marketing firms for agricultural products must be added to these resources. The Arab Bank of Oman-Jordan, for instance, is thought of by commentators as belonging to the PLO.[5] With an estimated capital of $4 billion, this bank is principally active in the United States and Western Europe. Financial capital is invested directly by the PLO in numerous banks all over the world.

This financial strength allows the Palestinian movement the capability to create and support training bases, to acquire weapons not offered by benefactors, and to establish a solid "in-exile" paramilitary framework in every refugee camp in the Palestinian diaspora. Important bases in the late 1970s were in Damascus, Baghdad, and Kwud Zarka in Tunisia. The major strongholds were in Lebanon—in western Beirut, Saida, Tyre, and the so-called Fatahland in the Southeast. Later, after the evacuation from southern and eastern Lebanon, bases were set up at Behahi and Nahar-al-Bard, north of Tripoli (Lebanon), in Tripoli (Libya), and at Shtura and Bal-Beck in eastern central Lebanon.

Specialized training was also offered to PLO recruits in the best ideological and military centers of the Soviet bloc, from the Patrice Lumumba University of Moscow to tank, aircraft, and missile bases in Czechoslovakia, East Germany, Cuba, and North Korea.

The PLO has also been supplied with a wide range of arms from varied origins. In 1982 it had, in Lebanon, about 130 to 160 antitank cannons of 122, 160, 85, and 57 mm; approximately 90 middle-range cannons of 115 and 130 mm; 70 to 80 BM-21, BM-11, and BM-14 missiles; 120 UR-416 and BTR-152 armored vehicles; between 80 and 100 Soviet-made T-34 tanks; and about 20 T-54 tanks.[6] The origins of these arms include Russia, China, and North Korea; some were imported directly, while others reached their destination by way of Libya, Syria, Iraq, and Algeria (see exhibit 7.1). A smaller quantity of equipment was of American and Western European origin, supplied by the Saudis and the world free market of weapons.

The resources at the PLO's disposal were also instrumental in its development of international terrorist activity against Israeli and Jewish targets abroad, as well as in its collaboration with most of the terrorist organizations of the world.

From July 1968 to December 1982, for instance, more than 336 operations were carried out by the PLO outside Israel and the territories.[7] The average number is 22 per year, but there are differences between years. In 1968 the figure was 2; in 1969, 14; in 1970, 15; and in 1971, 16. There was a sudden increase in 1972 (34) and 1973 (40), followed by a decrease in the two following years (14 and 9, respectively). From 1976 to 1978, the number fluctuated quite sharply (10, 14, 24), jumping again

Exhibit 7.1
Bombs from Libya in Boxes of Spare Tractor Parts

Source: IDF Spokesman, July 1982.

in 1979 (41). Two more restful years (20 and 17) were followed by a new peak (56 in 1982).

These fluctuations are a function of a variety of factors. Problems of organization after the Six-Day War explain the low rates after 1967; the necessary reorganization after the destruction of networks by Israeli and European antiterror warfare accounts for the figures of 1980 and 1981. The PLO leadership's interest in international terrorism has varied at different periods; the organization was particularly reserved after it achieved undeniable respectability in the early 1970s. Political circumstances, however, have also had the opposite effect: in the aftermath of the signing of the Camp David Agreements, for instance, the PLO again resorted to international terror in order to challenge the new peace.

Among PLO organizations, the Fatah is prominent in the realm of international terror, as well as in other fields of activity. Hence, among the 196 operations of which the executors' organizational affiliation was identified, 63 were carried out by members of the Fatah and 39 more by members of the Fatah-related Black September (52 percent in all). The PFLP is also responsible for a significant share—25 percent—and the small Abu Nidal group accounts for no less than 9 percent of Palestinian international terrorist acts. These achievements contrast with the relatively restricted part played by Naief Hawatmeh's DFLP (1 percent); other major participants have been the Saiqa (9 percent) and the PFLP-GC (5 percent).

The most dramatic case of Palestinian terrorism was the 1972 attack on the Israeli delegation at the Munich Olympic Games carried out by Black September. However, many of this group's operations, like those of Abu Nidal, are turned against Arab targets. In total, from 1965 to 1982, Palestinian international terrorism caused 45 Israeli deaths and 59 wounded, respectively 15 and 42 for non-Israeli Jews. Gentile victims were more numerous: 226 persons were killed, 667 wounded.

International terrorism raises ideological debates. George Habash and the PFLP, especially, consider this the most appropriate strategy under the conditions of the Palestinian struggle to annihilate the "Zionist entity." Accordingly, this group has invented new tactics and patterns, particularly the systematic campaign of hijacking. Although Habash himself eventually became somewhat less enthusiastic about these methods, his direct associate, Wadi Haddad, split from the PFLP to continue and to amplify them.

Wadi Haddad is today the most illustrative case of a Palestinian international terrorist.[8] Born in 1927, he belongs not to the younger protest generation but to that of the professional activists. Haddad grew up in Jerusalem and studied medicine in Beirut, together with George Habash. After splitting from the PFLP, he gained the confidence of Libya, Iraq, and South Yemen and set up his own network. His principal operations include the hijacking of an El Al airliner to Algiers (July 1968), of a TWA to Damascus (August 1969), and of three planes simultaneously (belonging to TWA, Swissair, and BOAC) to Jordan (September 1970). Haddad also stood behind the massacre at the Lod airport in Israel by three members of the Japanese Red Army (twenty-six were killed and seventy-six wounded in May 1972). He directed "Carlos" 's attack on the Vienna OPEC Conference (December 1975), as well as the hijacking of an Air France plane to Entebbe, Uganda (June 1976), which was later rescued by IDF commandos. Expanding his activity, Haddad got in touch with terrorist organizations in Europe and beyond. These include the Bader-Meinhof gang in Germany, the Japanese Red Army, and Iranian, Turkish, Irish, Latin American, and Eritrean movements. In this respect, Haddad has been very successful to enlisting collaborators without formally involving the mainstream of the PLO.

Palestinian nationalism has, in effect, been a major axis of worldwide cooperation between the numerous terrorist movements of the mid-1970s (see exhibit 7.2).[9] PLO bases in the Middle East have trained people of diverse origins (see exhibit 7.2); Haddad himself ran a camp located in South Yemen for this purpose. In return, the PLO enjoyed numerous channels for conveying weapons, explosives, and grenades all over Europe.

In one instance, grenades stolen by the Bader-Meinhof gang from an American base in Germany were found in July 1975 in a Paris flat owned by a PLO member; grenades of the same type were used in 1974 in an attack against a Champs-Elysées drugstore. Another form of mutual aid concerns the manufacturing of false passports, as shown by the discovery of most varied identity papers in "Carlos" 's hideout in the French capital (June 1975). Eventually, members of different national organizations also collaborate in specific operations: Japanese terrorists carried out the Lod massacre; Germans participated in the Air France hijacking to Entebbe.

Layla Khaled, a famous PFLP woman who took part in two hijackings, put it bluntly to a Turkish journalist: "My organization has sent an experienced officer to Turkey in order to train Turkish fedayeen in the art of urban guerrilla tactics, hijacking, and other patterns of action. He is the one who trained the men arrested recently [in Turkey]."[10] The Israeli consul in Istanbul, Elrom, was killed in May 1971 by the Popular Army of the Liberation of Turkey, while the Fatah declared its open support for the Turkish underground. Fourteen Turkish terrorists were arrested on a Fatah-owned boat on May 24, 1972, on their way back from a Palestinian camp. Several Turks were killed on May 30, 1973, in an Israeli attack on a PLO base in Lebanon.[11]

Similarly, the PLO's ties with the anti-Shah underground were always very close (see Exhibit 7.3). On July 13, 1971, for instance, Radio Baghdad

Exhibit 7.2
The Tyre PLO Training Bases for Foreign Movements

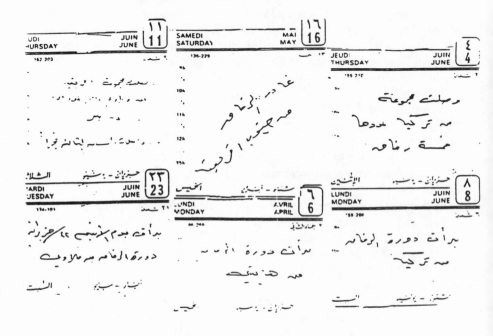

Translation:

11.6:   10 persons have arrived from Malawi

23.6:   the Malawi course has started

16.5:   the Southern-African comrades have left

6.4:   the Haitian course has started

4.6:   a five-man Turkish group has arrived

8.6:   the Turkish group has started

Source: Diary of Tyre PFLP Camp—IDF source.

Exhibit 7.3
Arab and Iranian Volunteers to the PLO

أ‌ــــــــــــــن الجــــــــوب

رئــــــم العــــــــــــادر   ع /٢٧٦

تاريـــــــ الدليـــــات   ١ ١ـ ١ـ ٨

مـــــــدر المعلومــــات

نسبــة دحــة المعلوـــــات

تحيـة الثـورة

ر / وصول بعـ. المقاتلين من جنسيات عربية ـ ايرانيــــة ٠ ـ

.٠ ـ

أفاد مصدر مقرب من الجبهــــة انه بتاريخ ١ ـ ٨ ل ٨ وصلـ. ديدة من المقاتلين الى الجبهة الشعبية
وهم متعددين الجنسيات وانأكد العدر، ان ١٠ : يعنيين عراقيين و ٢٥ من الايرانيين.و ١٥ من ال مانيين
وبعلمين الارتيريين وقد :لقوا تدريباتهم في معسكرات الجبهة في سوريا التحقوا في قواعد ال يـ.ة نـــــــي
الجنـــــوب ٠

رقم المندوب ٥٠ /٨٤٠ ٠٠
أ‌ــــــن الجنـــــوب

Translation
                Blessings of the Revolution!
Arrival of several fighters of Arab and Iranian nationality
A source close to the Popular Front has unveiled that on August 1, a new
group has arrived, of numerous nationalities, to the Popular Front camp in
Syria and has now joined the Front's bases in the South. Representative
No. 845, Security of the South.

Source: IDF Spokesman, Sheleg documents, September 28, 1982.

broadcast a joint declaration of the Fatah and the National Iranian Front, stating, "the Iranian hero Ali Akhbar Parkhany has died following torture in an Iranian jail. Parkhany has been trained in a fedayeen camp and has taken part in actions against the Zionist enemy . . . he became an officer before he joined the Iranian Front." In the same line, the Algerian newspaper *Al-Shab* announced, on October 22, 1971, "the Iranian Revolution has created a Palestinian group of forty-five Iranians to fight with their Palestinian brothers." Similar relations existed with the Eritrean Front of Liberation and the Japanese Red Army.[12] Well-informed sources reveal that besides the Lod massacre, PFLP members participated with Japanese terrorists in the hijacking of a Japanese plane to Libya (July 1973) and the occupation of the Japanese embassy in Kuwait (September 1973). When the Christian Phalangists in Lebanon took over the Palestinian camp of Tel al-Zatar in Beirut (July 1976) they found and captured a member of the Japanese Red Army.

C. THE ADVANTAGES OF A MINI-PALESTINE

The main advantage that the Palestinians have enjoyed from their benefactors, however, has been the possibility of setting up "mini-Palestines," that is, external territorial bases. In Jordan, until 1970 the PLO was given the opportunity to establish headquarters, to organize training courses, and to form its operational units within the refugee camps and in urban neighborhoods. Similarly, from 1968 on, groups of fedayeen slowly imposed themselves in Lebanon's refugee camps, occasionally clashing with the national army (April, August, October 1969). In the southeastern area of Marj Uyun and Hazbaya, the PLO even succeeded in creating an operational area, the "Fatahland," thanks to the direct support of the Syrians. The Cairo Agreement of November 3, 1969, concluded under the pressure of President Gamal Abdel Nasser, confirmed Beirut's acceptance of the autonomy of the PLO in all Palestinian concentrations. Nevertheless, some clashes did continue, mainly with the Christian-Maronite militia, the Phalange. On March 1970, these Phalangists attacked the PLO in Hala (a village on the Beirut-Damascus road) and in Tel al-Zatar.

The Palestinian presence in Lebanon was drastically increased during 1970 and 1971, with the liquidation of the PLO's bases in Jordan. Under pressure from the Arab League, the Lebanese government allowed the PLO to expand its action and to develop its politicomilitary structures to a complex degree. A center was established in West Beirut in the vicinity of the large Palestinian camps of Burj al-Barajneh, Sabra and Shatila, and Tel al-Zatar. This center developed welfare services, educational institutions, a research center, and sport clubs. From here, squads of fighters were sent to act throughout Europe against a variety of Israeli and Jewish targets. From this center, also, dozens of diplomatic delegations were dispatched throughout the world.

The assets that the PLO was able to accumulate constituted a major factor of the 1975–76 civil war in Lebanon. They definitively altered the power relations between the Christians, who enjoyed the largest share of political authority under the Lebanese constitution, on the one hand, and the Muslim, Sunnite, Shiite, and Druze comunities, who constituted the majority of the population, on the other.

In the late 1970s, the Palestinian movements, mainly the Fatah and the PLA, were even able to develop quasi-regular forces. A traditional military hierarchy crystallized alongside the political apparatus. The story related in exhibit 7.4 shows that the Supreme Command of the Fatah was still accessible to the ranks; it even handled such trivial matters as a junior officer's request for promotion. The issues themselves, then, are those of any normal army, as are the bureaucratic proceedings by which they are taken care of.

From 1965 to 1982, the numerous operations against Israel launched from Fatah, PLA, and other bases in Jordan and Lebanon caused the deaths of 1,066 persons in Israel and the administered territories (307 Israeli soldiers, 367 Israeli civilians, 392 Arab inhabitants of the territories) and 5,671 wounded (1,333; 2,361; and 1,977, respectively).

On the Lebanese border, the average number of incidents per year from 1969 to 1982 was 83, with peaks in 1969 (150), 1970 (110), 1974 (109), 1975 (118), and 1981 (135). The PLO used artillery equipment that made it possible to hit civilian settlements in Galilee from behind the Lebanese border. This equipment, the famous Katyusha rocket, is lightweight and can be focused on any spot; it can be automatically regulated and operated. Thus any response by artillery or air aimed at the point of shooting is in vain. Therefore, Israel had to retaliate on other targets, beyond its borders, which unavoidably entailed international condemnation. Escalation was easily set in motion: more Katyushas evoked more massive retaliation; more retaliation was followed by sharper accusations in the world community. On the other hand, the hostilities against Israel and the intensified responses also led to the exodus of civilians from the field of confrontation, southern Lebanon. Paradoxically, cities like Saida, Tyre, Nabatyeh, and Hazbaya were soon controlled by the PLO, while thousands of Lebanese Christians, Sunnites, and Shiites fled northward.[13] This was the direct context of the 1978 Israeli Litani operation, which "cleaned up" the PLO presence in the territory spreading between the Israeli border and the Litani River. UNIFIL, the United Nations force, took charge of the security of the area after the Israeli withdrawal. However, the escalatory process was renewed after the pullback, the PLO now using forty-kilometer-range Katyushas.

The deep rooting of the PLO and its various affiliated organizations

Exhibit 7.4
Application for Promotion of a Fatah Pilot in Air Force No. 14

سيادة اللواء الـ... رئاسات / القيادة العامة لقوات الجو الفلسطينية

تحية القوة والنضال

... أنا المناضل محمد رزا... رقم ٦٢١١ التحقت بجبهة فتح في ١/٣/١٩٦٨ لعمر ٣١ ...

الواجبه التكليف مع مدرسة اللعبه الارتال ما... في تلقيت دورة تدريب على عدة ...

من الاسلحه الاثراله (لمبرلا وصطفة) في معسكر الـ... لك تحت اشمر سامع الرامي ...

وابو جبر رئيس التدرج التحته بالقلاع الدرع وهو عطا لاع الوع احمر جبلا لا...

وفي عام ١٣٦٩ التحقت بالرؤم بدورة الكوادر ... منتقل ستها اشمر ربيع ...

إلى القلاء الوسط تابعة ... ع.٠١ باسم الاخ الرئيم نعيم . وفي عام ١٩٧٠ ستها ...

... حملة تفاكد على الطلاع من ١٧ ... الاسلحه الكلاك وروسن بردنية لربو٢! ...

امرطليب . والدوا ... م الذي تخرج كنرته سـ سرع ... الهليكبتر وجبا برة ...

وفي عام ١٩٧٢ رجع الاسلحه ابوكمال وجورة الا دفشه سـ بع بشكلم مع معتمد ...

بانتجي انا والدفع ... بابو حليج ... سترا عد الدفعه في ... تماموا ابتستيل ...

العلومات المتعلق بعم في الاداء السكندر رقم ١٤ ... في نكون نخبه لتواجد ...

... الجزائر وفي عام ١٩٧٤ صقنا عد الجزائر لطلبـ ... القيادة افسـ ... وفنا ...

جيتنا لك عام ... وجعنا بنزها الى اللسام والبناتيم جيتة عبت طلبا لعا في انداد...

لابو الاخ ابو الحكم .

سيدة القائدالعام زرملئ ارسـ برتبه نقيب اعتبا اسم ١/١/١٩٧٦ ...

وانا وصلاء امرحليب . لم ترل برتبه بدرسم الكوزله لعدم وجود سيى لنا في الدوا ...

والمه ١٤ سرع تاخذ الاتتابه بنتج ... والعلوا ت التو ذكرت ... تبن سفر ... ...

بترجبرا التقرم بالنظرف عتعو الرتبه اسومؤ بزرملط ...

واتقبلوا خالص ...

وبرئيم مع الله .

الادع القائد العام لقوات القوه الفلسطينية

لجنة الترقيه

الوصن يا جو حى دراسـ سبنل العنه العنـ

سم كانفة مرائبه نبل البند نته

... لعبره رؤب للعنا .

١٩٧٧/١١/١٨

الاجنه المنظم/ الردان لعد

لوسط بالرأس

٦٢ ١١١/٧٧

Exhibit 7.4
(continued)

Translation

To: Yasser Arafat, the General command of the Forces of the Palestinian
     Revolution.

I am the fighter Mahmud Kazaz nr. 43161. I joined the Fatah on 1.4.68
after a group of Turkish and Palestinian students, including myself, was
expelled from the Turkish University. We had a three month training
course together with the Turkish group (the Mustafa group) at the Esakhne
camp under the command of Abu-El... and Abu Geber. After the course I
joined the central front-line, the "Akko unit" under the command of Nebila
(Mahmud Alesh...). In 1969 I joined the cadres course for six months and
I came back to the central front-line, the 201 camp, under the command of
Nakim. In 1980 I went with other comrades to Algiers as a candidate for
the pilot course. I completed the course of Mig-17 pilots with the comrades Abu Kurkhal and Yusuf Brefith ("George") and Salaman Abu Khalib and
the comrade Awasama who finished the course for helicopter pilots, and
Khulab who was a navigator. In 1973 Abu Kurkhal and George went back to
Damascus because of some problem with the headquarter's representative.

Salaman Aba-Khalib and I remained. When the comrades were in Syria they
registered everything at the military command and the Force 14. We did
not register because we were in Algiers. In 1974 we left Algiers in
accordance with the command's order and we went to Uganda for one year.
From there we went back to Lebanon where I worked in the area under the
command of Abu Elmattsem.

    General Command! My colleagues hold now the rank of hakiv ("cap-
tain") since the date of January 1, 1976, while I and Salaman Khalib are
still mlazem awal ("lieutenant"). Because of the absence of any registration for us at the military command and Force 14, besides the date of our
joining the Fatah and before our travel to Algiers, I ask you to give me
the same rank of Mlazem awal, as my comrades, Mahmud Kazaz.

To the General Command of the Forces of the Palestinian Revolution, the
matter needs a thorough inquiry.
18.11.77, Abu Khatzer

To the Unified Committee,
For examination 19.11.77, Yasser Arafat

Source: IDF source and translation from Arabic.

account for the fact that on the eve of the 1982 Israeli invasion, about 15,000 "regular" fighters belonged to the various Palestinian units.

D. THE WORLD DIPLOMATIC SCENE: PLO SUCCESSES AND ISRAELI SETBACKS

On the international diplomatic scene, the PLO's achievements have been even more impressive. In the United Nations, the Arab states unanimously sustained the PLO's claim for recognition, and they sponsored a relentless campaign against Israel. They were unconditionally backed by the Soviet bloc, which, with the sole exception of Romania, had cut off its diplomatic relations with the Jewish state since the Six-Day War. The Communist states were followed, in the early 1970s, by the wide majority of Africa, which, though quite close to Israel during the 1960s, was subjected to heavy Arab pressure. The Arabs, moreover, even managed to shake the traditional pro-Israeli attitude of many Latin American countries and to create an international conjuncture that induced several Western European governments to take a more pro-Palestinian stand. PLO missions—whether full-fledged embassies, as in Athens or Moscow, or merely "bureaus de liaison," as in Paris—multiplied; they were soon three times as numerous as the Israeli delegations in the world.

Anti-Israel and pro-PLO decisions of the UN and related bodies were not the only result of these developments.[14] In November 1974, UNESCO equally condemned South African apartheid and Israeli Zionism, in a motion supported by 63 states against 33, with 27 abstentions and 14 absentees. A majority of 48 against 33 (31 abstentions and 25 absentees) decided that Israel could no longer be a member of the organization, because it was not accepted by its own regional group, Asia. In parallel, the General Assembly of the UN recognized the PLO, and by a majority of 109 out of 138, it invited the Palestinian organization to participate in its debates as an observer. This decision opened the doors of almost all UN bodies and agencies to the PLO. In the footsteps of the February 1975 General Assembly, the World Congress for Human Rights condemned Israel for a long list of PLO claims. In May 1975, the World Health Congress expressed, by 145 votes, "its deep concern for the degradation of the conditions of health among the Palestinian refugees in the occupied territories." In June, the International Work Organization accepted the PLO as an observer. On November 10, the UN General Assembly declared Zionism a form of racism and discrimination.

Other events of this period, such as the Biafran genocide, the massacres of Africans in southern Sudan, the Iraqi repression of the Kurds, the Soviet invasion of Czechoslovakia, the Vietnam War, and the civil war in Lebanon, were of no less international consequence. None of these matters were ever on the agenda of the UN, evidently because they were not viewed with the same near-unanimous attitude as that created by the Palestinian conflict.

The sharpest anti-Israel and pro-PLO decisions were those received by the Arab League and Third World conventions. In 1975, the Arab summit of Jedda decided to fight for the exclusion of Israel from any international body; on August of the same year, the Lima Congress of the Non-Aligned States decided to collaborate actively with the PLO in order to outline a strategy for the total liberation of Palestine. In October, Idi Amin Dada of Uganda called explicitly for the physical destruction of Israel. In 1975, the UN created a Committee for the Exercise of the Inalienable Rights of the Palestinian People.

In the forum of the United Nations, operative decisions are the privilege of the Security Council, where the five permanent members each have the right of veto. The United States has been willing to use this right against any decision implying sanctions on Israel. Moreover, at that time, some international bodies were still dominated by traditional friends of the Jewish state, such as the Socialist International, notwithstanding the strong pro-PLO sympathies of some figures, like the Austrian chancellor, Bruno Kreitzky. Yet this support among the socialist parties of the Continent did not necessarily mean that European governments would back Israel in the same way that the United States did. Many Europeans were tempted to demonstrate their independence of the United States through their attitude toward the Third World and the Soviets. Often inspired by France—and somewhat pressured by their dependence on Arab oil—they sometimes found it profitable to display some reservation toward Israel and more sympathy than the United States for the Arab world. In 1980, the European Venice Conference of the Common Market was ready to call publicly for a settlement of the Palestinian national problem through cooperation with the PLO.

These worldwide relations also offered the Palestinians new opportunities to obtain diverse assets, including military aid. (see exhibit 7.5). The existence of multiple international bodies that characterizes world diplomacy today lent greater impact to the lack of balance between the support for Israel and the sympathy for the Palestinians.

However, what seemed definitive in the 1970s might (and, in fact, would) be shaken by further developments. These developments were inherent in the primary power-building process that elevated the PLO to its international status, that is, the very linkage of non-Palestinian Arab interests to the Palestinian cause.

E. THE PROFITABILITY OF VIOLENCE AND THE PERPETUATION OF THE CONFLICT

The Palestinian conflict has become, for the PLO, a source of gain (in terms of military equipment, financial prosperity, diplomatic standing,

Exhibit 7.5
PLO International Cooperation in Military Matters (Examples of Reports
from the Press)

Media	Date	Report
Economist Foreign Report (London)	June 14, 1978	Agreement signed with Arafat to provide training in East Germany for the PLO
A-Watan al-Arabi	August 17, 1978	32 pilots and 60 mechanics return from training courses in the Soviet bloc
Ahar Saa (Egypt)	September 13, 1978	500 PLO members to Cuba for training
Economist Foreign Report	July 11, 1979	PLO personnel to Bulgaria for training
Ash-Shark Al-Awsat (London)	September 13, 1979	150 PLO men trained as pilots in the Soviet bloc
New York Times	September 20, 1979	Khaider, who participated in PLO raid, admits he participated in a 6-month military course in U.S.S.R.
Phalangist Radio (Beirut)	November 11, 1979	North Korea trains PLO spies
Economist Foreign Report	November 28, 1979	PLO cooperates with Cuba in training Central American squads
Express (Paris)	January 13, 1981	East Germany offers the PLO 50 advisors to help train fighters
Al-Liwa	February 8, 1981	PLO-Yugoslavian military agreements concluded in Belgrade
Radio Monte Carlo	January 17, 1981	Hundreds of Palestinians hold Soviet rank of brigade commander
Voice of Palestine	March 16, 1981	15 Czechoslovakian experts in sabotage train Fatah men in South Lebanon

Source: IDF Spokesman, 1981.

and international prestige) that may well be superior to the profit represented by the concessions Israel might be ready to make in the framework of negotiations. This is true at least in terms of the benefits sought by the upper stratum of Palestinian nationalism, that is, the senior officers in the various fedayeen organizations, the diplomats who serve in the diverse capitals of the world, and the politicians who appear both in the media and at conferences. These individuals would probably be ill at ease at the head of a small state located between Israel, the Hashemite Kingdom, and Egypt, and probably even more so if that Palestinian entity were limited in its sovereignty and had to accept federative bonds with Jordan, as is suggested by most of the peace plans designed in Washington or the European capitals.

This aspect of the Israeli-Palestinian conflict is congruent with the PLO's definition of the aim of the conflict, namely, the total destruction of the Zionist state. Such a definition, indeed, gives the conflict a basis that makes its solution quite unrealistic. When endorsed in the mid-1960s, this definition was a function of the conflict's link to the Israeli-Arab struggle.

Over the years, the PLO has accumulated a wealth of assets. The unrealistic definition of the conflict now prevents the movement from taking a realistic approach to the achievement of national goals within the limits of the possibilities. On the other hand, it perpetuates—on the behalf of the combat—that very situation of "profitability of violence." Herein lies a partial explanation of the reluctance of the PLO to translate its impressive assets into conceivable Israeli concessions.

Moreover, the very scope of these external profits also accounts for the fact that the Palestinians have to adjust their aspirations to interests that are not necessarily identical to their own. In this respect, the unrealistic definition of the conflict reflects the limits of the autonomy of the indebted contender and measures the control of the PLO's benefactors over the conflict.

The profitability of violence may thus lead to a situation where it perpetuates the conflict rather than contributing to its resolution.

NOTES

1. See E. Gilboa and M. Naor, eds., *The Arab-Israeli Conflict*, (Tel Aviv: Matkal ed., 1981 [Hebrew]); N. Safran, *The Israeli State and Its Relations with the U.S.* (Tel Aviv: Shocken, 1979 [Hebrew]).

2. D. Dishon, "Inter-Arab Relations since Yom Kippur," in Gilboa and Naor, 148.

3. H. Shaked, "The Middle East since 1973: Continuity and Change," in *Between War and Arrangements: The Israeli-Arab Conflict after 1973*, ed. A. Har-Even (Tel Aviv: Zmora, Beitan, Modan, 1977 [Hebrew]).

4. IDF Spokesman, *The PLO: A Setting of Terror and a History of Blood*, IDF

(Hebrew), 1982; J. W. Amos, *Palestinian Resistance: Organization of a Nationalist Movement* (New York: Pergamon Press, 1980).

5. S. Shamgar, *Yediot Aharonot,* May 9, 1983 (Hebrew daily).

6. IDF Spokesman, *The PLO.*

7. IDF Spokesman *PLO Activities,* IDF (Hebrew) and other current mimeographed publications of the IDF Spokesman, 1981, 1982.

8. IDF Spokesman, *Special Publication,* October 20, 1977, IDF (Hebrew).

9. *New York Post,* February 5, 1976.

10. *Haryet* (Turkish daily), May 26, 1971.

11. *Haber* (Turkish News agency), May 30, 1973.

12. See the Libyan *Al-Hakuka,* June 16, 1972, and the Lebanese *Al-Osboa,* June 5, 1972.

13. IDF Spokesman *The PLO Organization in Lebanon,* IDF (Hebrew), 1982.

14. Har-Even; *Haaretz,* October 21, 1979, 9 (Hebrew); See also *Skira Khodshit,* December 1976–January 1977, December 1975, August 1979 (Hebrew).

8 Curses

A. THE BENEFACTORS' LIMITED LIABILITY

The support of powerful allies has given the PLO great advantages. However, the same support may cause the Palestinian insurgents to act on the basis of considerations that are not necessarily their own. Because the Palestinian issue is a weapon used on various scenes—the Arab League, the UN bodies, superpower interrelations, Third World conventions—the desire of the mentors to control their protégés is always present. Sanctions may even be taken against the PLO when it tries to enhance its autonomy of action.

In Algiers (1973) and Rabat (1974), the PLO obtained full recognition from the Arab world as the "sole legitimate representative of the Palestinian people." This completed the process that had started ten years earlier in Cairo when the Arab League created the organization. During this decade, the Palestinian cause in the territories conquered by Israel had taken on the classic syndrome of liberation movements; the fedayeen had taken over leadership of the PLO from the politicians appointed by President Gamal Abdel Nasser; and the Arab nations had succeeded in presenting the case to the world as a central contemporary issue. In 1979, no less than 106 states recognized the PLO, and a 1974 UN decision (No. 3236) officially legitimized its struggle. In Moscow the PLO now had a full-fledged embassy; even American officials contacted it, albeit in secrecy. A closer look at the attitudes of the PLO's benefactors, however, reveals that these assets are by no means definitive or unconditional.[1]

Egypt, for instance, has done more for the PLO than any other state and has also shown the greatest hostility toward it. Nasser's initiative in sponsoring a Palestinian national movement was dictated by the Egyptians' own interests as the head of the Arab "progressive" camp. Moreover, after the blatant failure on the battlefield in 1967, the support of the PLO was a welcome alternative as a vehicle of the continued struggle. However, the Egyptians also knew when and how to ignore their Palestinian allies.[2] The Yom Kippur War was an intermediate step toward a new situation, the *paix des braves* in Gaulish vocabulary, which excluded—or at least minimized—the Palestinian cause as a relevant factor. Sadat's "Palestinian policy" was mainly to pressure the PLO to follow in his footsteps by creating an in-exile government and entering into negotiations with Israel. To punctuate his advice, the PLO's freedom in Egypt was drastically reduced and its broadcasting facilities were suppressed.

After the main clauses of the Camp David Agreements were implemented, that is, after Israel withdrew totally from Sinai, the Egyptians again wooed the PLO, this time in the hope of weakening the case for their ostracism by the Arab League, which had come in reaction to the agreements. For this purpose, they exploited the most difficult hour of PLO history—its expulsion from Tripoli, Lebanon, by Syria and its Palestinian allies (1983), following the earlier expulsion from Beirut by Israel (1982). At this point, Yasser Arafat could no longer refuse an invitation from President Hosni Mubarak, Camp David notwithstanding. The visit of the PLO leader was subsequently exploited further by Cairo on the Arab scene.

Jordan, too, was successively the PLO's "worst enemy" and its "best friend." The annexation of the West Bank in 1948 had been, along with the creation of Israel, the greatest blow to Palestinian nationalism. This "Jordanization" of Palestine, however, was halted by Israel's conquests in 1967. That the Palestinian nationalists aspired now to "Palestinize" Jordan—two-thirds of the population of the East Bank defined themselves as Palestinians—is related to Jordan's expulsion of the PLO in 1970, in which hundreds of fedayeen were killed and thousands wounded and tortured. Revealing the acuteness of this issue, in September 1975, the PLO's newspaper, *Shohon Palestinya*, cried, "the regime in Amman should be liquidated and, instead, a fatherland for the Palestinians established on the East Bank" on the way to the liberation of the occupied territories and the annihilation of Israel.[3]

In fact, Amman had by no means given up her ambitions regarding the West Bank; it maintained its position: "Both banks constitute one family."[4] King Hussein aspired to obtain the support of the Americans vis-à-vis Israel by recognizing its existence and sovereignty. This strategy seemed the only realistic way to bring about an Israeli withdrawal from the territories which, in turn, should convince both the Arab capitals and the Palestinian population to comply with this policy. The PLO would finally have no choice but to provide Hussein with the necessary backing to progress toward negotiations with the Israelis in view of the reannexation of the West Bank by Jordan. In the context of this strategy, a wide range of diverse and apparently contradictory moves have been undertaken. For instance, in the mid-1970s Hussein did not refuse an alliance with Syria and Iraq aimed at the creation of an eastern anti-Israeli front. In return, a Syrian statement in December 1975 still considered the PLO the legitimate representative of the Palestinians but omitted the word "sole." Exploiting its strengthened position in the Arab League, Jordan also created a National Consultative Council. This council, established by royal decree on April 16, 1978, numbered 60 members, half of them West Bankers.[5] In the same line, Jordan's foreign minister proposed to the European Council, in January 1980, the creation of a "national entity"—and not a state—"for the Palestinians through a global peace negotiation process whereby the PLO could play its part."[6] Ironically enough and notwithstanding the bitter memories of Black September, in 1984 Jordan hosted the National Palestinian Council itself. Arafat thus found that shelter was still available to him in Amman, at a time when the PLO was experiencing a sharp internal rift and grave tension with another friendly enemy, Syria.

Syria, indeed, has not always been the PLO persecutor that it seemed after the murder in Amman (December 29, 1984) of Fahd Qawasmeh, who was a member of the executive committee of the PLO. Syria supported Nasser in the creation of the Palestinian movement and was the very first benefactor of the Fatah. Almost all fedayeen groups were allowed to establish training bases and political bodies in Damascus, although Syria rarely allowed any action against Israel from its borders. On the other hand, Syria has always tried to patronize both the PLO and its individual movements. It even created a Palestinian movement of its own, the Saiqa, composed of Syrian officers. It also, however, combatted any movement that did not respect Syrian interests. The PFLP, for a time, was severely repressed in Damascus because of its sympathy for the Iraqi Baathist regime; George Habash was even imprisoned in this context. Al-Saiqa's platform reveals Syria's real interest in the Palestinian revolution: the general unification of the Arab world, based on Syrian Baathism.[7]

Syria's short-term considerations are more pragmatic. Syria took advantage of Lebanon's civil war in the mid-1970s to invade that country and to assume the position of referee of the multiple ethnic rivalries. It shifted alliances several times in order to prevent any contender from becoming "too strong." Later it became the most dedicated benefactor of the PLO, which it controlled by virtue of its physical presence in Lebanon. Using this position to enhance its status in the Arab League— Egypt was excluded after Camp David—in 1979 Syria formed the Steadfastness Front with Algeria, Libya, Iraq, South Yemen, and the PLO. After the Israeli invasion of Lebanon in 1982, the greatest "danger" in

President Hafiz Assad's view was that the PLO, suffering heavy losses, might become more compromising vis-à-vis the conflict. Therefore, Damascus systematically attacked Arafat's leadership in order to strengthen the radicals, who were closer, both ideologically and politically, to the Syrians.

To sum up, the backing of Egypt, Jordan, and Syria, which permitted the PLO to achieve what it did in the Middle East and in the world, remained essentially bound to their own respective interests, policies, and challenges. These might be foreign to the Palestinian cause itself— even contradictory and conflicting with it. These facts, are fully acknowledged by the interested parties themselves. As quoted by Helena Cobban from a PLO figure:

There are two kinds of Arab regimes. There are those who believe that they represent the leadership of all the Arab world—including everybody, including even the animals!—and this monopoly type of thinking means that they think that they have the right to take the decisions and nobody else has the right to take the decisions. . . . The other regimes only believe in their own small countries and they don't want anyone to interfere and they don't interfere in the affairs of the others: like the Moroccans, the Tunisians, the Algerians, the Sudanese, the Gulf—the Saudis.[8]

B. THE "SECOND-BEST FRIENDS" AND THEIR CONSIDERATIONS

Practical considerations also dictate the extent of support and the way it is offered to the PLO by other benefactors, that is, those who are not directly involved in the Middle East conflict. The Saudis, for instance, granted about $200 million to the PLO between 1967 and 1981. Their motivation lies in their self-image as the guardians of Arab unity and solidarity—which, on the other hand, also accounts for the limits of their support.[9] If necessary for the Arab cause—as they understand it—they do not hesitate to castigate the PLO and to turn their sympathy to those who, like the Syrians, repress the Palestinians because of their "lack of responsibility." Moreover, once the Saudis became anxious for their regime, in the face of the radical Muslim fundamentalists inspired by Iranian Khomeiniism, they made drastic changes in their attitude toward the Israeli-Arab conflict in order to assure stability in the area. They suggested plans for the rapid and practical resolution of this conflict in spite of the PLO's opposition. This was the case at the Arab summit of 1982.[10]

Though the interests themselves differ, Iraq's attitude is similarly motivated by self-interest. With Saddam Hussein's rise to power in 1968,

Iraq became a staunch supporter of the Palestinian issue for several years. The Kurdish revolt was then at a standstill, and Iraq's Baathist leaders aspired to a central role in the Arab world. Also urged on by an ideological rivalry with Syrian Baathism, Baghdad, like Damascus, financed the creation of a Palestinian fedayeen organization of its own, the Arab Liberation Front. Nevertheless it also channeled aid to other PLO groups, mainly to the radical fronts. Iraq hosted PLO bases and, more particularly, the Abu Nidal network, which is well known for its extremism (this network seemingly murdered several moderate PLO figures including Hammami in London and Ali Yasin in Kuwait). However, since the Iraq-Iran war, Baghdad has split from the Steadfastness Front and become closer to Egypt and Jordan. Since then, it has also moderated its aid to the PLO.

Libya's Palestinian policy[11] is also moved by the ambition of unifying the Arabs under its leadership. With the purpose of destabilizing the regimes hostile to him, Col. Muammar Qaddafi is particularly supportive of the radical wing of the PLO. Imitating Syria and Iraq, Libya has also tried to create its own Palestinian group, the small, extremist National Arab Youth for the Liberation of Palestine (NAYLP). This group claimed it blew up the house of the Israeli ambassador in Cyprus, attempted to hijack an Israeli plane on the island (April 9, 1973), and killed four and wounded fifty-four in an attack on a TWA plane arriving in Athens from Tel Aviv (August 5, 1973). In its attack on a Pan Am jet in Rome (December 13, 1973), thirty-one were killed and forty wounded. It took credit for the explosion of a TWA plane in the air over Athens, in which eighty-one were killed (March 9, 1974).

On June 19, 1981, the Libyan *Al-Siad* disclosed the creation of the Arab Organization for National Liberation, which is probably a new attempt by Tripoli to establish a Palestinian group dedicated to its policy. Tripoli deliberately encourages the radicals and interferes incessantly with the PLO's decisions. It publicly grants monetary awards to those who carry out "tough" operations, such as hijacking; it is prepared to provide asylum for the perpetrators of any anti-Jewish or anti-Israeli act. This policy has caused a deep crisis in Libya's relationship with the "too-mild" Arafat since 1979.

The PLO cannot hope either for unconditional backing from its Soviet friends or other non-Arab supporters. Russia and its allies recognize the state of Israel; during the late 1940s and the early 1950s, their relations with the Jewish government were quite cordial. The results of the successive military coups in Egypt, Syria, Iraq, and, later, Libya, which replaced pro-West conservative regimes with nationalist juntas, however, led the Soviets to reassess their policy in the Middle East. The fervent anti-Israeli pan-Arabism of these new regimes induced the Russians to harden their attitude toward the Jewish state. This development may also be detected in the use of anti-Zionist slogans in the trials of Jewish Communists in Eastern Europe in the mid-1950s. The Soviet bloc gradually aligned itself with the essentials of the Arab position. Although they did not question Israel's right to exist, the Six-Day War and the "conquest of Arab land" were enough to complete the rupture of all diplomatic relations with Jerusalem (with the exception of Romania).

When the Palestinian problem became a more central issue in the rhetoric of the Arab states, the Soviets, who had always neglected this aspect of the Middle East situation, reformulated their position.[12] The adoption of policies took time; the PLO's first Communist ally was China. Only after the all-Arab recognition of the PLO as the sole legitimate Palestinian representative in 1974 did Moscow abandon its last reservations about ties with the PLO. From then on, the PLO was granted regular diplomatic status in Russia, as well as generous material aid (see exhibits 8.1 and 8.2). Soviet-PLO meetings multiplied, and Palestinian leaders traveled frequently to Moscow. Similar relations were established between the fedayeen and the Eastern European nations.

The token "legitimate rights of the Palestinian people" was now current in official statements, accompanied by its corollary, the "imperativeness of an independent Palestinian state." Moscow, however, declared its condemnation of the use of terrorism on the international scene. Armed struggle, according to Radio Moscow, is the way to fight on a local scene; on the international scene, political action should dominate.[13] Moreover, the Soviets were cautious enough to avoid any explicit definition of future borders of the Palestinian state-to-be.[14]

Basically, according to Russia, the PLO should aspire to a mini-state—that is, Palestinian sovereignty in Judea, Samaria, and the Gaza Strip—and give up the expectation of destroying Israel. No wonder that a PLO leader dared complain, "The socialist states explain to us their position and hope we can agree so that we can collaborate in the combat against imperialism. Yet, despite their enormous contribution, we still do not know if they stand on the Palestinian side in the Revolution's fight over the liquidation of the Zionist entity."[15] This question has been debated at numerous meetings held by the Palestinians with Communist leaders in Moscow, Paris, Rome, and Lisbon, but without tangible results. The contrast between the Soviets' moderation with respect to strategic goals and their frequently radical tactics add confusion to this debate. The Communists in the administered territories, for instance, have allied themselves with the radical fronts and not the Fatah. This is partly accounted for by the fact that the radicals endorse the Communists' desire for official recognition by the Palestinian revolution.

The Soviets, in fact, have exhibited unexpected behavior at the hour of the gravest challenges for the PLO. On the one hand there were vigorous Soviet initiatives regarding any major Israeli-Arab crisis: in

Exhibit 8.1
Foreign Certifications of PLO Fighters

Exhibit 8.2
Intelligence Relations between the PLO and the USSR

‏- رقم / ۲.۷ / ع
‏رسـ: / ۲۱ / ۸ / ۱۹۷۱
‏'الجون / السلحة بحرية للعدو الاسرائيلي

‏المعلومات المتوافرة لدى الملحق العسكري الروسي في بيروت تفيد ان العدو الاسرائيلي يسعى جاهداً
‏'الحصول على صواريخ بريطانية المنشء و بحرت و رش باسم (سى ـ كات) ومدافع بحرية بريطانية الصنع
‏ايضا ميار ۰.۰۱۱ انش لتسليح وحدات البحرية الحربية بها وان الضدم البحرى الاسرائيلي سموئيل برانز
‏جبائر الى سنغافورة ومالطة على راء بعثة عسكرية اسرائيلية لاجراء اتصالات حول الحصول على شحنات
‏من هذه الاسلحة ولم يحدد بعد موعد هذه الزيارة وان كانت المعلومات الاولية تفيد بانها ستتم بالنصف
‏الاول ـ الشهر المقبل ايلول ۱۹۷۱

‏للعلم

‏شابة الامن

‏نسخة للحفظ

```
Translation
Aə/308
Date: 25.8.81
```

Matter: maritime weapon of the Israeli enemy

According to information from the USSR military attaché in Beirut the
Israeli enemy tries to obtain sea missiles S-Kat and sea cannons of
British make. An Israeli navy officer, Tsmuil Brany, is to head a military delegation to Sangapor and Malta for this purpose. The date has not
been fixed yet but the information speaks of the first half of September
1981.

For your information
Copy for the file

Security officer

Source: IDF Spokesman, 1982 (document seized in Lebanon by IDF).

1956, joint action was initiated by the Russians and the Americans to force Israel to retreat from Sinai; in 1967, Russia knew how to induce the Security Council to stop the Israeli advance into Egypt, Syria, and Jordan; in 1973, the Russians even resorted to a threat of direct intervention against Israel when the IDF, overcoming its initial weakness, undertook a counteroffensive into Egypt and Syria. On the other hand, and in blatant contrast to this intense activity, little conviction was shown by the Soviets at the PLO's difficulties in 1970 in Amman, in 1975 in Beirut, and in 1982 in Lebanon. The support given to the PLO during the entire period seems to be better explained as an exploitation of political realities than as the expression of an unambiguous commitment.

C. HOURS OF TRUTH

Arafat's own status, according to Joseph Neyer,

has rarely been secure even in his own guerrilla group, al-Fatah. . . . [In] January 1971, he was voted out of office during a meeting of Fatah's . . . "revolutionary council" in a secret ballot election, when he was challenged by the left wing of the group [sustained by Syria]. Arafat recovered his authority by demanding an open vote. . . . After the revolution of 1966 in Syria . . . it soon became evident that the Syrians intended to take over Arafat's organization, and the job was assigned to a Palestinian officer in the Syrian army, Captain Yussuf Urabi. When the captain informed all Fatah units that Arafat was dismissed, he was promptly murdered by one of Arafat's agents. Not long after this event . . . the Fatah-Syrian honeymoon was concluded by the imprisonment of the top Fatah leaders, including Arafat. . . . As late as 1965, Nasser reacted to the Syrian-Fatah alliance and to the first sabotage operation of Fatah against Israel by referring to Arafat as "an agent of imperialism."[16]

A few years later, in Jordan, the self-appointed "homeland of the Palestinians," the PLO again discovered the meaning of "conditional support." For three years, from 1967 to 1970, the Hashemite Kingdom was the main base for PLO operations against Israel. The guerrilla-inspired strategy consisted of de facto unification of the two banks of the Jordan River; dozens of bases were created in East Bank villages, from which the fedayeen crossed the river, hid among the inhabitants of the West Bank, organized the local population into cells, and directed sabotage operations. This model could not be implemented without the collaboration of the Jordanian army, which watched the borderline, offered artillery protection against Israeli counteractions, and was willing to accept unconventional military forces within the area of its responsibility.

Such collaboration effectively existed during these years, as illustrated in Karameh when the Israelis attacking this PLO stronghold sustained

many casualties from Jordanian artillery situated on the hill. The relations between the PLO and the Jordanian army deteriorated with the
strengthening of the Palestinians. Paradoxically, a semilegal "mini-Palestine" was in the making on the soil of the self-declared "homeland of
the Palestinians," and it was achieving wide autonomy. By the end of
1969 Amman housed a well-established PLO headquarters, propaganda
structures, and varied offices, while some eight thousand armed men
and several thousand officials freely circulated throughout the country.
The Hashemite dynasty, traditionally allied to the Bedouin minority,
could not compete with the PLO as a focus of national identification
among the Palestinian majority of the country. The PLO's autonomy
within Jordan was, therefore, of high revolutionary potential. Seeing
the danger, Hussein decided to suppress the PLO's presence altogether.
For eleven days, beginning on September 17, 1970, the Jordanian army
attacked the fedayeen. Although some groups, like the PFLP, initially
responded eagerly to the challenge, their defeat was rapid. An Israeli
ultimatum backed by the United States kept Syrian and Iraqi troops at
a distance. Hundreds of PLO fighters crossed the river, preferring to
hand themselves over to the Israelis rather than be taken by Hussein's
soldiers and sent to a Jordanian jail. Many others fled to Lebanon.

For several years, Jordanian institutions became the target of PLO
revenge. Sponsored by the Fatah, the hard-terrorist Black September
group multiplied its attacks on Alyah Airways, Jordanian embassies all
over the world, and senior officials of the Amman government. Wasfi
Tal, the prime minister of the Amman government, was killed while on
a visit in Cairo; an unsuccessful attempt to murder Hussein was made
in Rabat in October 1974.

However, in the late 1970s, the PLO and Hussein were compelled to
reconsider their relations. The strength of the radicals in the administered territories and their serious political work attracted most of the
dedicated nationalists. The Sadat peace initiative, on the other hand,
attracted the more moderate Palestinians, those who would otherwise
have supported the Fatah or Jordan. Many of these more moderate public
figures accepted invitations to Cairo during 1978 and 1979. A de facto
reconciliation between the PLO and Amman became, therefore, imperative. This trend was further encouraged by Jordan's friendly (at that
time) relationship with Damascus, the actual protector of the PLO in
Lebanon.[17]

The history of the PLO's relations with Syria on Lebanese soil is no
less painful and paradoxical. In 1967, many Lebanese were apprehensive
about the growth of a fedayeen power in their country, a power that
would unavoidably upset the equilibrium among groups within the local
population. This population consists of a large minority (35–40 percent)
of Christians (mainly, but not only, Maronites), Sunnites (20–25 percent),

Shiites (17–22 percent), Druzes (6–8 percent), and Palestinian refugees (7–9 percent). The figures are only a rough estimate, since they vary widely from one source to another, representing a political issue in itself. The diverse communities, indeed, have been virtually at war with each other since the imposition of the confessional-based constitution by the French authorities on the eve of their departure.[18] Demographic realities do not correspond to the dominant power granted to the Christians. Remembering the 1958 first civil war, the Christians thus feared that a strengthening of the Palestinians, who are Sunni Muslims, would definitely shift the balance to the advantage of the anti-Christian coalition. This shift could endanger not only the Christians' political status but even their physical security.

The diplomatic intervention of Syria and Egypt in the late 1960s was sufficient, however, to impose the Lebanese government's acceptance of a Palestinian paramilitary presence. After September 1970, the same forces obliged Beirut to allow the PLO to establish training camps and bases in any Palestinian neighborhood as well as new strongholds in the South which became later a "Fatahland."

Crises soon erupted. In May 1973, the fedayeen's determination to carry their weapons freely and to set controls on roads in the vicinity of their bases awakened a virulent quarrel with the national army. In turn, the army's relations with the militias of the Druze and Muslim communities deteriorated. Syria sent its own troops to sustain the PLO and even suspended all economic relations with Lebanon until the conclusion of the quarrel. The two-week crisis ended with an agreement that only partially satisfied Beirut's claims.

One year later, in May 1974, another dispute erupted. A Palestinian commando had infiltrated into Israel and had taken over an elementary school in Maalot, a small Galilean town. The Israeli rescue unit was unable to prevent a massacre (twenty-four civilians killed and sixty-two wounded). Massive reprisal air raids were launched against PLO strongholds in Lebanon. These raids reawakened intense intra-Lebanese frictions about the PLO's presence. On April 13, 1975, these tensions finally became a generalized civil war. An attempt to assassinate Pierre Jemayel, the aging leader of the Christian Phalangists, while he was inaugurating a Maronite church in Beirut (Eyn Romana) killed four people. The Phalange retaliated immediately by attacking a PLO bus on its way back from a march to the Tel al-Zatar camp; twenty-two fedayeen were killed. During the following days, Druze, Shiite, and Sunnite militias joined the PLO against the Christians in multiple incidents. The national army was falling apart along confessional lines. In January 1976, the PLA battalions of the Syrian army crossed the border and joined the PLO forces.

The Christian situation was critical; most unexpectedly, Syria shifted alliances and sent several thousand soldiers to aid the Phalangists. As a result of the logistic support that these troops provided, the Phalangists conquered Tel al-Zatar in August 1976, killing hundreds of PLO fighters. By October, the balance of forces was again favorable to them. A small Arab summit in Riyadh decided upon a compromise, assigning Syria the role of referee in the Lebanese situation; its army was to be strengthened by symbolic contingents of several other Arab countries.

The human price of this civil war up to then was 40,000 killed and 150,000 wounded, but new developments soon occurred.[19] In order to remain an effective referee, the Syrians turned against their former allies, the Christians, who had become "too strong." Thus, from February 1978 on, clashes multiplied between Syrian soldiers, on the one hand, and the Phalangists and the remnants of the national army, on the other. Lebanese institutions fell apart, dismantled.

Under Syrian protection, the PLO was now allowed to rebuild its political and military centers and to expand the area of the Fatahland. The subsequent increase of PLO raids against Israel, including the massacre of the passengers of a bus near Tel Aviv, provoked the Israeli Litani operation. All the land between the Israeli border and the Litani River was temporarily conquered. This operation did not result in any serious physical weakening of the fedayeen, since they could flee and avoid combat with the IDF. The main outcome was the creation of a border strip controlled by UN soldiers and the widening of an area ruled by a pro-Israeli Christian militia on the eastern boundary.

The Litani operation, however also sharpened the antagonisms within Lebanon. The Syrians were now openly hostile to the Christians; in September 1978, they shelled East Beirut, the Christian part of the city. Several Phalangist strongholds were conquered by Assad's army. Nevertheless, a relatively calm situation reigned for almost a year. During this period, the Christians multiplied their secret contacts with Israel, which provided them with training and equipment. The IDF even intervened in Zakhleh in April 1981 by air to sustain the Phalangists in their stand against repeated Syrian attacks. This Israeli intervention was abruptly met by Syria's establishment of bases of powerful SAM-6 ground-to-air missiles; this represented a genuine escalation in the level of hostilities in the area. An international crisis followed, with Israel threatening to destroy the new Syrian system. The crisis was calmed down only by American mediation through Philip Habib. Still, the struggle was prolonged by violent artillery combat between Israel and the fedayeen on the border and by Israeli air attacks against PLO objectives in Beirut. These tensions were released by Habib's mediation as a tacit agreement of cease-fire was concluded. Yet in the following year there were 190 PLO operations; most of them took place abroad, but 57 occurred in Israel, killing 29 and wounding 271. The peak of this era was the attempt in London to assassinate Israel's ambassador to Great Britain, Shlomo Argov.

Up to this point, the PLO in Lebanon had known times of distress but also a general strengthening. Within Lebanon, the PLO found foes and friends; Syria had been both. The extraordinary benefit of all these vicissitudes had been the maintenance of a mini-Palestine, where political and military structures could crystallize, plan their action and, mainly, serve as a focus for the accumulation of resources all over the Middle East and the world.

These circumstances explain Israel's invasion of Lebanon in June 1982. This was a chance for the Israelis to liquidate in a single operation the manifold structures of Lebanon's mini-Palestine and to create a totally new and much more advantageous conjuncture of the conflict.

For tactical reasons, the Israelis first presented the "Peace for Galilee" (Sheleg, a Hebrew acronym that forms a word meaning "snow") operation as aimed at limited goals, that is, moving the PLO forty kilometers away from the border and thus setting the Galilee settlements outside the range of the Palestinian Katyushas. In fact, the means and patterns used by the IDF were much more ambitious.[20] Attacks were launched by armored columns along three northbound axes, west, central, and east; air bombing weakened the force of resistance of the PLO strongholds; and the navy shelled fedayeen bases along the shores. At numerous points along the shores, infantry troops were landed to the north of targets that were simultaneously attacked from the south. This time, then, in contrast to the Litani operation, the PLO fighters were prevented from escaping northward. Obliged to remain in place, they had to fight back until death or surrender. Syria's troops in Lebanon were also assaulted, after a sudden air strike that totally destroyed their SAM-6 missile bases.

The peak of the operation was the blockade of West Beirut, where the PLO headquarters were still operating. This blockade continued for several weeks while the Israelis controlled the Beirut-Damascus road. Heavy air raids were launched on the Lebanese capital until American mediation finally stopped the hostilities, in return for the evacuation of Beirut by the PLO and the Syrians. This evacuation to eight different Arab countries by boat and by truck started on August 21 and continued until September 1. It involved 14,398 persons—8,144 PLO fedayeen of the various allegiances, 2,651 Syria-linked PLA soldiers, and 3,603 Syrian soldiers. Concomitantly, enormous quantities of weapons were seized by the Israelis all over the territories they occupied—including hundreds of tanks, 1,320 vehicles, and 5,630 tons of ammunition.[21]

The new political situation in Lebanon seemed, for a while, to serve the Israelis even beyond their strategic goals. The Lebanese Parliament elected Bashir Jemayel as president of the state. The leader of the Phalangists, however, was assassinated several weeks later, causing great harm to Israel's position in the country. Moreover, the subsequent reprisals of Christian militias on Palestinians in the Sabra and Shatila refugee camps caused one of the gravest crises of confidence among the Israelis vis-à-vis their own government. A State Commission of Inquiry was appointed to investigate whether plans for these reprisals had received tacit approval from some officials in Jerusalem. Its conclusions led to the dismissal of several senior IDF officers and the resignation of Arik Sharon from his position as minister of defense.

In the context of the invasion of Lebanon, the raids on Beirut, and the Sabra and Shatila massacre, the accusation of Israel and the moral sympathy for the PLO were now almost unanimous in the world community. Moreover, Israel's casualties were heavy (517 killed and 2,462 wounded up to August 19, 1984), and in winter 1985, the IDF confronted Shiite guerrillas in the "quagmire" of southern Lebanon. The original settlement with the Lebanese government, which had been obtained with the help of the United States, was vetoed by Damascus and cancelled by Beirut. Only in spring 1985 did the Israeli troops finally leave for home.

All this notwithstanding, however, the fact remains that the PLO mini-Palestine no longer existed, and the bases granted them in Tunisia and Syria were by no means of comparable operational and political value to those of Lebanon. The PLO consequently lost much of its importance as a political actor within the Arab world, while without political-military center, it was hardly able to maintain a coherence of action among its various components. Indications of this weakening were already evident during the Israeli operation, when the repeated calls of Arafat, Habash, and Hawatmeh for an Arab summit remained unanswered for several months.[22]

The Syria-backed Abu Musa revolt within the Fatah against Arafat's authority was also of significance in this respect. This revolt broke out in May 1983 in response to the nomination, by the Supreme Command, of several officers at the head of troops in eastern Lebanon, a territory controlled by Syria. Abu Musa (or Said Mara), who had previously held the highest rank within the Fatah of the area, refused to acknowledge the nominations and proclaimed Arafat's leadership illegitimate. He was backed by such old-timers as Abu Salah and Samih Abu Quik ("Katzri"), both leftist members of the Central Committee of the Fatah, as well as by Abu Mahgy, Abu Khaled, Asif Aryat (Abu Raad), and Zyada Zahi, all senior officers of the Fatah in Lebanon. Syria fully supported the revolt and actually demanded the dismissal by the Fatah and the PLO of Arafat, accusing him of "mildness" and "betrayal." Within a few days, all premises of the Fatah in Syria and the Syrian area in Lebanon were taken over by the revolt. Fatah fighting units gradually gave in to the insurgents, and Arafat and his followers were pushed to Tripoli, Lebanon. A blockade however, was placed on the city by Musa's men, with the aid of other groups (the PFLP-GC, the Saiqa, and the Syrian PLA battalions) and Syrian artillery. The blockade resulted in a second evacuation of Arafat from Lebanese soil.

In 1986, Palestinian nationalism was still deeply divided. The National Council of the PLO was unable to reunite the splinters.

D. CHANGES IN RULES

The same factors that explain the unprecedented strengthening of the PLO before Sheleg also explain its drastic loss of power afterward. Before Sheleg the support of and dependence on benefactors who had interests of their own in the Israel-Palestinian conflict account for the fact that huge resources were accumulated by the PLO and that, at the same time, they could not be exchanged for Israeli concessions. The road to power was becoming a via dolorosa every time the fedayeen were tempted to assume genuine autonomy of action. Thus, the very scope of the accumulation of benefits on the international scene made the conflict a goal in itself.

Israel could not ignore the opportunity to exploit the vulnerability of the PLO that resulted from the visibility of its strength within the Lebanese mini-Palestine. Both the Palestinian quasi-conventional military alignment and its political headquarters were now exposed to Israeli action. This situation provided a unique chance for the IDF, as a regular army, to quash an enemy that was a guerrilla force.

As a result of Sheleg, the conflict has been rendered less profitable for the PLO. The achievement of greater profits—or lesser losses—might well reside in its resolution, through some kind of compromise with Israel. If the PLO takes this direction, however, it cannot but hurt the interests of some of those who have invested in it. This should, and in fact does, find expression in related tensions. In sum, the PLO faces the dilemma of "Whom should we fear more?" or "What strategy should be avoided as the most costly?" Taking into account the in-the-field conflict scene, the interests of the incumbents, and those of the respective benefactors of both sides, one has to ask, "What now?"

NOTES

1. See *Publications from Arab Newspapers*, edited by the Shiloah Institute (Hebrew); J. Goldberg, ed., *The Middle East: Tendencies and Processes* (Tel Aviv: Shiloah Institute, 1982 [Hebrew]).
2. S. Shamir, *Egypt under Sadat's Leadership* (Tel Aviv: Dabir, 1978 [Hebrew]).
3. A. Sasser, "The Stand and Status of Jordan in the Israeli-Arab Conflict,"

in *Between War and Arrangements: The Israeli-Arab Conflict after 1973*, ed. A. Har-Even (Tel Aviv: Zamora-Beitan-Modan, 1977 [Hebrew]), 67.

4. Ibid., 73.

5. A. Yodfat and Y. Arnon-Ohanna, *PLO Strategy and Tactics* (London: Croom Helm, 1981), 43–44.

6. M. Guemer, ed., "The Statement of the Minister without Portfolio for Foreign Affairs of Jordan, at the European Council on January 31, 1980," in *The Negotiations about the Instituting of Autonomy (April 1979–October 1980), Major Documents* (Tel Aviv: Shiloah Institute, 1981 [Hebrew]).

7. J. Amos, *Palestinian Resistance: Organization of a Nationalist Movement* (New York: Pergamon, 1980), 101.

8. H. Cobban, *The Palestinian Liberation Organization* (Cambridge: Cambridge University Press, 1984), 199.

9. Radio Riyadh, May 16, 1981; Qatar News Agency, May 19, 1981; *Akhat,* October 28, 1981.

10. *Information Briefing,* June 1981, "The Saudi Arabian-PLO Connection," Jerusalem: Israeli Information Center.

11. IDF Spokesman, *Libyan-PLO Relations* (Tel Aviv: IDF, September 1982 [mimeograph; Hebrew]); *All Roads Lead to Libya* (Tel Aviv: IDF, December 5, 1976 [mimeograph]).

12. IDF Spokesman, *PLO Ties with the USSR and other Eastern Bloc Countries* (Tel Aviv: IDF, September 1981 [mimeograph; Hebrew]).

13. Radio Moscow, May 25, 1975.

14. G. Golan, *The Soviet Union and the PLO*, Adelphi Papers 131, 1976; M. Maoz, *The Palestinian Guerrilla Organizations and the Soviet Union* (Jerusalem: Harry S. Truman Research Institute, 1975).

15. *Publications from Arab Newspapers* (from a Kuwaitian newspaper, *Elikta*).

16. J. Neyer, "The Emergence of Arafat," in *The Palestinians: People, History, Politics,* ed. M. Curtis et al. (New Brunswick, N.J.: Transaction Books, 1975), 129–30.

17. Informal sources.

18. I. Rabinovitch and H. Zamir, *War and Crisis in Lebanon, 1975–1981* (Tel Aviv: Shiloah Institute, Tel Aviv University, Kibbutz Hameukhad [Hebrew], 1982).

19. M. Gabay, *Lebanon Fights for Survival: Israeli Interference in Lebanon* (Givat Haviva: Institute for Arab Studies, 1983 [Hebrew]).

20. Office of the Higher Officer for Education and Information, *The Peace for Galilee Operation* (Tel Aviv: IDF, 1982 [Hebrew]).

21. IDF Spokesman *Data about the Peace for Galilee Operation and Lebanon* (Tel Aviv: IDF, 1983).

22. D. Dishon, "The Inter-Arab Scene during Sheleg," *Skira Khodshit* (Hebrew) June 1982.

Part IV   Perspectives

9 What Now?

A. NEW ATTITUDES

Until the early 1970s, radical hostility toward Israel was consensual among the Arabs. Jordan was then an exception because of its vested interest in the pre-1967 status quo, when the existence of Israel justified the Hashemite ambition to unify the West Bank and the East Bank. Yet, Jordan could not escape the commitments involved in the belligerent position of the Arab League which, in Algiers (1973) and Rabat (1974) recognized the PLO as the "sole legitimate representative of the Palestinian people."

This recognition, however, and the respectability it granted Palestinian nationalism on the international scene, soon compelled the PLO to both limit its support of transnational terrorism and to understate the ultimate goal defined by the Palestinian Covenant: the liquidation of Israel. The idea of a Democratic Palestine was formulated in terms which allowed more Jews—according to the date of their immigration to Israel—to be a part of the future "secular Palestinian state." Moreover, the PLO leaders spoke now of a step-by-step strategy and declared themselves ready to take over any piece of "liberated land" until the "total liberation" of Palestine. In reaction to these attitudes, in September 1974 the PFLP and other leftist groups created an oppositionist Rejection Front within the PLO.

The radicals, however, were unable to prevent ever more compromising formulas being advanced by PLO figures. Walid Khalidi, in 1978, and Khalid al-Hasan in 1980, proposed an Israeli withdrawal from the territories to be followed by the creation of a Palestinian state with East Jerusalem as its capital, in the framework of a general Israeli-Arab peace. The new Palestinian entity should then replace the Covenant by a new constitution. This readiness to accept the existence of Israel alongside a

Palestinian state constituted a drastic change in the PLO's traditional position. Nevertheless, as emphasized by Shaul Mishal, the establishment of the Palestinian state prior to the renunciation of the Covenant in effect "released the PLO from the burden of revising its national goal as a prerequisite." Moreover, nothing excluded that "the new constitution would express the same political desires." These proposals, henceforth, enabled the PLO "to maintain its commitments to its ultimate goal, and at the same time to demonstrate its willingness to accept a settlement based on two states in Palestine."[1]

Ambiguity was now the major trait of the position of the PLO's central leadership. The reaction to the 1981 Russian plan constituted the best example. This plan, proposed by President Leonid Brezhnev, called for an international conference to be held with the participation of all interested parties: the PLO, Israel, the Arab states, and the great powers. This conference was to reach a definite settlement of the Israeli-Arab dispute through mutual Israeli-Palestinian recognition, an Israeli withdrawal from the territories, and the creation of a Palestinian state alongside Israel.

The PLO was far from unanimous in its positive reaction but it "preferred not to express its reservations explicitly."[2] Yet, in March 1982, Ibrahim Sus, the PLO's representative in Paris, declared that the alteration of the Palestinian Covenant to omit the explicit intention to annihilate Israel, was totally unjustified.[3] At the end of May, Abu Jafer, the head of the PLO's political department, accused the United States of being "the most intransigent state in the world against the Palestinian people."[4] Similarly, one month later, Said Kamal, the PLO representative in Cairo, reiterated the necessity of mobilizing all the Arabs against Israel and the Americans.[5]

A plan formulated by PLO Isam Sartawi, however, called now for talks with those Israelis who accepted a return to the 1967 borders and recognized the Palestinian right to a sovereign state alongside Israel and the PLO as exclusive representatives of the Palestinian people. Because these propositions recommended Palestinian recognition of Israel only after the implementation of these principles,[6] they were still less compromising than the Saudi plan—known as the Fahd plan—which implicitly acknowledged the right of Israel to exist in security while also reaffirming the need for a Palestinian state.[7] This plan, submitted unsuccessfully to the 1981 Arab summit of Fez, was endorsed one year later by the same forum, including the PLO. In fact, Sidqi Danjani, a prominent PLO figure, had already stated that a Palestinian government in-exile should be established following the fedayeen's exit from Beirut; this government should negotiate with the United States for a peaceful settlement of the conflict.[8] The same Danjani met with the Egyptian foreign minister, while further PLO-Jordan contacts led the authorities in Amman to declare, "Jordanian-Palestinian relations are stronger than Jordan's relations with any other Arab party."[9] In November 1982, Nabil Shath, a chief assistant to Arafat, openly accepted the principle of some linkage between the future Palestinian entity and the Hashemite kingdom. He further stated that Palestine would not include what is now Israel.[10] In January 1983, Arafat stated that he was ready for a union with Jordan after Palestine was created. In parallel, it was announced that "Egypt now has the closest day-to-day contacts with the PLO."[11]

An agreement between the PLO's chairman and the Jordanian king now accepted an a priori recognition of Israel in order to start a negotiation process. On these grounds a Jordanian peace offensive in 1985 attempted to reach a secret understanding with Israel and called for an international conference in the framework of which a Palestinian-Jordanian delegation could start direct talks with the Israelis and the Americans. The move failed because the PLO was not ready yet to go this far in maintaining the Arafat-Hussein agreement. However, the way covered during the last twelve years is impressive; this development is to be understood as related to the evolving of the conflict's context.

B. CHANGE OF CONTEXT

Soviet influence in the Middle East had progressed in the footsteps of the militant anti-Zionist and anti-West regimes of the region. This influence became dominant in Tripoli (Libya), Damascus (which also meant Beirut), Algiers, Baghdad, Aden, Khartoum, and, mainly, Cairo. These also were the principal participants in the race for leadership among the Arab nations. Egypt's move of briskly leaving the Soviet area of influence for integration with the United States constituted the first major Russian setback in the area since the mid-1950s. This turnabout, moreover, took place concomitantly with negotiations with Israel and thereby served as the vehicle for a genuine revolution of Middle Eastern realities. From then on, despite the positions of governments, a decisive military confrontation of Arab states with Israel was quite out of the question: Egypt, the most populated Arab country, has always been the principal belligerent in Jewish-Arab wars.

The Iran-Iraq war was another factor that, beginning in the late 1970s, contributed to the change of face of the area. Syria tacitly supported Iran, because the rulers in Damascus are Shiite, like the Iranian majority; its Russian allies were also interested in maintaining Khomeini's virulently anti-American regime. Iraq, as a result, drifted closer to the pro-Western camp, that is, to Jordan, Saudi Arabia, and Egypt. The 1984 renewal of diplomatic relations between Baghdad and Washington, which had been broken in 1967, was accompanied by moderate statements from Iraq about the conflict with Israel.

Against this background, Sheleg's real political meaning may be analyzed. Soon after the beginning of the operation, the Syrians saw their antiaircraft missile system, supplied by Moscow, totally destroyed by Israeli planes. The pro-Soviet camp received an additional setback when Syria, though still very influential in Lebanon, no longer occupied Beirut militarily. The drastic weakening of the PLO was another blow for both Damascus and Moscow. Moreover, outside Lebanon, the Fatah-led PLO, though much weaker, stood far from Damascus' direct control and could rethink its interests and goals more freely than before. Power relations in the Arab world between the pro-Western moderates and the pro-Eastern radicals were rapidly evolving with an irreversible impact on dominant attitudes toward the Israeli-Arab and Israeli-Palestinian conflicts.

In the meantime, pro-Western Saudi Arabia had also become progressively more moderate vis-à-vis Israel after Ayatollah Ruholla Khomeini's rise to power in Iran, which endangered its traditional regime and strengthened its interest in calming any crisis and tension. In these circumstances, the ostracism of Egypt by the other Arabs that followed Camp David was soon broken. Syria and Libya were the ones to be isolated among the Arab nations. "Peace plans" now multiplied. After the Fez summit of 1982 endorsed the Fahd plan, the Arafat-led PLO National Council met in November 1984, under the auspices of Amman itself. The council heard King Hussein give an elaborate speech about the imperative of peace and compromise.

On the other hand, the Sheleg operation paradoxically caused deep cleavages among the Israelis. For the very first time, the role of the IDF was a subject of debate in Israel. In the light of the six hundred soldiers who had been killed by the beginning of 1985, the deafening international outcry against an operation that was not justified by direct self-defense, and the moral crisis following the Sabra-Shatila massacres (perpetrated by Christians against Palestinians with the tacit consent of the Israeli authorities), many Israelis considered Sheleg a painful page in the country's annals. However, the picture is different when one looks at Sheleg's impact on Israel's status in the context in which the operation took place, that is, the international dimension of the Israeli-Palestinian conflict.

The condemnation encountered by Israel at the time of the bombing of Beirut and in the aftermath of Sabra-Shatila progressively gave way in Western capitals to a reappraisal of the new Middle East realities. It soon became evident to Europe and the United States that the Israeli operation had weakened the pro-Soviet camp in the Arab world. The United States, France, Italy, and Great Britain tried to make the situation more concrete by organizing a common force (the international peace-keeping force), which provided conditions of security for the departure of the PLO. This force, however, was unable to protect Beirut's new sovereignty or to withstand the hostility of local groups (Shiites, Palestinians, and Druzes) that was encouraged by Syria. In Washington, Paris, London, and Rome, governments were unwilling to pay a price of blood for the sake of Western influence in Lebanon. The withdrawal of this force made it clear that Israel was the major Middle Eastern pro-Western power that could be relied on to counter pro-Soviet Arab radicalism. The importance of this role increased with the realization of the limits to the sacrifices that the West is willing to make for the sake of maintaining its assets in the area.

The anti-Israeli overtones frequent in the speeches of Western European politicians and media were gradually tempered. The new climate was best illustrated by an official visit of Shimon Peres, the Israeli prime minister, to Paris in December 1984. Similarly, within the Third World diplomatic relations with Israel were renewed by Zaire and Liberia during 1983; at a minor level, by Sri Lanka in 1984; and by the Ivory Coast in 1986. More astounding is the unofficial information related by the world press of important arms deals and economic contracts concluded between China and Israel.

C. THE PLO TODAY

Initially, however, the PLO was the moral victor of the Israeli invasion of Lebanon. During the months following June 1982, there was an overwhelming growth of popularity of the Palestinian cause. A landmark of this period was Yasser Arafat's reception by Pope John Paul II on September 15, 1982. Similarly, several of Israel's traditional friends changed their attitude toward the Jewish state and exhibited a new cordiality vis-à-vis the PLO. This was the case of Canada and of the regional government of Quebec, where the PLO was recognized (December 1982) as the "sole legitimate representative of the Palestinian people."[12] In other capitals, such as Athens, where Israel is represented, it was attacked in particularly vigorous terms.

However, the reappraisal of Middle Eastern realities by the Western powers generated gradual changes in the international standing of the PLO.[13] After his expulsion from Tripoli, Lebanon, Arafat was unable to land in Western Europe or America. Even the publication of his biography in London in December 1984 was insufficient to eliminate the obstacles to a private visit to Great Britain. Information about the PLO in major newspapers, from *Le Monde* to the *New York Times*, was mostly relegated to inside pages; PLO offices around the world no longer multiplied, and their activity slowed down. The clearest expression of this change concerns the PLO's relations with its major benefactors.

As for the USSR, before 1982 it had considered the PLO an essential factor in its policy.[14] Sheleg, however, transformed this situation. Initially, the USSR's major worry was to prevent an outbreak of violence between Syria, its principal ally in the area, and Israel; such a confrontation could escalate uncontrollably into a Russian-American clash.[15] Russia therefore pressured the Syrians to limit their involvement in the opposition to the Israeli invasion and did not hesitate to strengthen its warnings by diminishing military aid at the height of the combat. For the same reasons, in blunt disagreement with Damascus, Moscow became more critical of the radicals within the PLO. On the eve of the November 1984 PNC session in Amman, George Habash, Naief Hawatmeh, and other opponents of Arafat were invited to Moscow in order to be sermonized—in vain—to rejoin the PLO's mainstream. A Russian statement about Soviet leader Yuri Andropov's talks with Arafat in January 1983 included a positive appraisal of future links between the Palestinian revolution and Jordan.[16] Furthermore, Moscow made efforts to improve its relations and collaboration with Jordan and even with Egypt. Related to these moves, in December 1984 Amman and Cairo agreed to call for a UN-sponsored peace conference for the Middle East; such a possibility would associate the USSR with the effort to resolve the conflict. The PLO then became aware that it had lost some of its privileges in Moscow.

Moreover, the PLO's relations with Syria were now fraught with difficulties. Damascus wanted to maintain its supervision over Palestinian nationalism and could not accept any prospect of a future settlement of the Palestinian conflict that would ignore its interest in being a unifying and leading power in the Arab world. Syria therefore pressured the radical wing of the PLO, whose headquarters were located in Damascus. The rift between this wing and Arafat's mainstream seemed definite.

In fact, the central PLO leadership was seeking pragmatic solutions. The salvaging of whatever territory and power could still be saved required a new attitude toward the Israelis and what they could accept. In other words, it must take into consideration the Israelis' determined opposition to the creation of a totally independent Palestinian state on the West Bank. From the American point of view also, the link of a Palestinian entity with Jordan was desirable, in light of the Hashemites' allegiance to the Atlantic world, on the one hand, and the PLO's relationships with the Soviet bloc, on the other. A Greater Jordan—including the Gaza Strip, which was never a part of the pre-1967 kingdom—would create a viable territorial-political entity. The Hashemites' formidable capability of survival would seemingly maintain this entity within Western influence. In light of both Israel's and the United States' motivations, then, the PLO might hope to achieve new assets only by moving closer to Amman.

The USSR's attempts to woo Jordan were now apparently intended to safeguard a role in forthcoming diplomatic games, while the same conditions also accounted for Syria's stubborn challenging of the legit-imacy of the PLO leadership[17] and its persecution of PLO figures in Damascus and Beirut.[18] This explains numerous events in 1983 and 1984: the delivery of anti-Assad and anti-Qaddafi speeches by PLO leaders in Algiers (February 1983) and Amman (November 1984) and the killings within the Fatah and between them and members of other organizations throughout the Arab world, including in the territories (Hebron and Bir Zeyt).[19] In the climate of hostility that existed in PLO-Syrian relations, the pro-Arafat *Al-Dustur*[20] did not hesitate to accuse Rifat Assad (the Syrian president's brother) of having secretly met with Ariel Sharon, Israel's defense minister, in order to liquidate together a Fatah officer, Abu al-Walid, in the Lebanese Valley.[21] In the same vein, Damascus was condemned for the murder of Fahd Qawasmeh, the moderate former mayor of Hebron and a newly elected member of the PNC (Amman, December 1984). In contrast, Egypt had sent an important delegation to the PNC session in Amman, where Hussein had presented his plan of a Palestinian-Jordanian collaboration without raising any opposition in the audience.

At this Amman session, however, 123 delegates were missing. These were the representatives of the radical groups, in particular, the PFLP, the DFLP, the PFLP-GC, the Saiqa, and the Communist party. The latter had participated at the PNC in Algiers (in 1983) and now boycotted, to show its solidarity with the Left and to prevent an expression of Syria-USSR divergencies.

These groups had been the most active within the administered ter-ritories for about fifteen years. The masses, whether in Gaza, Hebron, or Halhul, however, had never identified ideologically with the radicals. Essentially, the population at large always wanted the Israelis to leave Arab land as soon as possible. Thus, though the Fatah's political activity among the population was less than those of the Communists and the radicals, its pragmatic outlook was a factor of powerful attraction to "ordinary people." It was Arafat, not Habash or Hawatmeh, who en-joyed the greatest public favor. Those who persecuted the members of the mainstream in the PLO were soon abhorred. After Syria's support of the 1982 rebellion of Abu Musa, Hafiz Assad, as well as the Fatah insurgents and the radicals, was generally criticized. In contrast, the concurrent rapprochement of the PLO with Hussein and Egypt raised among the inhabitants the expectation of realistic moves that might lead to practical solution of the conflict. The strength of this general opinion caused numerous figures identified as radicals to publicly decry Abu Musa and Assad and to sign petitions in favor of the Amman PNC session.

To be sure, the Hashemite Kingdom was strengthened by these de-velopments, which enhanced the position of local figures who combined

PLO allegiance with pro-Hashemite sympathies. At the hour of Palestinian nationalism's greatest weakness, this development constituted a serious challenge to it. Possibly because of this challenge, the central PLO leadership could not endorse up to its ultimate limit King Hussein's 1984 peace offensive. However, the crisis that followed in Jordan-PLO relations only deteriorated the Palestinians' status on the Arab scene further. The poor relations with Syria as well, and the deep divisions among fedayeen factions were feebly compensated by developments in Lebanon. The Palestinians were now more or less secretly rebuilding bases in the refugee camps of Beirut, Tyre, and other places, taking advantage of the enduring ethnic war in Lebanon. Above all, the animosity which was now the rule in PLO-Jordan relations was causing confusion in the territories where pro-Fatah and pro-Jordan elements were striving in common against the influence of the pro-Syrian leftist fronts.

The retreat from political initiatives thus seemed temporary. Moreover, in autumn 1985 Israel raided PLO bases in Tunisia and in early 1986 the United States retaliated against Libya for Qaddafi's backing of anti-American terrorism on behalf of the Palestinian cause. These developments added to the conclusion that in present circumstances there was no profitable alternative to diplomacy.

D. FORMULATING A SCENARIO

At the end of 1984 and the beginning of 1985, terrorist activity was at its lowest level ever within the administered territories, in Israel, and abroad. It received a new impetus in the last months of 1985 and early 1986. Yet, in Samaria, Judea, and the Gaza Strip, the tumultuous period seemed to be over, though erratic demonstrations and incidents still occurred. An Israeli government of national unity included the right wing as well as the Labor party; no new settlement was planned for the near future, while the contacts between Israeli officials and Palestinian leaders were more numerous than in the recent past. As for the PLO, though deeply divided, its majority followed Arafat, who was both tempted by and reluctant to start a common diplomatic initiative with Hussein in order to open negotiations with Israel through the United States. What ending may be expected to this fifty-year-old conflict?[22]

More than ever, an Arab-Palestinian military victory over Israel does not seem likely as a future conclusion of the conflict. It would require a set of exceptional conditions contrasting with present reality. It would need, above all, the total devotion to the Palestinian cause of a coalition of states and movements controlling stronger forces than those Israel has already confronted and overcome in the past: the seven-state coalition in 1948, the three-state alliance in 1967, and the two-state offensive in 1973. After Camp David, which has removed Egypt from the arena of belligerence, there are no indications of a new, stronger alignment.

The parallel development of the Arabs and Israel still preserves a qualitative gap in favor of the Jews in military capability, technology, and social-ideological cohesion.[23] Israel, moreover, is a strategic asset for the West; it is supported by the solidarity of Jews over the world; its political regime is a democracy. For all these reasons, it seems that the Jewish state may rely on the United States for survival if challenged by its enemy, probably even if this enemy is directly supported by its principal outside benefactor, the USSR.[24] Furthermore, since Israel possesses a nuclear weapon, to be used in a desperate situation, both the US and the USSR would be highly interested in preventing the occurrence of such a conjuncture in order to avoid any chance of a nuclear confrontation between themselves.

Present circumstances, however, make the possibility of a decisive Israeli victory over the PLO quite unlikely as well. The Palestinian issue is a fact of the world's consciousness. Even in Israel, only a few deny the existence of this problem.[25] Moreover, the Palestinians have a wide diaspora from which to recruit militants. By no means is Israel capable of reacting to everyone everywhere, and the Israeli-Palestinian conflict can hardly find a definitive solution *manu militari*. In the administered territorities, the Israeli's ideal of a state of a Jewish character prevents the normalization of the existence of a wide national minority. Even if a relatively calm situation reigns in this area at given times, it could not be considered an end to the conflict.

A permanent end to the conflict can be achieved only through compromise.[26] The Camp David Agreements, concluded four years after the Yom Kippur War, seemed at their time unbelievable; they showed that, all obstacles notwithstanding, peace processes cannot be excluded from Middle Eastern forecasts. As mentioned above, qualitative changes have been taking place in this respect since the late 1970s, following the Israel-Egypt treaty. Moderate statements issued by Amman, Riyadh, and even Beirut reveal these changes. Moreover, after Sheleg, the PLO's benefactors are less generous while territorial autonomy, even in the frame of a Palestinian-Jordanian linkage and even within the limited space of the West Bank and the Gaza Strip, may be viewed as better than paralysis and impotence.

This is even more the case as the possibility of a settlement seems at hand. Most probably, as with President Jimmy Carter's response to Sadat's 1977 initiative, a move toward peace and negotiations coordinated with Jordan from the PLO side would be received positively by the Americans. The United States is interested in widening its influence in the area by any means that do not jeopardize Israel's existence. Once this aspect is settled (that is, once there is a possibility of peace that

Exhibit 9.1
Close versus Open Patterns of Conflict Relations

Aspects	The Close-Relations Syndrome	The Open-Relations Syndrome
1. Political goals	"final" strategies	intermediary goals
2. Patterns of rewarding	stable	changing
3. Attitudes toward actors	stable	flexible
4. Images of contender	ill-intended, treacherous	also human
5. Points of reaction to contender	low	high

includes the acceptance by Arabs of the existence of Israel), the Americans would probably use the Jewish state's economic and military dependence on them to get from it the territorial and political concessions necessary to meet the Arabs' exigencies and to firmly anchor their influence in the area.

More specifically, it may be said that recent developments have entailed precise qualitative changes in the Israel-PLO conflict. The contemporary attitude of the PLO regarding the "final goal" hints at a readiness to make do with a Palestine alongside, not instead of, Israel. Israel's officials have endorsed an autonomy scheme in the Camp David Agreements for a five-year period in the administered territories until a definitive settlement is reached by consensus. Both developments represent moves from "final" strategies to intermediate goals.

In the background, the PLO's present benefactors are less numerous and less committed than in the past. In parallel, Israel is more vulnerable to American pressures. The invitations of Israelis, journalists, and leftist politicians to PLO meetings are signals of this new era; another such signal is the lack of any legal action by Jerusalem against these men. At the same time, contacts have been renewed between Israeli officials with figures in the administered territories who are well known for their sympathy to the PLO. Both sides now show a greater flexibility regarding their images of each other. Israel today is less sensitive to and more understanding of the Palestinians' identification with the PLO and their desire to manifest this identification, and the PLO sympathizers are less reactive to every move of the incumbents. Exhibit 9.1 summarizes these changes under the form of two differentiated syndromes of conflict relations.[27]

In view of the reluctance of the PLO and Israel to recognize each other for the time being, however, a more pragmatic agreement might take the more limited path of "passive arrangements."[28] Such arrangements mean that despite contradictory interests, ideologies, and commitments, adversaries accept de facto a given status quo. With time this would lead to a new compromise. Some steps that might be taken are a total freeze of Israeli settlement plans in the administered territories, a practical intensification of the inhabitants' ties with Jordan, some reactivation of local political bodies, and informal contacts between Israel, Jordan, and the Palestinian external leadership. All these could gradually merge into some federative or confederative scheme.

E. THE PEACE FORMULA

If the two sides are to reach the shores of a real peace, they must answer the requirements of the following formula:[29]

	(i)		(ii)		(iii)		(iv)
A basis for	balanced		balanced		balanced		balanced
a truly	= power	+	aspirations	+	objective	+	international
stable peace	relations		and perceptions		circumstances		conjuncture

i. Balanced Power Relations

Obviously, a sharp dissymmetry characterizes the Israeli-PLO power relations today, in which a well-armed and cohesive state opposes a movement rooted in a subordinate population. Still, Israel is deeply dependent, economically as well as militarily, on external benefactors. Moreover, some balance does exist in that each side is able to prevent the other from achieving its goals. To Israel's capability to bear the situation indefinitely, the PLO responds with its power to survive within the population of the territories as well as in the Palestinian diaspora.

ii. Balanced Aspirations

An end to the conflict by means of peace also requires that both contenders sincerely aspire to it. Each side is still far from such a deliberate will. For the Palestinians, the situation is an enormous injustice perpetrated by a people that in Islamic tradition is only to be "tolerated." For the Jew, the negation of Israel's legitimacy by a nation that numbers more than twenty states is associated with the Jewish history of persecutions. Nevertheless, the story of the Israeli-Egyptian relationship shows that images, feelings, and resentments are a function of political and practical realities.[30] Similarly, tens of thousands of inhabitants of the administered territories work in Israel, and incidents between them and Israelis are very rare. In Nablus and Hebron, moreover, Jewish-Arab relations are quick to improve when political tensions become calm. The peace process, once started, may thus create new mutual orientations among the two populations, the Jewish and the Palestinian, thereby contributing to balanced aspirations.[31]

iii. Balanced Objective Circumstances

Objective material and geographical circumstances are, however, also important in the creation of peaceful relations. In this case, especially, the whole conflict is related to territorial concepts, the land of Israel versus Palestine. Both are national and cultural myths and concomitantly bear crucial security and strategic meanings. The Israelis believe that a major factor of the 1967 war was the lengthy and sinuous Israeli-Jordanian border, which at certain points reaches the vicinity of the most populous centers of Israel.[32]

On the other hand, a "Palestinian homeland" in the administered territories would face the absence of natural resources and heavy social problems (10 percent of the West Bank's inhabitants and more than 40 percent of those in the Gaza Strip are 1948 refugees). Total separation from the Israeli economy would endanger this entity's ability to survive. Yet to remain bound to Israel would signify the development of an explosive neocolonial situation, while a Palestinian anti-status-quo state surrounded by two more powerful neighbors, Israel and Jordan, could be tempted to challenge the weaker Hashemite Kingdom on the East Bank, where the population is mostly Palestinian anyway. The most stable, peaceful solution of the Israeli-Palestinian conflict could then well reside in some federative scheme including the PLO and Jordan, even a confederative framework that would leave room for Israel as well. Such a scheme would actually not be very far from the Democratic Palestine advocated by PLO propaganda or from the Greater Israel claimed by militant Jews.

iv. A Balanced International Conjuncture

As discussed above, the interests of the major world powers also play a role in this conflict. These interests are of crucial importance in the development of the contenders' hostile relations; they should be of no less importance in the search for peace.[33]

In principle, both the United States and the USSR want a peaceful resolution of the conflict, though their positions differ on almost every aspect involved. The Russians are interested in a pro-Soviet Palestinian state, which would weaken both Jordan and Israel. If this state were created by means of UN intervention, it would associate the USSR both with the sponsorship of the new arrangements and with future international initiatives in the region. The United States prefers a Palestinian autonomy, which would strengthen Jordan and set Israel more at ease. Bilateral talks excluding Russia but under Washington's auspices would also affirm American influence as the major axis of peacemaking in the region.

The United States and the USSR are closer to agreement on some other points, however. Both refuse any substantial annexation of territories by Israel and recognize the necessity of solving the Palestinian problem. Both seek primarily to avoid the degeneration of the Middle East problem into a world war. In the context of this strong common denominator, it seems plausible that a compromise between the Americans and the Russians could also include the Israelis and the PLO.

This eventuality is not to be excluded, particularly in light of the Russians' cautious behavior during Sheleg, their reserve toward Syrian extremism, and their systematic support of Arafat against the Palestinian leftists. The Soviets have apparently drawn their conclusions from the new political map of the Middle East that developed following the Camp David Agreements, during the Iran-Iraq war and as the outcome of Sheleg. The Russians might, indeed, fear that solutions may be found more easily today than in the past, without their help and in spite of their opposition.

Edward Said's forecast of 1979 seems more farsighted than ever in the mid-1980s, both despite and because of its cautiousness:

Two things are certain; the Jews of Israel will remain; the Palestinians will also remain. To say much more than that with assurance is a foolish risk. I have little doubt that the United States will press on with negotiations between Israel and Egypt over Palestinian autonomy, or that in the short run Jordan will not join in. . . . Saudi Arabia and Jordan are in a peculiarly acute position at present, and that too is bound to change . . . will the effect of Iran's revolution make itself more strongly felt? . . . it is far too tempting to say confidently that a Palestinian political initiative will emerge, and will carry the whole region forward. In many ways such an eventuality would be a positive result of the Egyptian-Israel treaty. But . . . we [also] must look forward realistically to much turbulence [yet to come].[34]

NOTES

1. S. Mishal, *The PLO Under Arafat: Between Gun and Olive Branch* (New Haven: Yale University Press, 1986), 67.

2. *Ibid.*, 83.

3. *Africa,* May 26, 1982.

4. *Al-Majallah,* July 24, 1982, 3/128.

5. *Mena* (Middle East News Agency), August 15, 1982.

6. S. Mishal, 69.

7. "Summary and Review of the Second Fez Summit," *Hatzav,* 843/069, September 29, 1982.

8. *Mena,* September 21, 1982; *Africa,* October 21, 1982.

9. *Al-Majallah,* November 13, 1982, 3/144.

10. *Mena,* January 24, 1983.

11. *Al-Nahur,* February 21, 1983, 7/8.

12. *Jerusalem Post,* December 28, 1982.

13. *Al-Watan Al-Arabi* 312 (February 4, 1983):48–49.

14. "PLO-Moscow Links: More Details," *Arab-Asian Affairs* 116 (December 1982), 1–9.

15. G. Golan, "The Soviet Union and the Israeli Action in Lebanon," *International Affairs* (London) 59, no. 1 (1982):7–16.

16. *Pravda,* January 14, 1983.

17. Nicholas Tatro, "Who Controls the PLO?" *Monday Morning* 11, no. 541 (November 22, 1982):46–47.

18. E. Rouleau, "Damascus Is Not Beirut," *Middle East Forces* 5. no. 5 (January 1983):2–3, 23.

19. *Economist* 282/722 (March 6, 1982):66–67.

20. *Al-Dustur* 12/259 (August 11, 1982):16–19; see also E. Jary, *Le Monde,* December 11, 1982.

21. *Middle East Newsletter,* 25/1324 (March 19, 1982):38–39 (Arabic).

22. A. Har-Even, "Is Another War Possible?" *Hotam (Al Hamishmar),* April 23, 1982 (Hebrew).

23. A. Yariv, interview (with the author's assistants), 1983.

24. Y. Harkabi, *Basics of the Arab-Israeli Conflict,* no. 110 (Tel Aviv: IDF Education and Information Department, 1971 [Hebrew]).

25. Yariv.

26. See D. Kama, *The Conflict: Why and Until When?* (Tel Aviv: Shakmuna, 1975), 113–22 (Hebrew).

27. T. Lanir, *Israeli Interference in Lebanon* (Tel Aviv: Tel Aviv University, 1980 [Hebrew]).

28. K. J. Holsti, "Resolving International Conflicts," *Journal of Conflict Resolution,* no. 3 (September 1976):272–96.

29. See also Kama.

30. A. Har-Even, "Are Relations of Confidence Possible?" in *Between Threat and Hope,* ed. A. Har-Even, 7–42 (Jerusalem: Van Leer Institute, 1980 [Hebrew]).

31. Harkabi, 87–89.

32. A. Yariv, "The Ground of Israel's Security Policy," in *The Arab-Israeli Conflict,* ed. E. Gilboa and M. Naor (Tel Aviv: IDF Headquarters, 1981 [Hebrew]), 295–305.

33. E. Gilboa, "The Big Powers' Policy in the Arab-Israeli Conflict: From the Yom Kippur War to Camp David," in Gilboa and Naor, 272–91.

34. E. Said, *The Question of Palestine* (New York: Times Books, 1979), 235–38.

10 Among Other Conflicts

A. THE GOAL OF THE ANALYSIS

The goal of this book was to analyze the Israeli-Palestinian conflict globally, from the viewpoint of guerrilla-conflict theory. In any guerrilla conflict, violence is employed as a means of changing power relations between a weaker contender and a political regime. From this point I developed the approach to guerrilla conflict that I have applied to the case under study.

In the context of this definition, it may be deduced that in a guerrilla conflict the "profitability of violence" for the weaker party is at stake. One can then delineate appropriate circumstances by elaborating on the concept of "inflation of power" and the non-zero-sum character of the conflict. In this chapter, the successive steps of the approach and the related aspects of the specific case at hand are summarized and concluded.

In the course of this discussion, however, I also briefly refer comparatively to the specific conflicts that were used to substantiate and exemplify the theoretical discussion in chapter 1, with particular emphasis on the FLN in Algeria and the EOKA in Cyprus. These two cases, indeed, share a number of common traits with the Israeli-Palestinian conflict in different respects. These comparative remarks should highlight the contribution of the study of the Israeli-Palestinian problem to guerrilla-conflict theory.

B. INFLATION OF POWER AND THE CONDITIONS OF PROTRACTED VIOLENCE

Protracted violence, we have seen, seriously threatens incumbents, particularly in societies that have undergone acute political and social crises and in which no effective institutionalized channels for the expression of dissent exist. If such a regime, despite superior strength, loses the commitment of wide segments of the population, it must resort to means of coercion in order to survive. However, the deterrent value of these means when they are imposed upon (and all the more so if they are drafted from) a hostile population necessarily declines, and ever more numerous means will be necessary to maintain the political status quo. This juncture illustrates the notion of the inflation of power of a political center. Violence initiated by dissenters from within the sociey provokes the incumbents to tighten their control over the potential supporters of the insurgency; this may be expected to further weaken the remaining power assets of the rulers.

Thus, this process would already represent undeniable profits from violence for the insurgents. These profits increase further if, as a result, wider civilian support is attracted to the dissenters, solidifying their own power assets. Furthermore, the highest degree of profitability may be attained if these assets are converted by the insurgents into elements of force, such as new fighters, intelligence structures, or financial aid. Hence a guerrilla conflict may be seen from this angle as an initiative of dissenters designed to "capitalize," by means of violence, on the inflation of the regime's power.

As in all four cases reviewed in chapter 1, the historical background of the Israel-Palestinian conflict provides an appropriate illustration for this theoretical outlook. During the British Mandate, a growing Arab-Palestinian nationalism, sustained by the neighboring states, confronted the Zionist movement and culminated in the 1936–39 revolt against Jewish immigration.

However, following the creation of Israel, most Palestinians lived in those Arab countries, mostly on the West Bank of the Jordan River, which had been annexed by the Hashemite Kingdom. Another major Palestinian population existed in the Gaza Strip under Egyptian rule. About sixteen years later, and in the context of inter-Arab rivalries, a Palestinian Liberation Organization was created.

Following the Six-Day War, an Israeli authority on the West Bank and in the Gaza Strip re-created, in sharper terms than when the British had served as referees, the pre-1948 direct confrontation between Jewish and Palestinian nationalisms. Palestinian nationalism was denied any political expression, because the new regime saw the conquest of these territories as the result of an interstate war that could be discussed only in interstate negotiations. This situation responded in a most extreme manner to what I have called the inflation of power. Violent acts, strikes, and other forms of protest multiplied against the forces Israel soon deployed.

C. MODELS OF ANTIGUERRILLA AND GUERRILLA ALIGNMENT

1. The Theoretical Possibilities

As a violent means of changing power and force relations, however, and as far as the setting of direct—or "in-the-field"—conflict is concerned, the incumbents are the strongest party, in least initially. As such, they are the ones whose reactions to the outbreak of violence are the major codifier of the confrontation.

Because this confrontation implicates power assets as well as the use of force, it questions both the regime's response to the population's lack of loyalty and its military action against the insurgents themselves. The dissenters, it is true, bring incumbents into a conflict in which socio-political realities are ultimately related to protracted violence. However, within this context, the antiguerrilla models employed toward the hostile population and the insurgents play a determining role in the shaping of the rebels' development as a political factor and as an armed force, respectively.

As for the rulers' possible reactions toward the population, the concept of inflation of power highlights the two basic alternatives. The first, the "penetration model," postulates the reduction of the rate of inflation. This refers to the creation of circumstances in which insurgents will be unable to accumulate power assets—and thereby, elements of force—within the setting. This type of policy may take the form of intensive "selling" of the regime's own ideological position by political, social, or economic reforms that may isolate the insurgents from their social basis and facilitate the regime's own legitimization within the population.

The second possible strategy, the "watching-over model," takes inflation of power as a given and perceives the insurgency as an alteration of the political reality only. It seeks principally to deter the inhabitants by coercion from translating their lack of sympathy with the regime into active support for the insurgents. The intention is less to prevent the insurgents from accumulating political power than to prevent the conversion of such assets into elements of force.

To some extent, each model may be used to increase the effectiveness of the other strategy. Nevertheless, the intensification of coercion or of penetration beyond a certain degree cannot but be counterproductive to the development, respectively, of commitments or of deterrence. Hence, these models constitute alternatives, and in any given case and at any given time, one of them is dominant.

One may ask now, however, in any specific case, what factors influence incumbents to prefer one model over the other? The answer is implicit in the definitions of the models themselves. Whatever the specific context of the incumbents' stand, the penetration model, in its desire to gain the loyalty of the inhabitants, expresses the regime's aspiration to remain the focus of legitimacy of the social order. The watching-over model, on the contrary, stresses force relations, indicating that, whatever the underlying reasons, the regime's interest lies primarily in the continuation of its sheer domination. Hence, the level of the incumbents' ambitions regarding the population determines whether they adopt a penetration or a watching-over antiguerrilla model. Whichever model is implemented by the incumbents, the scope of the resources at their disposal accounts for the sophistication of the means they utilize and thereby for the practical effectiveness of the strategy.

The scope of available resources, however, is significant mainly with respect to the military confrontation. From this perspective, the major issue is the extent to which the regime possesses—despite the inflation of its power—sufficient means not only to adopt a static, defensive posture (which is essential in any case) but also to engage in appropriate offensive moves. This military dimension combines with the model adopted vis-à-vis the population, according to the level of the regime's ambitions, in the overall characterization of the antiguerrilla alignment.

We may consider the impact of the various types of antiguerrilla strategy upon the development of the guerrilla force, as both a political and a fighting organization. Whatever the guerrillas' power assets within the population at the beginning of the conflict, they will have difficulties maintaining these assets, let alone increasing them, in the face of a vigorous penetration model implemented by the incumbents. Things are different when the antiguerrilla combat takes the form of watching-over model and does not compete with the insurgents for the population's loyalty, thus creating a political vacuum among the inhabitants. In this case, the guerrilla movement may succeed in establishing meaningful political mechanisms that could gain control over the population or over given segments of it.

The logic of the military confrontation is the same as for the political dimension. The incumbents enjoy a superiority at the beginning of the conflict in any case; the question, however, is whether their antiguerrilla force is militarily strong enough to combine both offensive strategy and defensive tactics. If this is the case, the insurgents have only very limited chances to convert power into force and to become much more than a terrorist group. When the antiguerrilla force is able only to maintain a defensive posture, violence may grow more instrumental for the dissenters. They may aspire at first to build a significant military force in areas that are weakly controlled by the incumbents. Then, gradually, they may also attempt to expand their control over the territory and the inhabitants and to physically weaken the incumbents' forces.

Hence, as far as the conflict setting is concerned, the profitability of violence for dissenters is a function of specific circumstances, which refer primarily to the incumbents and which account for the particular forms the conflict assumes (see exhibit 1.2).

2. The Israeli Policy and Alignment

Within the conflict setting constituted by the administered territories, the Israeli authorities represent a *metropole*, Israel. This *metropole* is strong enough to provide a comprehensive military response to the guerrilla movement. Grounded in the Israelis' usual paramount concern for any matter implying security problems, this response combines defensive tactics to the extent of a wide and complex alignment along the borders and an offensive strategy that includes highly mobile units and appropriate technological means.

The situation becomes more complex when the incumbents' ambitions and policies toward the Palestinian population are considered. The symbolic historical and religious significance of sites in Judea and Samaria explains why many Israeli Jews feel that these areas should be annexed. Moreover, in the eyes of maximalists as well as most minimalists, security considerations preclude agreeing to a total withdrawal to the vulnerable pre-1967 borders. The same attitude applies to the creation of a sovereign Palestinian state, which presumably would adopt an anti-status-quo orientation because of its tiny size. Yet to many it is also obvious that territorial concessions are a necessity, while the Zionist conception of the Israeli state makes the annexation of the Arab population an unattractive prospect.

This background must be kept in mind when analyzing Israel's antiguerrilla policy in the administered territories and its alterations over time. For a whole decade (1967–77), a period mostly dominated by the rule of the left-of-center Labor party, the final status of the Palestinians was conceived as an issue to be settled with the neighboring states (principally Jordan). The lack of commitment of the Palestinian population to the Israeli authorities was taken for granted. The major objective was the maintenance of Israel's hold over the territories until such an agreement could be achieved.

In light of these limited ambitions, the coercive watching-over model was the most appropriate. Its aim was to deter the population from actively supporting the PLO without trying to "buy" its loyalty. Yet two additional features account for the peculiarities of the watching-over model applied, namely, the geographic proximity of the *metropole* to the conflict setting and Israel's own liberal regime. Hence, though by no means a basic aim of the antiguerrilla policy, an impressive economic boom took place in the territories. In parallel, open bridges between the administered territories and the Arab world were maintained and juridical privileges endowed.

Camp David in 1979 introduced new elements into the political equation. The peace treaty recognized the "legitimate needs" of the Palestinians. "Full home rule" was to be implemented for a five-year interim period, during which a definitive solution was to be negotiated. Armed with a "calling," the incumbents tried to enlist anyone who kept his distance from the PLO, such as the pro-Jordan notables and, mainly, the various Associations of Villagers.

These moves, however, were not free of contradictions. The rightist government then in power in Israel aspired to the annexation of the West Bank and Gaza in the long run and encouraged the settlement of Jews much more actively than had the former government. Further deterioration of Israel's relations with the local Arab population was therefore inevitable. The Israeli policymakers were not prepared to make the extensive investments necessary for generating drastic changes and new, favorable sociopolitical alignments among this population. Hence, despite several significant efforts in the direction of the penetrative model, in the final analysis, the watching-over perspective remained dominant.

3. The PLO's Infiltration and Action

The PLO's evolution within the conflict setting has been congruent with these theoretical statements. From the military viewpoint, the organization was confined to a small terrorist network in the face of an antiguerrilla policy combining defensive tactics and an offensive strategic alignment. The Gaza Strip refugee camps, more resistant than the West Bank, were finally neutralized by energetic IDF campaigns. Since then, the PLO's acts on the local scene have consisted mainly of placing bombs in buses and public sites and of killing individuals at random.

Beyond the PLO's military weakness, however—and in keeping with theoretical expectations—one may refer to the antiguerrilla watching-over model: the PLO has been allowed a wide range of freedom for political articulation. The general deterrence policy of the regime only increases the population's sympathy for the insurgents and, in effect, legitimizes their use of coercion against "collaborators" with the Israelis. The pro-Hashemite notables cannot constitute an effective obstacle to the PLO. Lacking the prestige of the fighting organizations, and vulnerable to their threats, they cannot stand in the way of the PLO's systematic infiltration of political circles, social clubs, and trade unions.

Exhibit 10.1
Antiguerrilla and Guerrilla Alignments in the Administered Territories

Characteristics of Incumbents	Profile of Anti-Guerrilla Alignment	Profile of Guerrilla Movement
Limited ambition vis-à-vis the population	Sophisticated watching-over model vis-à-vis population	PLO becomes an omnipresent political force
+	+	but
Strong and determined metropole vis-à-vis insurgents	defensive and offensive military	militarily remains a terroristic network

This model of military and political antiguerrilla policy, which accounts for a given profile of guerrilla development "in the field," in fact duplicates the case of Cyprus as outlined in chapter 1. There, too, the *metropole*, Britain, had limited ambitions vis-à-vis the population, although, at the same time, it was able to draft sufficient resources for the armed struggle to indulge in both defensive and offensive strategies. Accordingly, anti-British activities on the part of *enosis* supporters— though powerful—were mainly of a political nature (demonstrations, boycotts, and the like), while the EOKA, as a paramilitary movement, soon evolved into a restricted network of urban terrorist cells.

In several respects, however, differences still exist between the Palestinian situation and that of the EOKA. In contrast to the Cypriots' unity, there are the numberless divisions of the PLO; moreover, the most radical groups, who are a minority in the movement as a whole, are a majority among the militants in the administered territories. These traits reflect the dynamics of the interaction of the local field with other aspects of the conflict.

D. EXTERNAL INTERFERENCE

1. The Span of Possibilities

An additional, and highly significant, dimension of the Israeli-Palestinian conflict, as of many other guerrilla conflicts, is its non-zero-sum character. More particularly, because the conflict challenges the regime of a sovereign state, it must also be considered within its wider international context.

Incumbents, for instance, who represent a *metropole* or who rely on foreign allies, might maintain their force of deterrence in spite of their eventual lack of power within the conflict setting. As a rule, however, a guerrilla conflict damages the international status of the incumbents. Unfriendly countries may then be tempted to support the insurgency. The conflict in itself becomes outstandingly profitable to the guerrillas if such support creates the possibility of setting up in-exile political and military structures.

On the other hand, external assets may also represent, for the insurgents, a problem as to their freedom of action. Disagreement among benefactors regarding issues concerning the guerrilla movement they commonly support could entail splits and disorder within that movement. Moreover, transnational terrorism against the incumbents (that is, on foreign soil), might inflict only limited actual harm, and far-reaching military strikes at the insurgents' external centers might create new, unexpected circumstances for each contender. These remarks are widely applicable to our present knowledge of the Palestinian issue.

On the other hand, when considered jointly with the cases of Cuba, Algeria, Indochina, and Cyprus, the Palestinian conflict illustrates the infinite variety of international contexts in which guerrilla conflicts may occur. Within this variety, any substantial theorizing about the modes of interference of these contexts would be in vain. Nevertheless, the Israeli-Palestinian case, in particular, shows that some generalizations may still be formulated. These statements may be seen as the major theoretical contribution of the analysis of this case to guerrilla-conflict theory. They concern the paradoxical attributes of the PLO's external "capital." Even when this capital is at its highest, illustrating impressive processes of accumulation, it is converted into assets that remain of limited relevance to the resolution of the conflict.

To systematically characterize this conflict from this viewpoint, one has to start from the fact that it belongs to a particular category of cases. In this category, external resources are not just significant at some stage of the conflict; *they actually amount to no less than the gains the insurgents may realistically expect over the incumbents as a result of the struggle itself.*

For this category of cases one may suggest two models of interference of foreign factors in guerrilla conflicts, which are, in fact, directly deduced from the rules of non-zero-sum game theory; they constitute two ideal types that may be understood as the parameters of the span of the theoretical possibilities.[1] In order to define such ideal types it suffices to assume that (1) for the incumbents a guerrilla conflict is always mainly a cost in terms of international standing, and (2) the international scene, if frequently favorable to insurgents, may also be a source of costs for them once assets have been accumulated. From these two assumptions, and seeking the opposite extremes, one obtains two well-known models.

The first is not usually associated with non-zero-sum game theory, though it may be viewed as one of its most appropriate illustrations. In this case, the external assets accumulated by the insurgents are disproportionate to the concessions that could be obtained from the incumbents; the conflict as such, therefore, comes to be an end in itself. This definition is essentially a rephrasing of what Lewis Coser, following Georg Simmel, calls a *nonrealistic conflict.*[2] The terms of this rephrasing permit the inclusion under this heading of conflicts that satisfy not only emotional drives—such as those considered by Simmel and Coser—but also sheer instrumental calculations. It particularly fits, obviously, a case where the benefactors' generosity toward the insurgents is accounted for by their interest in the very perpetuation of the conflict.

The ideal type at the opposite extreme is the case where, for the insurgents no less than for the incumbents, the continuation of the conflict implies costs that are disproportionate to the price each contender would pay in a realistic conclusion. This model is none other than the *prisoner's dilemma,* the classic example of non-zero-sum conflict.[3] It is especially relevant to cases in which both sides are crucially dependent on their respective benefactors, who are able and willing to reach an understanding among themselves about the issues at stake and to impose it, by appropriate sanctions, on their protégés.

In the external arena, then, the nonrealistic conflict represents the highest degree of profitability of violence for insurgents, while in the prisoner's dilemma situation, the cost of violence becomes extremely problematic for both insurgents and incumbents. Accordingly, it is possible to analyze the development of any empirical case involving critical external factors by considering the chain of relevant events in terms of the relative proximity to these two poles.

2. The Nonrealistic Phase

Above we have seen the generous support of the major Arab states for the PLO. Since its very inception they permitted, over time, the establishment of mini-Palestines in countries surrounding Israel. In Lebanon, particularly, genuine state structures were developed, while funds were supplied by the Saudis, Kuwaitis, Libyans, and many others. Arab backing also got the PLO increasing Soviet aid, the sympathy of numerous Third World countries, and the understanding of many a Western country.

Diplomatically, Israel has been defeated by its adversary. Its few remaining international ties are mainly with Western countries, and even with them it does not always enjoy completely positive relations. Israel's dependency on the United States is increasingly critical. In the final analysis, however, the nature of the PLO's declared aims is radical, as is the challenge represented by the larger struggle of Israel with the Arab world over its legitimacy and recognition. The Jewish state, therefore, has remained quite insensitive to the deterioration of its international standing, since the United States, as the leader of the Western world, could not renounce its commitment to its existence.

As for the PLO, the existence of numerous generous benefactors with changing interests in the Palestinian cause has resulted in several problems. The multiplication of guerrilla organizations directly reflects the great number of benefactors and has permitted the solicitation of resources from governments that are constantly in conflict with each other. Yet the same multiplication of groups also implies difficult problems of coordination. This aid to the PLO, moreover, has been, for the Arab states, a major aspect of their own conflict with Israel as well as a lever of their mutual rivalries and competitions. Because their Palestinian policy is intimately bound to their particular interests, many of the benefactors have made their aid conditional upon their control over the PLO. This has been periodically revealed when the mini-Palestines' aspirations to an autonomy of action were relentlessly repressed by these very benefactors.

These facts help explain the PLO's inability to translate its assets into Israeli concessions. Through its insistence on maintaining Israel's destruction as its ultimate aim, the PLO has been unable—and apparently unready—to use the "invincible" weapon wielded so adroitly by Anwar Sadat in 1977, that is, the recognition of Israel. Sadat was able, by offering peace to the Jewish state, to regain the entire Sinai Peninsula. His very offer pressured the Americans to exploit the Jewish state's dependency on them in order to obtain for Egypt the necessary concessions. In the background there is the endless competition of Americans with the Soviets, who have been able to penetrate the Middle East on behalf of the Arab and Palestinian causes. The Americans, therefore, cannot afford to sacrifice their interests in the area by backing Israel to the detriment of the Arabs once Israel's existence is not at stake.

The PLO's redefinition of its political aims in realistic terms would probably have results quite similar to those of Sadat's initiative. Recognition of Israel by the Palestinian leadership would probably entail recognition of the PLO by Washington, and heavy American pressures on the Jewish state would then probably lead to the creation of a Palestinian entity in the administered territories bound in some way to the Hashemite Kingdom. The continuing radical stand of the PLO, up to the late 1970s excluded this perspective; against the background described above, this can be related to the fact that the conflict in itself was, for the PLO, an extraordinary source of profits within the context of the wider Israeli-Arab antagonism. Moreover, it seems that for reasons of their own, none of the organization's decisive benefactors—neither

Syria, Libya, nor the USSR—were interested in any practical conclusion of the conflict.

3. Toward a New Dilemma

From the late 1970s on, however, drastic changes took place in that wider context of the conflict. The protracted Iran-Iraq war widened the split between Syria, which sided with Iran and pro-Western Saudi Arabia, and Jordan, which assisted Iraq. The collapse of the anti-Israeli Arab front, which followed Egypt's withdrawal from the Soviet camp, was a severe setback for Soviet influence. At the same time, the Camp David Agreements represented, for the Arabs as a whole, the end of any expectation of overcoming Israel militarily. The Israeli invasion of Lebanon, moreover, caused the decimation of the PLO as far as Beirut and further confirmed the retreat of Soviet influence.

Looking more closely at the contemporary PLO and Israeli power settings, it appears that their dependence on the moderate Arab states and the United States, respectively, has increased. The PLO, although it enjoys the prestige of the martyr, has lost, together with its Lebanese mini-Palestine, a major asset that made it an actual actor on the inter-Arab scene. Its future is quite difficult to forecast; it is now the object of Syria's hostility. On the other hand, Amman's goodwill toward the Palestinian nationalists implies the price of a revision of PLO's strategic goals concerning both Israel and its future relations with the Hashemites.

As for Israel, it has always been heavily dependent on the United States, both economically and militarily. Having achieved an undeniable success by eradicating the Lebanese mini-Palestine, its dependence on the United States is greater than ever before. The action in Lebanon has represented a great hardship on its precarious economy and, for a time, the most severe blow to its diplomatic standing.

All these signify that the Palestinian conflict has entered a new stage, with both the Arab moderates and the United States able to assume leading roles in resolving the conflict. Hence, the Saudi plan was accepted by the Arab League. In parallel, a Reagan plan has taken a "middle-of-the-road" position between Israel's interests (it emphasizes the need for defensible borders) and the Palestinians' ambition to achieve political sovereignty (it advocates a federative scheme with Jordan).

Israel and the PLO might well be coming close to a prisoner's dilemma. This would be the case if (a) an understanding between their respective benefactors is effectively operating, or (b) if the rejection by either party of such a plan were to lead to sanctions against it by the United States (in the case of Israel) or the Arab benefactors (for the PLO) that would assure the ultimate implementation of such an understanding.

Exhibit 10.2
Possible PLO and Israeli Attitudes toward a U.S.–Pro-Western Arab Understanding

I – Israel	II – PLO	
	rejects	accepts
rejects	I (a)/II (a)	I (a)/II (b)
accepts	I (b)/II (a)	I (b)/II (b)

More precisely, a prisoner's dilemma would come into being when the following are true within the context of an agreement between benefactors: if (I) Israel (a) rejects the understanding between benefactors, it would probably lose many of the advantages it receives from the United States and would also, finally, be compelled to withdraw from most (if not all) of the administered territories. In the case that it (b) accepts the understanding "in time," it would still have to abandon the territories but would be in a position to request substantial compensations.

On the other hand, if (II) the PLO (a) rejects the proposed solution, the Palestinian entity might well be created without its participation; if (b) it accepts it, there would be no further obstacle to its official recognition by the United States and its participation in the shaping of the Palestinian entity.

If rational calculations were the rule for both Israel and the PLO, the most probable outcome, with each side losing the least, would be box I(b)/II(b) in exhibit 10.2.

In summer 1986, the crystallisation of a prisoner's dilemma in the near future seems ultimately dependent on Jordan's determination to reach an agreement with the United States—the PLO's opposition notwithstanding—about the creation of a Palestinian entity linked to Amman, in the framework of a peace treaty with Israel. Today's Middle East should not rise up in an overwhelming protest. Many other factors, however, may still also interfere—unexpected Russian moves, political changes in Arab countries, American hesitancy to compel Israel to accept difficult choices, or mass emotional reactions of the Israelis. Both Israel and the PLO may be led to "crazy" actions in the hope of ruining an eventual mutual understanding among their respective benefactors. Yet, it remains that the prisoner's dilemma has become a potential component of the conflict's evolving, and the "nonrealistic" stage seems over.

At this juncture of the international scene, Algeria, not Cyprus, is the closest analogy to the Israeli-Palestinian conflict among the cases overviewed in chapter 1. Like the PLO—though to a lesser extent—the FLN has been supported by major international forces: the Soviet bloc and the Third World. It was directly taken over by the Arab states and offered the opportunity to set up territorial bases in neighboring Morocco and Tunisia. Unlike the PLO, however, these external resources could never counterbalance the enormous benefit represented by control over a huge country like Algeria.

On the other hand—and quite like Israel, though to a lesser extent—France suffered heavy costs in international standing as a result of the conflict. It even tried, without success, to hit at the heart of the FLN's international backing, Egypt, in the 1956 Suez operation. The operation was a failure, and France's isolation in the world brought it to the greatest concessions despite the fact that in Algeria itself, the antiguerrillas were clearly dominant. A prisoner's dilemma was actually quite characteristic of France's position, since it had to choose between possibilities representing heavy sacrifices in all cases. On the one hand, it could try to invest great efforts in Algeria in order to maintain its hold there, with a high cost in terms of international standing. On the other hand, it could recover a role in world politics while giving up its colony and confronting the domestic consequences.

The Algerian case is, however, still several steps behind the Middle Eastern conflict, where external resources are impressive not only in scope but also in terms of their spectacular fluctuations. These mark two distinct periods that imply another extreme situation, the nonrealistic conflict and the prisoner dilemma. In this sense, the Israeli-Palestinian conflict contributes to guerrilla-conflict theory: it permits an elaboration of this non-zero-sum game aspect of the guerrilla conflict by outlining relevant models that narrow down its possibilities.

4. Interactions between Arenas

The question that arises now concerns the interactions between the internal and the external spheres of the conflict, first, during the conflict, and second, in its aftermath. This question can hardly be answered at a theoretical level, because one of its factors, the international scene, depends on conditions that are of infinite variability. However, one can elaborate on the question. Because of the scope of their external assets, the insurgents do not need to enlist material resources from the population of the administered territories; on the contrary, they distribute financial aid on the behalf of the *tsumud*. The insurgents' international status strengthens the inhabitants' identification with the PLO. The Arab summits that have proclaimed the PLO the "sole legitimate representative of the Palestinian people" have contributed their part to the weakening of non-PLO parties within the administered territories. In turn, the great sympathy of the inhabitants for the PLO further enhances its legitimacy in world public opinion.

An additional point of interest, however, is that the PLO's external leaders, though themselves interested in dissidence in the territories, have tried for long to prevent the growth of a strong local leadership because of their own distance from the "field" and their fear of losing control of those acting on their behalf. This fact was the key for minority groups within the PLO—the radical fronts and the Communists—to achieve predominance for many years. In turn, this fact compelled the Fatah-led PLO to join forces with the pro-Jordanians in becoming the leading power, not only among the masses but among the organized elements as well.

In 1986, however, the attention of all parties focused mainly on Washington, Amman, Riyadh, Cairo, and Jerusalem. Hence, the international context in this case overshadows local events. This fact implies that *in a guerrilla conflict where an external front exists alongside the local one, each of these fronts achieves its relative importance in the overall development of the conflict according to the scope of interests it involves.* It also follows that the conclusion of a guerrilla conflict does not necessarily reflect in a direct manner the "simple" evolution of factors in the field.

Before this summary concludes, another aspect must still be considered. The cases of Cyprus and Algeria share a common denominator that distinguishes them from the Israeli-Palestinian case: unlike the latter, each has reached an end. A question arises in view of an eventual settlement of the conflict in a way that would—hypothetically—constitute a Palestinian entity in the administered territories. What political reality may be expected here, in terms of comparison to the cases of Cyprus and Algeria?

In Cyprus, the military aspect of the insurgence, on the internal scene, was gravely weakened by the forceful military alignment of the incumbents. At the same time, the local political leadership accumulated power, thanks to the political vacuum left by the antiguerrilla watching-over model. Thus, this leadership naturally inherited the position of the incumbents, once they left the scene. In a similar antiguerrilla model, the PLO developed strong political structures and public figures in the administered territories that had no counterpart at the head of the local paramilitary activity.

On the other hand, with regard to the Algerian FLN, the role of external military and political leadership must be emphasized. This leadership was the direct outcome of the scope of external resources accumulated. The configuration of power that these external resources created for the FLN was quite different from that in the case of the PLO. Nevertheless, the common aspect is the creation of given foci of power—external structures—within the guerrilla movement as a result of the drafting of external resources. Beyond this similarity, the main differences consist in the profusion of such resources that multiplied the PLO's splits. Since Lebanon, moreover, a large part of the PLO's military strength, which separated itself from the central leadership of the movement, has been neutralized. Hence, the end of the Palestinian conflict might witness (1) the sharpening of intergroup rivalries, (2) the development of antagonism between military and civilian factors that now operate on the outside, and (3) the emergence of specific interests of local politicians diverging from those now in exile. From this diversity of groups and elements, one might expect difficult—even harsh and spectacular—confrontations recalling those which tore apart the nationalist party in Algeria in the aftermath of its victory.

E. IN CONCLUSION

These considerations bring us back to the preliminary discussion, in which the weak theoretical elaboration characterizing the scholarly literature of guerrilla conflicts was emphasized. The major difficulty in this respect is that this type of conflict often takes place simultaneously in both a given conflict setting and the international scene and involves a political as well as a military dimension. Hence, the construction of an appropriate theoretical framework requires the simultaneous application of different sets of concepts. Moveover, the degree of potential theoreticization varies among the many spheres to be focused upon.

In this book, we have confronted the analysis of the local scene, including background conditions, through the theory of inflation of power. From this perspective, we were able to discern alternative antiguerrilla models and point out their foreseeable impacts upon the development of the guerrilla movement as a political power and a military force. The various antiguerrilla models were formulated in terms from which one could also easily derive general assumptions concerning the theoretical conditions of their respective implementation.

Regarding the external aspects of the conflict, the formal theory of the non-zero-sum game is a useful conceptual framework. The degree, scope, and way in which the international scene interferes with the local conflict cannot be formulated a priori, in light of the numerous possibilities. However, their impacts on the development of the conflict in this arena can be seen as "additional costs" or "profits" for the parties and may be analyzed as such.

The justification for using these different sets of concepts, drawn from distinct perspectives, lies in their unifying common denominator. Both perspectives, indeed, are capable of showing the profitability of violence for a weaker party attacking a political regime as the very stake of the conflict. This constitutes the essence of a guerrilla conflict. The theoretical elaboration of these possibilities, it seems, has permitted the presentation of a coherent explanation of the two major paradoxes of the Israeli-Palestinian conflict: (1) both within and outside the conflict setting, military superiority and political advantages are each bound to different contenders; (2) costs, and not benefits, for both parties may well be the key to their reconciliation.

NOTES

1. M. Shubick, *Game Theory and Related Approaches to Social Behavior* (New York: Wiley, 1964).

2. L. Coser, *The Functions of Social Conflict* (London: Routledge & Kegan Paul, 1965), 48–50; G. Simmel, *Conflict and the Web of Group Affiliation* (New York: Free Press, 1966), 27.

3. R. Boudon, *Effets pervers et ordre social* (Paris: PUF, 1979), 100–101.

Appendixes

Appendix 1:
PLO Actions with Casualties in Israel and the Administered Territories (1967–1981)

Date	Place	Action and Fate of Perpetrators (when known)	Killed Military	Killed Civilian	Injured Military	Injured Civilian
1967						
June 12	Tel-Reim	car and ambulance on road mines		3		4
Sept.19	Jerusalem	bomb in hotel				4
-----25	Ometz	explosion of bomb in private home		1		
Dec. 29	Petah-Tikva	rockets from mountains on neighborhood				1
1968						
Feb. 8	Jordan Valley	tractor on mine		4		
March 3	Yad Mordechai	jeep on mine		2		
----- 7	El Hama	fire from ambush on military truck			2	2
-----18	Ber Ora	bus on mine		2		28
-----28	Massada	tractor on mine		4		1
April 4	Tel Aviv	bomb near private home				4
May 19	El Arish	fire on vehicle				1
Aug. 3	Gaza	bomb under jeep		1		2
-----18	Jerusalem	2 bombs discovered, 1 other exploded				14
-----28	Jerusalem	bomb near private home				.5
Sept. 4	Tel Aviv	bomb in the central bus station		1		59
----- 9	Gaza	grenade thrown at the market				16 (14 locals)
-----17	Beit Shean	Katyusha rockets from over border				8
Oct. 9	Hebron	grenade in Fathers' Tomb Synagogue				45
-----27	Beit Shean	5 Katyushas				1
-----28	Ramya	tractor on mine		2		
Nov. 2	Eilat	Katyushas from Jordan				3
----- 4	Hebron	bomb in Fathers' Tomb Synagogue				6 (4 locals)
-----22	Jerusalem	car explosion in the market		12		53
Dec. 17	Gaza	bomb under private car				3 (2 locals)
1969						
Jan. 1	Kiryat Shmona	5 Katyushas from Lebanon		3		1
-----27	Beer Sheva	train on mine				3
Feb. 14	Porya	Katyusha from mountain				1
-----21	Jerusalem	bomb in supermarket		2		12
March 6	Jerusalem	bomb in cafeteria, university				29

Source: IDF Spokesman, October 1981 (mimeograph).

Date	Place	Action and Fate of Perpetrators (when known)	Victims			
			Killed		Injured	
			Mili-tary	Civi-lian	Mili-tary	Civi-lian
1969 (continued)						
Apr. 8	Eilat	Katyushas from Aqaba				13
-----28	El Hama	bus on mine		1		21
June 5	Hamadya	Katyushas from Jordan				7
-----30	Tel Aviv	bomb on private car				10
July 22	Hebron	grenade on truck				8
-----23	Petah Tikva	bomb near bus		1		
-----24	Haifa	bomb in shop				1
Aug. 11	Hebron	grenade on truck				8
-----31	Haifa	bomb near cinema				1
-----26	Jerusalem	bomb near a bank		1		1
-----30	Ramat Shalom	guards of factory attacked		1	1	
Oct. 6	Afula	bomb in market		1		27
-----22	Haifa	bombs near several private homes		2		21
-----23	Haifa	bombs on public sites		1		6
1970						
Feb. 23	Jerusalem	bus attacked in ambush		1		3
Apr. 23	Nablus	grenade on public site				27
May 20	Avivim	bus attacked in ambush		12		19
June 1	Beit Shean	Katyushas from Jordan		1		8
----- 7	Hanita	horses on mines				2
-----25	Beit Shean	Katyushas from Jordan				1
Aug. 1	Beit Shean	Katyushas from Jordan				2
-----11	Ramat Magshimim	vehicle on mine		2		
-----19	Jerusalem	grenade in restaurant				11
Nov. 6	Tel Aviv	bombs at central bus station		2		33
-----13	Hebron	grenade on military vehicle		12		
1971						
Feb. 2	Baram	stepping on road mine				13
Mar. 21	Beit Djobrin	tractor on road mine		1		
July 7	Petah Tikva	Katyushas from mountains on hospital and school		4		16
Sept.19	Jerusalem	grenade on group of tourists		1 (local)		11 (4 locals)
Oct. 9	Jerusalem	grenade in street				16 (16 locals)

Date	Place	Action and Fate of Perpetrators (when known)	Killed Military	Killed Civilian	Injured Military	Injured Civilian
1972						
Jan. 5	Netanya	grenade in street				2
----- 5	Kfar Saba	bomb at central bus station				3
----- 6	Ramat Hagolon	murder of traveller by infiltrators from Syria		1		
March 1	Ahihud	truck on roadmine				13
Apr. 13	Al Arish	bomb in restaurant			1	1
-----23	Ein Hashlosha	car on road mine		2		
May 30	Lod	3 Japanese Red Army attack passengers (2 killed, 1 prisoner)		16		76
June 20	Hermon	bazooka rocket on bus, from Lebanon				2
July 11	Tel Aviv	bomb at central bus station				11
Nov. 8	Ramat Hagolan	tractor on road mine				1
-----11	Nablus	bomb in street				2
1973						
Feb. 14	Maalot	truck on road mine				2
Mar. 30	Hadera	central bus station				4
Apr. 9	Tel Aviv	bomb in private yard				2
June 14	Tel Aviv	bomb on street				1
July 19	Jerusalem	bomb in market				5
Oct. 5	Gaza	grenade on police car	1		2	
1974						
Feb. 9	Dan	bazooka rocket on car		1	1	
Apr. 2	Jerusalem	bomb in garden				1
----- 5	Tel Aviv	bomb in bus		1		5
-----11	Kiryat Shmona	3 fedayeen from Lebanon shoot at civilians (all 3 killed)	2		4	12
-----15	Jerusalem	bomb in bus				1
-----17	Jerusalem	murder of taxi driver		1		
-----18	Pardes Katz	bomb in agricultural plant				13 (12 from territories)
May 14	Kiryat Ata	shooting at vehicle		1		6
-----15	Maalot	3 fedayeen attack school, take hostages	1	24	4	62
June 13	Shamir	4 fedayeen from Lebanon attack kibbutz (all 4 killed)		3		
-----24	Naharia	3 fedayeen attack private home (all killed)	1	3	5	1
Aug. 25	Kfar Saba	bomb in garbage can				2
Sept.21	Jenin	murder in street		1		
-----30	Ein Yahav	fedayeen from Jordan kills Bedouin and is killed by soldier		1		

Date	Place	Action and Fate of Perpetrators (when known)	Victims			
			Killed		Injured	
			Military	Civilian	Military	Civilian

1974 (continued)

Date	Place	Action and Fate	Killed Mili-tary	Killed Civi-lian	Injured Mili-tary	Injured Civi-lian
Nov. 19	Beit Shean	3 fedayeen attack house (all killed)		4		18
Dec. 1	Kfar Rihemja	2 fedayeen attack house (1 killed, 1 wounded)		1		1
----- 6	Rosh Hanikra	fedayeen attack kibbutz (1 killed)				1
-----11	Tel Aviv	bombs in cinema		2		66
-----20	Jerusalem	bomb discovered on public site		2		18
-----22	Jerusalem	grenade on tourist bus				1

1975

Date	Place	Action and Fate	Killed Mili-tary	Killed Civi-lian	Injured Mili-tary	Injured Civi-lian
Jan. 5	Jerusalem	bomb in cafeteria				2
Feb. 26	Petah Tikva	bomb in market				2
Mar. 5	Tel Aviv	8 fedayeen take over hotel; IDF attack; 7 killed, 1 prisoner	3	8	5	6
-----28	Jerusalem	bomb in bus				11
Apr. 10	Jerusalem	bomb in car				1
May 4	Jerusalem	bomb in street		1		3
----- 6	Jenin	shooting on truck		1		
-----11	Bar Giora	train derailed				1
-----17	Al-Bireh	bomb in truck				1
-----17	Ein Paskha	bomb on swimming spot				20
-----20	Jerusalem	murder in street		1		
-----26	Afula	bomb in private car				2
June 5	Jerusalem	grenade on police checkpost				2
-----15	Kfar Yuval	fedayeen take over school, attacked by IDF (4 killed)	1	2	3	3
-----15	Naharia	Katyushas from Lebanon				2
-----23	Nablus	bomb on public site				3
July 4	Jerusalem	bomb in old refrigerator on public site		15 (3 locals)		62
----- 7	Jerusalem	bomb on archeological site				1
Aug. 5	Kiryat Shmona	Katyushas from Lebanon				1
----- 5	Kiryat Shmona	Katyushas from Lebanon				2
-----16	Tel Aviv	bomb in synagogue				3
Oct. 3	Tel Aviv	bomb in street				2
-----27	Jerusalem	car explodes near hotel				8
Nov. 13	Jerusalem	car explodes on public site		7		41
Dec. 2	Kiryat Shmona	Katyushas from Lebanon				2
-----26	Keren Shalom	car on road mine		1		2

Date	Place	Action and Fate of Perpetrators (when known)	Killed Military	Killed Civilian	Injured Military	Injured Civilian
1976						
Jan. 9	Jerusalem	bomb in supermarket				6
Apr. 28	Jerusalem	bomb in street explodes while being dismantled	2		4	
May 3	Jerusalem	bomb in street				33
-----11	Tel Aviv	bomb in cinema				3
-----25	Lod	bomb in suitcase in passenger hall of airport		1		10
June 25	Megiddo	bomb in square				1
July 18	Ramat Gan	bomb in bus				10
-----29	Jerusalem	bomb in street				2
Aug. 7	Hebron	shooting at bus				2
Nov. 11	Petah Tikva	bomb in supermarket				4
-----21	Kfar Saba	attack on civilians at bus station				1
1977						
Jan. 26	Beit Hanina	shootings at taxi				1
Apr. 24	Kiryat Gat	bomb in bus				31
July 6	Petah Tikva	bomb in the market		1		22
-----20	Naharia	bomb in street				5
-----27	Tel Aviv	bomb in the market				11
-----27	Jerusalem	bomb under car, in street				2
-----28	Beersheba	bomb in market				28
Aug. 16	Kiryat Shmona	bomb in bus				8
-----25	Natanya	bomb in street				5
Sept.11	Beersheba	bomb in parcel department of central bus station				9
Oct. 14	Jerusalem	bombs on public sites				3
Nov. 4	Jerusalem	bomb explodes in bus station office after being found on bus				1
----- 7	Naharia	bombs from Lebanon		1		5
Dec. 31	Jerusalem	bomb in street				7
-----29	Netanya	bomb in street		2		1
1978						
Jan. 8	Jerusalem	grenade explodes behind a bus				3
-----13	Tel Aviv	bomb in street		2		
-----29	Ramallah	bus driver assaulted with knives		1		
Feb. 14	Jerusalem	bomb in street		2		41
Mar. 11	Tel Aviv	13 fedayeen land from sea, take over bus, drive to Tel Aviv		35		80
-----17	Upper Galilee	Katyushas from Lebanon		2		2
-----19	Gaza Strip	cars stoned				6
Apr. 26	Nablus	grenade at tourist bus		2		7
May 4	Akko	bomb in central bus station			3	2

Date	Place	Action and Fate of Perpetrators (when known)	Killed Mili-tary	Killed Civi-lian	Injured Mili-tary	Injured Civi-lian

Date	Place	Action and Fate of Perpetrators (when known)	Victims Killed Military	Victims Killed Civilian	Victims Injured Military	Victims Injured Civilian
1978 (continued)						
June 2	Jerusalem	bomb in bus		1		9
-----29	Jerusalem	bomb in market		2		28
Aug. 3	Tel Aviv	bomb in market		1		49
-----30	Tel Aviv	road mine				1
Sept. 5	Bethlehem	bomb fixed at fuel reservoir	1			1
-----16	Jerusalem	bomb in public site				7
-----19	Jerusalem	bomb in bus from Jericho		4		37
-----19	Tel Aviv	bomb in street				2
-----25	Bethlehem	explosion at bus station				1
Dec. 17	Jerusalem	explosion in bus				18
-----20	Jerusalem	explosion in the street				4
-----21	Kiryat Shmona	4 Katyushas		1		7
1979						
Jan. 13	Maalot	3 fedayeen attack rest home all 3 killed		1	1	2
-----18	Jerusalem	explosion in the market				19
-----21	Upper Galilee	Katyushas from Lebanon				2
-----28	Natanya	explosion on public site				33
Feb. 27	Jerusalem	explosion in the market				6
Mar. 7	Allenby Bridge	explosion in tourist bus				12
-----23	Jerusalem	explosion on public site		1		14
-----27	Lod	explosion in the market		1		20
Apr. 5	Jerusalem	explosion on the street				13
----- 7	Jerusalem	explosion in a restaurant				16
-----10	Tel Aviv	explosion in the street		3		20
-----11	Kiryat Shmona	Katyushas from Lebanon				1
-----18	Upper Galilee	Katyushas from Lebanon				1
-----22	Naharia	4 fedayeen land and take over house, try to escape with hostages (2 killed, 2 taken prisoner)	1	3		4
-----25	Upper Galilee	Katyushas from Lebanon				1
-----25	Kfar Saba	explosion in bus station				2
May 14	Tiberias	explosion in bus station		2		31
-----23	Petah Tikva	explosion in bus station		3		11
-----24	Kiryat Shmona	shootings from Lebanon				2
-----24	Jerusalem	explosion in supermarket				1
-----28	Haifa	explosion in street				1
June 3	Jerusalem	explosion in bookshop				3
-----24	Tel Aviv	car explodes at central bus station (2 fedayeen killed)				4
-----28	Upper Galilee	shooting from Lebanon				4
July 6	Jerusalem	explosion near a monument				3
-----23	Kfar Saba	explosion near a school				1
-----25	Beit Lid (Netanya)	explosion at a crossroad				12

Date	Place	Action and Fate of Perpetrators (when known)	Killed Military	Killed Civilian	Injured Military	Injured Civilian
1979 (continued)						
Aug. 15	Kfar Saba	explosion near the municipality				2
-----21	Tel Aviv	two explosions at exhibition park				4
-----25	Kiryat Shmona	Katyushas from Lebanon				2
-----29	Jerusalem	explosion near government office				1
Sept.14	Bat Yam	bomb discovered, exploded			1	
-----15	Bat Yam	bomb in private yard				1
-----16	Jerusalem	murder near a church		1		
-----19	Jerusalem	explosion in street		2		38
-----27	Tel Aviv	two explosions in street				9
Oct. 23	Tel Aviv	explosion near cinema, central bus station				3
-----26	Tel Aviv	bomb discovered at central bus station			1	
Nov. 1	Tel Aviv	grenade at central bus station		1		
----- 7	Kfar Giladi	murder of pedestrian by fedayeen from Lebanon		1		
-----19	Jerusalem	explosion in bus				4
-----19	Jerusalem	explosion in bus				8
Dec. 3	Ashkelon	explosion in square				1
1980						
Feb. 3	Rehovot	explosion in street				6
-----11	Petah Tikva	explosion in street				11
-----16	Gaza (12.00)	grenade thrown at vehicle, public site		2		5
-----16	Gaza (13.30)	grenade thrown at vehicle			2	4
Apr. 6	Misgav Am	5 fedayeen from Lebanon take over house in kibbutz with hostages (all 5 killed by IDF)	1	2	11	5
May 2	Hebron	group attacked by fedayeen on way home after praying at Fathers' Tomb	3	3	9	7
-----21	Hebron	Molotov cocktail thrown at vehicle				1
June 22	Gaza	explosion under car at market				2
-----23	Pardes Katz	explosion near grocery				2
-----25	Netanya	murder of Israeli intelligence agent	1			
Aug. 9	Jerusalem	explosion in a park				5
-----19	Kiryat Gat	explosion near bus station				1
-----24	Abu Gosh	explosion at gas station		1		11
Oct. 18	Jerusalem	Molotov cocktail thrown in street				1
-----26	Ramat Gan	explosion at bus station				1
Nov. 6	Upper Galilee	Katyushas from Lebanon				5
-----25	Nablus	fedayeen set up ambush on road, shoot at bus				2
Dec. 4	Jerusalem	explosion in street				10
-----26	Jebaliya	driver of local workers attacked by ambush				1

Date	Place	Action and Fate of Perpetrators (when known)	Killed Military	Killed Civilian	Injured Military	Injured Civilian
1981						
Jan. 10	Wadi Gaza	grenade thrown at car				3
-----11	Jebaliya	attack on taxi driver at garage		1		
-----28						
-----29	Kiryat Shmona	Katyushas from Lebanon				7
-----30	Kiryat Shmona	Katyushas from Lebanon				3
Feb. 7	Gaza	grenade thrown at car		2	2	20
-----10	Hebron	assault in the casbah				1
-----21	Jerusalem	a watchman prevents car of fedayeen from entering a hospital				1
-----23	Tel Aviv	explosion in grocery				1
Mar. 2	Kiryat Shmona	Katyushas from Lebanon				3
----- 9	Jerusalem	bus attacked by 2 fedayeen				1
-----14	Jerusalem	bus attacked by fedayeen				1
-----29	Tel Aviv	explosion at central bus station				4
Apr. 8	Jerusalem	grenade thrown at wedding party		1		2
-----21	Upper Galilee	Katyushas from Lebanon				1
May 1	Jerusalem	bomb discovered in cafe			1	
-----26	Khan Yunis	grenade thrown at vehicle		1		1
July 10	Kiryat Shmona	Katyushas from Lebanon				6
-----15	Nahariya	Katyushas from Lebanon				2
-----15	Upper Galilee	Katyushas from Lebanon		3		14
-----17	Upper Galilee	Katyushas from Lebanon				2
-----17	Western Galilee	Katyushas from Lebanon				5
-----18	Upper Galilee	(2.05) Katyushas from Lebanon				5
-----18	" "	(2.30) Katyushas from Lebanon				1
-----18	" "	(6.10) Katyushas from Lebanon				1
-----19	" "	Katyushas from Lebanon				15
-----20	" "	Katyushas from Lebanon		1		1
-----21	Western Galilee	Katyushas from Lebanon				1
Aug. 24	Upper Galilee	Katyushas from Lebanon		1		12
-----29	Maaleh Hamishmar	bus attacked by fedayeen				4
Sept. 3	Jerusalem	tourist attacked in Old Jerusalem		1		
-----12	Jerusalem	grenade thrown at group of tourists		2		22

Appendix 2:
PLO and PLO-linked Actions Abroad (July 23, 1968–October 7, 1981)

Date	Place	Action and Victims	Fate of Perpetrators	Affil.*
1968				
July 23	Algiers	3 fedayeen hijack El Al plane	freed with exchange	PFLP
Dec. 26	Athens	El Al plane attacked on ground, 1 killed, 2 injured	arrested and freed after hijacking of Olympic plane July 22, 1970	
1969				
Feb. 18	Zurich	El Al plane attacked on ground, 1 killed, 5 injured	1 killed, 3 arrested and later freed after hijacking of Swissair plane	PFLP
May 22	Copenhagen	plot against Ben Gurion airport of Lydda	3 fed. arrested freed after no proof found	PFLP
Aug. 18	----------	bomb found in Israeli tourist office		PFLP
-----18	London	explosion at Marks & Spencer's		PFLP
-----23	Izmir	bomb explodes in hands of fed. intended for Israeli exhibition	1 killed, 1 arrested	DFLP
-----23	Tehran	explosion in Jewish school		-
-----25	London	grenade thrown at office of Zim Israeli Navigation Co. 1 injured	fed. succeeds in escaping	PFLP
-----29	Damascus/ Rome	TWA hijacked to Damascus 2 Israeli passengers freed in exchange for Syrian prisoners		PFLP
Sept. 8	Brussels	grenade thrown at El Al office locals wounded	2 escape, 3rd later released to Libya	PFLP
----- 8	The Hague	grenade thrown at Israeli embassy	1 fed. caught and later released to Libya	PFLP
----- 8	Bonn	grenade thrown at Israeli embassy	2 fed. escape	PFLP
Nov. 9	Berlin	bomb found in Jewish Center		PFLP
-----27	Athens	grenade at El Al office, 1 killed, 14 injured	2 fed. arrested, freed with hijacking of Olympic plane, July 27, 1970	PSF
Dec. 12	Berlin**	bomb at El Al office dismantled but another exploded in American club		Bader Meinhof PFLP
-----21	Athens	3 fed. plan hijacking of TWA	fed. arrested before hijacking, freed in return for Olympic plane, July 22, 1970	PFLP
1970				
Feb. 10	Munich	ground attack on El Al passengers 1 killed, 8 injured	3 fed. arrested later freed for hijacked plane	-
-----13	Germany	asylum for Jewish elderly persons in fire		
-----21	Zurich	Swissair to Tel Aviv explodes in air, 47 killed	fed. escape	PFLP-GC

Source: IDF Spokesman, *The Sabotage Organizations: Thirteen Years of Terorism Abroad (1968–1981)*, October 1981.

* not filled in when (1) no information is available about the group, (2) the label that is known does not correspond to a known organization and only serves as a cover

** actions carried out with the collaboration of non–Middle Eastern movements

*** actions not directly aimed at Jewish or Israeli targets

Date	Place	Action and Victims	Fate of Perpetrators	Affil.*
1970 (continued)				
Feb. 21	Frankfurt	explosion in Austrian plane, no casualties	fed. escape	PFLP-GC
-----24	Frankfurt	two parcels with explosives sent to Tel Aviv and neutralized	fed. escape	PFLP-GC
March 7	Guatemala**	grenade thrown at yard of Israeli Consul		local group
Apr. 24	Istanbul/ Izmir	bombs explode at El Al office in Istambul and Pan-Am office in Izmir		PSF
May 4	Paraguay	armed attack on Israeli consulate, 1 killed, 1 injured	fed. caught, in prison	-
July 22	Athens/ Beirut	Olympic plane hijacked	fed. and others in Greek prisons, released to Cairo	PSF
Sept. 6	Jordan	Pan Am, TWA, and BOAC with 400 passengers hijacked to Cairo & Zarka		PFLP
----- 6	London/	Attempt to hijack El Al plane	1 fed. killed, 1 inj. fed. arrested, later freed	PFLP*
	Lod	checked by Israelis in battle in plane, 4 inj.,	in BOAC deal	Nicaragua movement
----- 8	Athens	Attempt to assault El Al office checked by security men	2 fed. arrested later freed in Olympic deal	-
----- 9	Bahrain/ London	Another BOAC plane hijacked and brought to Zarka, Jordan		-
Oct. 6	London	Envelopes with explosives sent to El Al and Israeli embassy		-
-----15	Berlin	Similar envelopes sent to Israeli exhibitions		-
1971				
Mar. 14	Rotterdam	Fuel reservoirs sabotaged by 5 fed.		Fatah
May 26	Rio de Janeiro	explosion in Israeli official office		
-----28	Turkey	murder of Israeli consul		Turkish Liberation Army
June 11	South Yemen	Israeli ship Coral Sea attacked at Bab-el-Mandeb	fed. escape by boat	PFLP
July 20	Rome***	explosion at Jordanian Air Alya Co. office		Fatah
-----23	Paris***	several Molotov cocktails thrown at Jordanian embassy	1 fed. injured caught	Fatah
-----24	Egypt***	Alya plane shot at on the ground		Fatah
-----28	Rome/Lydda	attempt to hit El Al plane in air with explosive suitcase	naive girl from Holland freed; fed. escape	PFLP-GC
Aug. 30	Algiers***	2 fed. hijack Jordanian plane		Fatah
Sept. 1	London/ Lydda	Attempt to blow up El-Al plane in air by explosive suitcase	Naive Peruvian girl freed	PFLP-GC

Date	Place	Action and Victims	Fate of Perpetrators	Affil.*
1971 (continued)				
Sept. 8	Jordan***	Jordanian plane hijacked to Libya	fed. set free	Fatah
-----16	Beirut***	failure of attempt to hijack Jordanian plane		Fatah
Nov. 28	Cairo***	Jordan's prime minister murdered by 4 fed.	All 4 fed. captured and set free later	Fatah-Bl Sept
Dec. 15	London***	Jordan's ambassador injured by boats	fed. escape	Fatah-Black Sept
-----16	Geneva***	explosion at Jordanian Embassy, 4 injured		-
-----28	Austria/ Yugoslavia	Envelopes with explosives sent to Israel, 1 injured		PFLP-GC
1972				
Feb. 5	Holland	two gas reservoirs sabotaged	fed. escape	Fatah-Bl.Sept
----- 6	Germany***	Electronic plant damaged		"
----- 6	Germany***	5 Palestinians and 1 Jordanian killed by fed.	fed. escape	"
-----19	Cairo***	unsuccessful attempt to hijack Jordanian plane		-
-----22	Hamburg***	pipeline sabotaged	fed. escape	Fatah-Bl.Sept
-----22	Europe-Asia***	Lufthansa hijacked and returned with ransom paid	fed. untouched	PFLP
Mar. 11	London***	attempt to hit Hussein's residence		Fatah-Bl.Sept
Apr. 29	Hanover	explosive parcel sent to Israeli stand of international exhibit		PFLP-GC
Aug. 4	Trieste***	attempt to sabotage oil pipes		Fatah-Bl.Sept
-----16	Rome/Lydda	recorder with explosives sent by El Al, minor damage caused	2 girls set free and two fed. liberated later	PFLP-GC
Sept. 5	Munich	8 fed. get hold of Israeli Olympic team. 11 sportsmen killed during operation	5 fed. killed, 3 caught and set free later in Lufthansa deal	Fatah-Bl.Sept
-----10	Brussels	attack on Israeli Embassy worker		Fatah-Bl.Sept
-----18	Amsterdam	envelopes with explosives sent to numerous Israeli institutions		"
-----19	London	Israeli diplomat killed by explosion of envelope		"
-----20	Buenos Aires	sabotage in synagogue		
Oct. 4	Malaysia	wave of envelopes with explosives to many Jewish and Israeli institutions		"

Date	Place	Action and Victims	Fate of Perpetrators	Affil.*

1972 (continued)

Date	Place	Action and Victims	Fate of Perpetrators	Affil.*
Oct. 13	Paris	bomb discovered in El-Al office		-
-----17	Rotterdam	bomb discovered in Israeli building		-
-----23	Holland	PLO representative arrested with explosive envelope on him	freed soon	PLO
-----29	W.Germany***	Lufthansa hijacked, returned with liberation of imprisoned men	fed. found shelter in Libya	PFLP
-----30	Singapore	explosive envelopes sent to Israel		Fatah-Bl.Sept
-----31	Nigeria	explosive envelope at Israeli embassy		-
Nov. 4	Frankfurt	explosive envelope at Zionist youth club		-
-----11	Geneva	5 explosive envelopes to local Jewish clubs		-
-----11	Gt.Britain	14 explosive envelopes; 1 causing injury to 1 person		-
-----13	Paris***	3 fed. kill Syrian journalist	fed. escape	Fatah-Bl.Sept
-----14	Ankara***	explosion at US information center		-
-----21	Toronto	4 explosive envelopes to Jewish leaders		-
-----25	Rome***	4 boxes with arms found at airport		
Dec. 7	Singapore	explosive envelopes sent to Israel		PFLP-GC
-----24	London	1 fed. caught with arms intended for coup against Israeli officials	still in prison	Fatah-Bl.Sept
-----28	Bangkok	4 fed. take over Israeli Embassy, 6 held hostage for 19 hours	sent to London	"
-----	Greece	several fed. arrested before boarding ship to Haifa	fed. sent back to Lebanon	-
-----	Lebanon/ Europe	explosive car from Lebanon to Europe in order to damage Israeli embassy		Fatah

1973

Date	Place	Action and Victims	Fate of Perpetrators	Affil.*
Jan. 1	Kuwait/ Jordan***	explosive envelopes to Jordan		Fatah-Bl.Sept
----- 8	Paris	explosion in Jewish Agency		"
----- 9	Cyprus	4 fed. caught on boat before getting to Haifa	expulsion to Lebanon	PFLP
-----19	Vienna	3 fed. try to hit Jewish emigration center	expulsion to Syria	Fatah-Bl.Sept
-----24	Greece	explosive envelopes to Israeli delegation over the world		"
-----26	Madrid	murder of Israeli citizen		"
-----26	Italy	3 fed. caught at Austrian border on their way to Vienna	expulsion	"

Date	Place	Action and Victims	Fate of Perpetrators	Affil.*
1973 (continued)				
Jan. 29	Turkey	explosive envelopes to Israel		Fatah-Bl.Sept
-----31	Rome	explosive envelopes to Israeli delegation in Ruanda		"
Feb. 5	Rome	explosive envelopes to Israeli embassy in Guatemala		"
----- 8	W.Germany	explosive envelopes to Israeli institutions in the world		"
March 1	Khartoum***	attack on Saudi Embassy - 3 Western diplomats murdered	8 fed. in prison	"
----- 3	Cyprus***	Cypriot boat sabotaged		PFLP
----- 6	N.Y.	3 explosive cars discovered in front of Israeli institutions		-
-----12	Cyprus	murder of Jewish businessman		Fatah-Bl.Sept
-----14	France	fed. caught before coup on Israeli embassy	2 fed. arrested	"
-----20	Rome***	4 boxes of weapons discovered		-
-----21	Singapore	explosion in Zim office		Fatah-Bl.Sept
Apr. 4	Rome	attempt to attack El Al plane;	2 fed. caught expulsion to Syria	PFLP
----- 9	Cyprus	bomb in Israeli ambassador's house attempt to hijack Israeli plane (Arkia)	fed. sent to Libya after KLM hijacking	-
-----11	Geneva	molotov cocktail on El-Al office		Fatah-Bl.Sept
-----12	Seoul	explosive envelopes to Israel		-
-----24	Rome***	grenades found at airport		Fatah-Bl.Sept
-----27	Beirut***	explosives found on French plane	3 fed. arrested	-
-----27	Rome	murder of Italian employed by El Al	1 fed caught and liberated	-
-----27	Bolivia	Explosive envelope to Israeli embassy		-
-----29	Costa Rica	molotov cocktail at synagogue		-
May 7	Paris	2 fed. try to take over room in house facing Israeli Embassy	fed. caught	-
June 8	Berlin***	explosion in weapons factory		Fatah-Bl.Sept
-----13	Italy	explosion in car in front of El Al office;	2 fed. wounded in the car and liberated	"
July 1	Washington	military diplomat of Israel killed in ambush		-
-----19	Athens	1 fed. fails in attempt to penetrate El Al office	fed. sent to Kuwait	PFLP

Date	Place	Action and Victims	Fate of Perpetrators	Affil.*
1973 (continued)				
July 20	Japan**	Japanese plane hijacked to Libya, plane blown up	1 fed. killed; other fed. arrested and later freed	PFLP + Red Army
Aug. 5	Athens	mass attack at airport (4 killed, 54 injured) on passengers from Israel	fed. freed to Libya	-
-----30	Beirut	fed. arrested before taking off to Czechoslovakia	2 fed. set free later	Saiqa
Sept. 5	Rome	unsuccessful attempt to hit an El Al plane by light missiles (SA7)	7 fed. arrested and freed later	Fatah-Bl.Sept
----- 5	Paris***	Saudi embassy taken over	5 fed. to Libya	"
----- 7	Berlin	Sabotage at Israeli stand in exhibition	1 fed. arrested set free	"
-----11	Australia			"
-----28	Austria	several fed. take over train of Jewish immigrants from Russia to Israel	fed. get plane to fly to Libya	Saiqa
Oct. 18	Berlin	fed. arrested with explosives intended for El Al plane	4 fed. set free later	Fatah-Bl.Sept
Nov. 25	Beirut***	KLM hijacked to Dubai	sent to Syria	-
-----27	Geneva	post office uncovers 5 explosive envelopes to Israel		
-----29	Holland	5 explosive envelopes to Israel		-
Dec. 14	Gt.Britain	9 explosive envelopes to Israel		-
-----17	Rome***	5 fed. attack Pan-Am passengers (31 killed, 40 injured) & Lufthansa hijacked to Kuwait (1 killed)	fed. to Egypt and later freed	-
-----19	Paris**	network uncovered which intended to kidnap Israeli diplomat	freed after short time	PFLP + Turkish group
-----25	Gt.Britain	fed. arrested before action	4 fed. sent to Syria	Fatah-Bl.Sept
-----30	London	Jewish leader to be attacked	fed. escaped	PFLP
-----31	Geneva***	6 explosive parcels seized at railroad station		
1974				
Jan. 20	London	Libyan citizen arrested - intended to attack El Al plane	expulsion	-
-----24	London	bomb at Israeli bank		PFLP
-----31	Singapore***	sabotage oil reservoir and take over boat	4 fed. fed. set free after Japanese embassy in Kuwait taken over	PFLP + Japanese group
Feb. 2	Karachi***	Greek boat taken over for liberation of men held in Greece	3 fed. sent to Libya	-

Date	Place	Action and Victims	Fate of Perpetrators	Affil.*
1974 (continued)				
Feb. 6	Kuwait***	Japanese Embassy taken over in Kuwait to secure liberty of fed. in Singapore	´5 fed. freed	PFLP Japanse group
Mar. 3	Beirut***	British plane hijacked to Amsterdam; plane blown up on ground	fed. freed after another hijacking	-
-----14	Beirut***	smuggling weapons onto KLM	6 fed. arrested and freed	-
-----29	Berlin***	explosion near Japanese air company		PFLP
July 26	Paris	Japanese citizen arrested with false id.	set free	PFLP + Japanese national
Aug. 3	Paris	3 cars explode, 1 near Jewish institution		PFLP
-----26	Frankfurt	explosion near Israeli office and at factory trading with Israel	PFLP	
Sept. 8	Greece	TWA from Lod exploded in air (88 killed)		-
-----13	The Hague***	French embassy taken over, 8 hostages for liberation of Japanese caught in France	3 fed. freed to Iraq	Japanese group
Oct. 1	Rabat***	plan to attack Hussein in Morocco	15 fed. arrested sent to Egypt	Fatah + Bl.Sept
Nov. 22	Dubai	hijacked British plane, 1 hostage killed	4 fed. taken over by PLO	ex-Fatah
1975				
Jan. 13	Paris	2 rockets on El Al plane, hurt Yugoslavian plane (3 injured)		PFLP
-----19	Paris	attack on El Al plane 20 injured	2 fed. to Iraq with hostages	PFLP
Feb. 10	Geneva***	explosion in W.German Consulate		
Aug. 4	Malaysia***	Japanese group takes over American Consulate & Swedish delegation - retract after 7 liberated by Japan		Japanse group
-----19	Berlin	explosive envelope to Jewish figures		-
Sept. 5	Holland	plan to attack train to stop Holland's aid to Jewish immigrants	4 fed. arrested 1 year prison	Saiqa
-----15	Madrid***	fed. take over Egyptian embassy require cessation of Israel-Egyptian arrangements	fed. sent to Algeria	Fatah,
Dec. 21	Vienna***	OPEC ministers held by fed. (4 killed, 1 injured)		PFLP + others
-----29	N.Y.***	explosion in TWA (14 killed, 75 injured)		-

Date	Place	Action and Victims	Fate of Perpetrators	Affil.*
1976				
Jan. 12	N.Y.***	3 bombs discovered before explosion		Haddad
-----25	Nairobi	attempt checked to hit El-Al with rockets	5 fed. caught and brought to Israel	group
Feb. 8	Berlin	explosion near Jewish institution		PFLP
Apr. 17	Paris	explosion near Israeli Embassy		-
-----27	Canada***	men arrested for carrying arms supposedly for Olympic Games	2 fed. in prison	-
May 30	Paris	explosion near Rothschild Bank		-
June 28	Athens	Air France hijacked to Entebbe, rescued by Israeli commando (6 killed, 9 injured)	fed. killed	Haddad
July 10	Paris	explosion in Jewish club		-
-----20	Rome***	explosion near Syrian Air Co.		-
Aug. 11	Istanbul	attack against El-Al plane checked (4 killed, 21 injured)	2 fed. in prison	Haddad
Sept. 4	Nice***	KLM hijacked	fed. to Libya from Cyprus	PFLP-GC
-----24	Lod	plan of attack against Paris-Tel Aviv flights revealed	2 Dutch citizens arrested in prison	PFLP + Dutch group
-----24	Rome	Israeli-Italian factory set on fire		-
-----25	Rome	bomb at Jewish institution		-
-----25	Lebanon***	bomb at Christian monastery		-
-----26	Damascus***	attack hotel in Damascus (4 killed, 34 injured) to deliver fed. held by Syria,	3 fed. executed	Black June
Oct. 4	Berlin	explosion in Israeli restaurant		-
-----11	Rome***	fed. against Syrian embassy	3 arrested	Black June
-----11	Pakistan	Group of fed. against Syrian embassy		"
Nov. 6	Istanbul	explosion in El Al building		-
-----17	Amman***	fed. attack hotel (4 killed, 4 injured)	3 fed. killed 1 caught	black June
Dec. 2	Damascus***	attempt to murder Syria's foreign minister		"
-----13	Istanbul***	attempt to hit Syrian embassy	fed. arrested	"
-----15	Paris***	manager of Arab library killed		
1977				
Apr. 20	Geneva	explosive envelope in Zim office		-
May 6	Beirut	Norwegian youngster arrested, intended to take Israeli-bound plane in Frankfurt, with arms	in prison	DFLP
-----12	Tehran	break into Jewish institution	2 fed. killed	Iranian group

Date	Place	Action and Victims	Fate of Perpetrators	Affil.*
1977 (continued)				
July 8	Beirut***	hijacked Kuwaiti plane to liberate fed. held by Arab regimes	6 fed. surrender to Damascus	Black June
-----12	Sweden***	plann to act against OPEC conference	. Japanese arrested	Japanese group
-----25	Washington	bomb set in house of Jewish leader		
Sept.28	Bangladesh***	Japanese plane hijacked-got ransom	fed. sent to PLO bases	Japanese group
Oct. 13	Majorca***	Lufthansa hijacked (1 killed); German commandos take over	3 fed. killed, 1 injured	Haddad + Bader Meinhof
Nov. 20	Cannes	bomb found in conference hall where Israelis participated	-	
-----27	Paris	explosion in Israeli bank		-
-----29	Ankara***	bomb uncovered at Egyptian Embassy		-
Dec. 6	Caracas***	explosion near Egyptian Embassy		-
-----25	Copenhagen***	fire at office of Egyptian Air company		PFLP

1978				
Jan. 1	Bonn***	bombs uncovered near gas balloons of Egyptian Embassy		-
----- 8	Belgium	2 bazookas pointing to Israeli embassy discovered		Haddad
-----12	Venezuela	bombs explode near offices of Jewish organization		-
-----16	France***	car of Egyptian ambassador sabotaged		-
-----20	W.Germany***	bomb uncovered near Egyptian office		-
-----26	Holland	signs of poisoning found in children who ate Israeli imported oranges		-
Feb. 1	Paris	explosion at Israeli bank		-
-----18	Cyprus***	Egyptian politician murdered and Egyptian aircraft taken over - Egyptian commandos take control (15 killed)	2 fed. surrender	Black June
Mar. 1	London	attempt to set fire to Israeli office		-
----- 4	Brussels***	explosion at Iraqi Embassy		Fatah
-----30	Berlin	bomb discovered in El-Al office		-
May 20	Paris	attack on El Al plane (2 killed, 2 injured)	3 fed. killed	PFLP
June 20	W.Germany	explosion in Israeli office in Frankfurt		-
July 24	Brussels***	explosion at Iraqi embassy		Fatah
-----28	London***	attempt to kill Iraqi ambassador	1 fed. arrested	Fatah

Date	Place	Action and Victims	Fate of Perpetrators	Affil.*
1978 (continued)				
July 31	Paris***	Iraqi embassy taken over (2 killed, 2 injured)		-
Aug. 2	Karachi***	Unsuccessful attempt to kill Iraqi consul		Fatah
----- 7	Brussels***	attack on Iraqi ambassador	fed. surrenders; in prison	"
-----20	London	El Al bus attacked (1 killed, 11 injured)	1 fed. killed, 1 in prison, 3 escaped	Haddad
-----22	Copenhagen	Molotov cocktail on Israeli embassy		-
Sept. 8	Copenhagen	explosive envelopes to several countries to Israeli institutions		-
-----30	Istanbul	explosion at Israeli consulate		-
-----30	Istanbul***	explosion at Egyptian consulate		
Oct. 15	Berlin	bombs found near Jewish institution		Saiqa
-----15	Berlin	bomb found near Jewish shop		"

Date	Place	Action and Victims	Fate of Perpetrators	Affil.*
1979				
Mar. 25	Damascus***	bombs thrown at American Embassy		-
-----26	Ankara	bomb thrown at Israeli consulate		Saiqa
-----27	Paris	explosion in Jewish restaurant (26 injured)		"
-----27	Paris	explosion in Jewish shop		"
-----29	Istanbul***	bomb thrown at American consulate		"
Apr. 1	Istanbul	attempt to sabotage El Al building		"
----- 2	Beirut***	rockets on U.S. Embassy		-
----- 3	Frankfurt	explosion in airport of parcel sent to Jewish school		Fatah
----- 5	Nicosia	explosion in Israeli embassy		Saiqa
----- 5	Nicosia***	sabotage in Egypt-linked office		"
----- 7	Paris	bomb found near Jewish cultural event		"
----- 8	Ankara	explosion at Israeli delegation office		"
-----16	Brussels	attempt to attack El Al plane; 12 injured	2 fed. caught 1 escaped	Fatah
-----16	Cairo***	plan of sabotaging government office	2 fed. caught	Saiqa
-----16	Beirut***	sabotage of Canadian center		-
-----19	Cairo***	explosion at post office (1 killed, 3 injured)		Saiqa
-----22	Vienna	explosion at Jewish center		"
-----26	Berlin	attempt to kill Jewish leader	8 fed. caught	Fatah
-----26	Rome***	explosives found at airport explosives	1 fed. caught 5 others on the spot arrested later	Fatah

Date	Place	Action and Victims	Fate of Perpetrators	Affil.*

1979 (continued)

Date	Place	Action and Victims	Fate of Perpetrators	Affil.*
Apr. 27	W.Germany***	transfer of dynamite to Holland with plan to sabotage oil reservoirs	2 fed. arrested	Fatah
-----29	W.Germany	transfer of dynamite at airport	2 fed. arrested	Fatah
May 11	Paris	1 fed. arrested at airport with dynamite	2 fed. arrested at border	"
-----14	Istanbul**	plot uncovered to kidnap Israeli and US consuls	2 killed, 2 arrested	Turkish group + Fatah
-----15	Ankara	shootings at Israeli Embassy		-
June 15	Frankfurt	sabotage of truck conveying Israeli products		-
July 13	Ankara***	attack on Egyptian Embassy; 2 injured	4 fed. arrested	Saiqa
Aug. 24	Beirut***	grenade against German Embassy		-
-----25	Beirut	explosion in Lufthansa Office		-
Sept. 4	Beirut	explosion in Lufthansa Office		-
-----27	La Paz	bomb thrown at Israeli ambassador's home	-	
-----27	La Paz	grenade thrown at Egyptian ambassador's home		-
Oct. 3	Buenos Aires	explosion at Jewish Theological College		-
Nov. 13	Lisbon**	attempt to murder Israeli ambassador, 1 killed, 3 injured		Portug. group
-----13	Berlin***	smuggled rockets with collaboration	fed. caught before action	PFLP
-----14	Italy***	of Red Brigade linked group	2 fed. arrested	-
-----21	Rome***	explosives found at airport	3 fed. arrested	-
-----30	Salzburg	sabotage in hall where Israeli evening was held (4 injured)		-
Dec. 4	Bahrain***	sabotage of KLM office		-
-----10	Rome	explosion near El Al office (9 injured)		-
-----12	El Salvador	explosion at Israeli embassy		locals
-----14	London***	Iraqi with dynamite intended for IRA caught	arrested	-

1980

Date	Place	Action and Victims	Fate of Perpetrators	Affil.*
Jan. 2	Istanbul	manager of El Al office murdered		Turkish group
-----17	London***	bomb explodes while being prepared for action	1 fed. killed, 1 injured	Haddad

Date	Place	Action and Victims	Fate of Perpetrators	Affil.*
1980 (continued)				
Jan. 29	Paris***	explosion at Syrian embassy (1 killed, 8 injured)		-
Feb. 16	Athens	plan to hit Israeli embassy and other institutions	11 leftists arrested	-
-----18	Rome	explosion near El Al office		Armenian group
-----27	Bogota***	Party of diplomats, including Israeli ambassador, taken as hostages by leftist group		locals
Mar. 3	Madrid	Jewish leader missed by fed. who instead kill non-Jew	fed. arrested	Black June
Apr. 21	Zurich	explosive suitcase infiltrated to El Al plane with naive passenger; uncovered in time	1 arrested, 1 escapes	Haddad
-----29	Cairo	explosion in synagogue		-
May 23	Guatamala	murder of Jewish leader		locals
June 14	Rome***	3 bombs exploded near Jordanian plane		-
-----	Paris	dynamite sent to South Yemen embassy	5 fed. arrested	Haddad + German group
-----20	Copenhagen	weapons for attack on El Al found	4 fed. arrested	PFLP-GC
July 18	Paris***	attempt to kill former Iranian prime minister	5 fed. arrested	Fatah
-----27	Antwerp	grenades at group of Jewish pupils (1 killed, 16 injured)	2 fed. arrested	-
Aug. 7	Buenos Aires	bomb explodes near Jewish school		-
----- 8	Istanbul	bomb discovered in building where Israeli consul lives		PFLP
Oct. 4	Paris	explosion near synagogue (3 killed, 20 injured)		
Nov. 25	Paris	travel agency dealing with Israel and Egypt attacked, 2 owners killed (1 injured)	fed. escape	-
Dec. 31	Nairobi***	hotel sabotaged (20 killed, 85 injured, mostly foreigners)		PFLP
1981				
Feb. 6	Beirut***	attack of leftists on Jordanian representative's house, man kidnapped		Saiqa
-----16	Cairo	attempt to sabotage Israeli embassy, and synagogue	5 fed. arrested	Fatah

Date	Place	Action and Victims	Fate of Perpetrators	Affil.*
1981 (continued)				
Mar. 2	Pakistan***	Pakistani plane hijacked	3 fed. receive asylum in Damascus	locals Fatah
May 1	Vienna	politician friendly to Israel murdered		black June
-----15	Rome	explosion near El Al office		-
-----16	Istanbul	explosion near El Al office		-
-----22	Athens***	travel agency attacked (2 killed, 70 injured)		PFLP
July 29	Vienna***	large quantity of weapons found	2 fed. arrested; expulsion	Fatah
Aug. 9	Rome	explosion near El Al office (1 injured)		-
----- 9	Athens	2 grenades thrown at Israeli embassy		-
-----10	Vienna	explosion in house neighboring Israeli Embassy		-
-----29	Vienna	attack on synagogue (2 killed, 19 injured)		Black June
Sept. 23	Limasol	grenades at Zim office (5 injured)		Black June
Oct. 7	Rome	explosion near El-Al office (8 injured)		-
----- 7	Rome	explosion in Jewish institution (2 injured)		-

Source: IDF Spokesman, The Sabotage Organizations: Thirteen Years of Terrorism Abroad (1968-1981), October 1981.

(*)   not filled in when (1) no information is available about the group, (2) the label that is known does not correspond to a known organization and only serves as a cover

(**)   actions carried out with the collaboration of non Middle Eastern movements

(***)   actions not directly aimed at Jewish or Israeli targets

Bibliography

1. GENERAL

Aston, C. C. "Restrictions Encountered in Responding to Terrorist Sieges: An Analysis." In *Responding to the Terrorist Threat*, ed. R. H. Schultz and S. Sloan, 59-92. New York: Pergamon, 1980.

Baechler, J. "Revolutionary and Counter-Revolutionary War." *Journal of International Affairs* 25 (Winter 1971):70-91.

Ben-Rafael, E., and Lissak, M. *Social Aspects of Guerrilla and Anti-Guerrilla Warfare.* Jerusalem: Magnes, 1979.

Blackstock, P. W. *The Strategy of Subversion.* Chicago: Quadrangle Books, 1964.

Bohonnan, C. T. R. "Anti-Guerrilla Operation." In *Unconventional Warfare*, ed. J. K. Zawodny, 19-29. Stanford, Calif.: Annals of the American Academy of Political and Social Sciences, 1962.

Boudon, R. *Effets pervers et ordre social.* Paris: PUF, 1979.

Boulding, K. *Conflict and Defense.* New York: Harper & Row, 1963.

Browne, M. W. *The New Face of War.* Indianapolis: Bobbs-Merrill, 1968.

Clutterbuck, R. *Guerrillas and Terrorists.* London: Faber & Faber, 1977.

Conner, W. "The Politics of Ethnonationalism." *Journal of International Affairs* 97 (1973):1-21.

Corsi, J. R. "Terrorism as a Desperate Game." *Journal of Conflict Resolution* 25, no. 1 (1981):47-85.

Coser, L. *The Functions of Social Conflict.* London: Routledge & Kegan Paul, 1965.

Crozier, B. *The Rebels.* London: Chatto & Windus, 1960.

Fairbairn, G. *Revolutionary Warfare and Communist Strategy.* London: Faber & Faber, 1968.

Fetscher, I. "Thesis on Terrorism Today." *Terrorism* 3, nos. 3-4 (1980):215-7.

Galula, D. *Counter-Insurgency Warfare.* New York: Praeger, 1966.

Gurr, T. "Comparative Study of Civil Strife." *The History of Violence in America.* New York: Times Books, 1969.

———. *Why Men Rebel.* Princeton, N.J.: Princeton University Press, 1970.

Heilbrunn, O. *La Guerre de partisans.* Paris: Payot, 1964.

Jenkins, B. *International Terrorism: A New Mode of Conflict.* Los Angeles: Crescent Publications, 1975.

Jenkins, B. M. *The Study of Terrorism: Definitional Problems.* Santa Monica, Calif.: Rand Corp., November 1980 (mimeo).

Johnson, C. "The Third Generation of Guerrilla Warfare." *Asian Survey* 6 (1968):435-47.

Kaufmann, J. *L'Internationale Terroriste.* Paris: Plon, 1977.

Kerstetler, W. A. "Terrorism and Intelligence," *Terrorism* 3, nos. 1-2 (1979):109-16.

Knorr, K. "Unconventional Warfare." In *Unconventional Warfare,* ed. J. K. Zawodny, 53-64. Stanford, Calif.: Annals of the American Academy of Political and Social Sciences, 1962.

Leites, N. "Understanding the Next Act." *Terrorism* 3/1-2, 1979:1-46.

Lustick, I. "Stability in Deeply Divided Societies: Consociationalism versus Control." *World Politics* 31 (1979):325-44.

McCuen, J. J. *The Art of Counter-Revolutionary War.* London: Faber & Faber, 1966.

Mao Tse-tung. *La Guerre révolutionnaire.* Paris: Union Générale d'Edition, 1955.

Marine Corps School. "Small Unit Operations." In *The Guerrilla and How to Fight Him,* ed. Col. Greene, 270-307. New York: Praeger, 1965.

Mickolus, E.; Heyman, E. S.; and Schlotter, J. "Responding to Terrorism: Basic and Applied Research." In *Responding to the Terrorist Threat,* ed. R. H. Schultz and S. Sloan, 189. New York: Pergamon, 1980.

Motley, J. B. "International Terrorism: A New Mode of Warfare." *International Security Review* 6, no. 1 (1981):93-123.

Ney, V. "Guerrilla Warfare and Modern Strategy." In *Modern Guerrilla Warfare,* ed. F. M. Osanka, 25-38. New York: Free Press, 1962.

Paget, J. *Counter-Insurgency Campaigning.* London: Faber & Faber, 1967.

Paret, P., and Shy, J. W. *Guerrillas in the 1960's.* New York: Praeger, 1966.

Parsons, T. "Some Reflections on the Place of Force in Social Processes." In *Internal War,* ed. H. Eckstein, 33-70. New York: Free Press, 1964.

Pustay, J. S. *Counter-Insurgency Warfare.* New York: Free Press, 1965.

Pye, L. W. "Roots of Insurgency and the Commencement of Rebellion." In *Internal War,* ed. H. Eckstein, 157-79. New York: Free Press, 1964.

Richardson, L. F. *Statistics of Deadly Quarrels.* Edited by Q. Wright and C. C. Licnan. London: Atlantic Books, Stevens and Sons, 1960.

Schultz, R. H., Jr. "The State of the Operational Art." In *Responding to the Terrorist Threat,* ed. R. H. Schultz and S. Sloan, 18-58. New York: Pergamon, 1980.

Shills, E. "Centre and Periphery." In *The Logic of Personal Knowledge,* 117-30. London: Routledge & Kegan Paul, 1961.

Shubik, M. *Game Theory and Related Approaches to Social Behavior.* New York: Wiley, 1964.

Simmel, G. *Conflict and the Web of Group Affiliation.* New York: Free Press, 1964.

Tanter, R. "Dimensions of Conflict Behavior within Nations, 1955-1960." In *Peace Research (International) Papers,* vol. 3, 1965, Chicago Conference 1964.

Thayer, Ch. W. *Guerrilla.* London: Michael Joseph, 1964.

Thompson, R. *Defeating Communist Insurgency.* New York: Praeger, 1966.

Timasheff, N. S. *War and Revolution.* New York: Sheed & Ward, 1965.

Trinquier, R. *Modern Warfare: A French View.* London: Pall Mall, 1964.

Wilkinson, P. "Terrorism: International Dimensions." *Conflict Studies* 113 (1979):1-22.

———. "Terrorist Movements." In *Terrorism and Practice,* ed. Y. Alexander, D. Carlton, and P. Wilkinson, 99-117. Boulder, Colo.: Westview Press, 1979.

Zawodny, J. K. "Guerrilla and Sabotage." In *Unconventional Warfare,* ed. Zawodny, 9-18. Stanford, Calif.: Annals of the American Academy of Political and Social Sciences, 1962.

2. CASE STUDIES: ALGERIA, CUBA, CYPRUS, AND VIETNAM

Barker, D. *Grivas: Portrait of a Terrorist.* London: Macmillan, 1959.

Bedjaoui, J. *Law and the Algerian Revolution.* Brussels: PIADL, 1961.

Bodard, L. *La Guerre d'Indochine.* Vols. 1 and 2. Paris: Air du Temps, 1963.

Bromberger, M. and D. *Les 13 Complots du 13 Mai.* Paris: Fayard, 1959.

Bromberger, S. *Les Rebelles algériens.* Paris: Plon, 1958.

Byford-Jones, W. *Grivas and the Story of the EOKA.* London: Robert Hale, 1959.

De Villiers, G. "L'Etat et la révolution agraire en Algérie." *Revue Française de Science Politique* 30, no. 1 (1980):112-39.

Drogat, N. *Les Pays de la faim.* Paris: Flammarion, 1963.

Dubois, J. *Fidel Castro.* Buenos Aires: Eudeba, 1959.

Duchemin, J. *Histoire du FLN.* Paris: La Table Ronde, 1962.

Eqbal, A. "Revolutionary War and Counterinsurgency." *Journal of International Affairs* 25, no. 1 (1974):23-56.

Fall, B. "Dien Bien Phu: A Battle to Remember." In *Vietnam,* ed. M. E. Gettleman, New York: Fawcett, 1960. 105-114.

Fanon, F. *Sociologie d'une révolution.* Paris: Maspero, 1967.

Grivas-Dighenis, G. *Guerrilla Warfare and EOKA's Struggle.* London: Longmans, 1962.

Gude, E. "Batista and Betancourt: Alternative Responses to Violence." In *The History of Violence in America.* New York: Times Books, 1969.

Guevarra, E. C. *Souvenirs de la guerre révolutionnaire.* Vol. 1. Paris: Maspero, 1967.

Hammer, E. J. "Genesis of the First Indochinese War." In *Vietnam,* ed. Gettleman, 15-23. New York: Fawcett, 1966.

Karol, A. *Guerrilleros au pouvoir.* Paris: Laffont, 1970.

Katz, M. N. "Origins of the Vietnam War." *Review of Politics* 42, no. 2 (1980):131-51.

Levy, R. *Regards sur l'Asie du Sud-Est.* Paris: Armand-Colin, 1952.

Quandt, W. B. *Revolution and Political Leadership: Algeria 1954-1968.* Cambridge, Mass., and London: MIT Press, 1969.

Royal Institute of International Affairs. *Cyprus, the Dispute and the Settlement.* London: Oxford University Press, 1969.

Saurel, A. *La Guerre d'Indochine.* Paris: Rouff, 1966.

Sauvage, L. *Autopsie du Castrisme.* Paris: Flammarion, 1968.

3. *THE ISRAELI-PALESTINIAN CONFLICT*

Aaroni, Y. "Hevel Yehuda Veefrayim" (The Area of Judea and Ephraim). In *Sefer Eretz Israel Hashlema* (The Book of the Greater Land of Israel), ed. A. Ben-Ami. Tel Aviv: Greater Israel Movement, 1977 (Hebrew).

Alexander, Y. "Terrorism in the Middle East: A New Phase?" *Washington Quarterly* 1, no. 4 (1978):115-17.

Amos, J. W. *Palestinian Resistance: Organization of a Nationalist Movement*. New York: Pergamon, 1980.

Avineri, S., ed. *Israel and the Palestinians*. New York: St. Martin's Press, 1971.

Bailey, C. "The Participation of the Palestinians in the Politics of Jordan." Ph.D. diss., Columbia University, 1966.

Bar-Haim, S. "The Palestine Liberation Army: Stooge or Actor." In *The Palestinians and the Middle East Conflict*, ed. G. Ben-Dor, 173-92. Ramat Gan: Turtledove, 1978.

Beeri, E. *Hapalestinayim Takhat Shilton Yarden* (The Palestinians under Jordanian Rule). Jerusalem: Magnes, 1978 (Hebrew).

Ben-Dor, G. "Mishtarim Tsfayim Baolam Haarvi: Sikuim ve Dfusim shel Maavar Lemimshal Ezrahi" (Military Regimes in the Arab World: Possibilities and Patterns of Transition to Civilian Rule). *Medina, Memshal Veyahasim Beinleumiim* 8 (September 1975):85-96 (Hebrew).

———. "Nationalism without Sovereignty and Nationalism with Multiple Sovereignties." In *The Palestinians and the Middle East Conflict*, ed. G. Ben-Dor, 143-72. Ramat Gan: Turtledove, 1976.

———. "The PLO and the Palestinians." *The War in Lebanon*, CSS Memorandum no. 8, Tel Aviv University (1983), 24-42.

Ben-Rafael, E. "Hebetim Khevratiim Shel Haconflict al Hashtakhim" (Sociological Aspects of the Conflict over the Territories). In *Habaaya Hapalestinayit: Sugiot Nivkharot* (The Palestinian Problem: Selected Aspects), 47-75. Tel Aviv: Tel Aviv University Press, 1982 (Hebrew).

Benvenisti, Y. M. *Preliminary Report no. 1*. West Bank Data Base Project (mimeograph, n.d., Hebrew).

Bernard, J. *British Rule in Palestine*. Washington D.C.: Public Affairs Press, 1948.

Blum, Y. "Hamaamad Hamishpati shel Yehuda Veshomron" (The Legal Status of Judea and Samaria). In *Sefer Eretz Israel Hashlema* (The Book of the Greater Land of Israel) ed. A. Ben-Ami, Tel-Aviv: The Greater Israel Movement, 1977 (Hebrew): 121-30.

Cobban, H. *The Palestinian Liberation Organization*. Cambridge: Cambridge University Press, 1984.

Cohen, A. "Does a Jordanian Option Still Exist?" *Jerusalem Quarterly* 16 (1980):111-20.

———. *Miflagot Bagada Hamaaravit Betkufat Hashilton Hayardeni* (Parties in the West Bank in the Period of Jordanian Rule). Jerusalem: Magnes, 1980 (Hebrew).

Curtis, M. "The U.N. against Israel." *Middle East Review* 13, no. 2 (Winter 1980-81):32-35.

Curtis, M.; Neyer, Y.; Waxman, C.; and Pollack, A., eds. *The Palestinians: People, History, Politics*. New Brunswick, N.J.: Transaction Books, 1975.

Dan, A. *Etsba Haelohim, Sodot Hamilkhama Bateror* (God's Finger, the Secret of Anti-Terror Warfare). Tel Aviv: Masada, 1976 (Hebrew).

Dayan, M. *Mapa Khadasha, Yakhasim Akherim* (A New Map, New Relations). Tel Aviv: Maariv, 1969 (Hebrew).

Dishon, D. "Hayakhasim bein-Aravim meaz Milkhemet Yom Kippur" (Inter-Arab Relations since the Yom Kippur War). In *Hasikhsukh Haisraeli-Aravi* (The Israeli-Arab Conflict), ed. E. Gilboa and M. Naor, 272-91. Tel Aviv: Matkal Ed., 1981 (Hebrew).

Dotan, S. *Hamaavak al Eretz Israel* (The Struggle over the Land of Israel). Tel Aviv: Ministry of Defense, mimeograph (Hebrew), 1981.

Dror, Y. "Manifest Mizrah-Tikhoni" (Middle East Manifesto). In *Bein Sikun Lesikui* (Between Threat and Hope), ed. A. Har-Even, 89-100. Jerusalem: Van Leer, 1980 (Hebrew).

Efrat, E. "Spatial Patterns of Jewish and Arab Settlement in Judea and Samaria." In *Judea, Samaria and Gaza: Views on the Present and Future*, ed. D. Elazar, 9-43. Washington: American Enterprise Institute for Public Policy Research, 1982.

———. *Haplitim Hapalestinayim: Mekhkar Kalkali Vehevrati 1949-1974* (The Palestinian Refugees: Economic and Social Research, 1949-1974). Tel Aviv: David Horowitz Institute, Tel Aviv University, 1976 (Hebrew).

El-Rayyes, R., and Nahas, D. *Guerrillas for Palestine*. London: Croom Helm, Portico, 1976.

Furlonge, G. *Palestine Is My Country: The Story of Musa Alami*. London: John Murray, 1969.

Gabay, M. *Levanon Neeveket al Kiuma: Meuravut Israelit Belevanon* (Lebanon Fights for Survival: Israeli Interference in Lebanon). Givat Haviva: Institute for Arab Studies, 1983 (Hebrew).

Garfinkle, M. Adam. "America and Europe in the Middle East, a New Coordination," *ORBIS*, Fall 1981.

Gazit, S. "Khamesh Shanim La-Shtakhim Hamukhzakim" (Five Years to the Administered Territories). In *Hasikhsukh Haisraeli-Aravi* (The Arab-Israeli Conflict), ed. E. Gilboa and M. Naor, 225-55. Tel Aviv: Matkal Ed., 1981.

Gemer, M, ed. *Hamasa Umatan al Kinun Ha-Autonomia* (*April 1979-October 1980*) (The Negotiations about Autonomy, April 1979-October 1980). Tel Aviv: Shiloah Institute (Hebrew).

Gerson, A. *Israel, the West Bank and International Law*. London: Frank Cass, 1978.

Gilboa, E. "Mediniut Hamaatzot Basikhsukh Haaravi-Israeli, Mimilkhemet Yom Hakippurim vead Kamp Deivid" (The Powers' Policy in the Arab-Israeli Conflict, from the Yom Kippur War up to Camp David). In *Hasikhsukh Haisraeli-Aravi* (The Arab-Israeli Conflict), ed. E. Gilboa and M. Naor, 272-91. Tel Aviv: Matkal Ed., 1981.

Gilboa, E., and Naor, M., eds. *Hasikhsukh Haaravi-Israeli* (The Arab-Israeli Conflict). Tel Aviv: Matkal Ed., 1981 (Hebrew).

Golan, G. *The Soviet Union and the PLO*. London: Adelphi Papers no. 131, 1976.

———. "Soviet-PLO Relations." *Jerusalem Quarterly* 16 (1980):121-36.

Golan, M. *Peres* (Peres). Tel Aviv: Shocken, 1982 (Hebrew).

Goldberg, J., ed. *Hamizrah Hatikhon: Megamot Vetahalikhim* (The Middle East:

Tendencies and Processes). Tel Aviv: Tel Aviv University, Shiloah Institute, 1982 (Hebrew).

Hadawi, S. *Bitter Harvest: Palestine, 1914-1967.* New York: New World Press, 1967.

Halabi, R. *Yesh Gvul: Hasipur Shel Hagada Hamaaravit* (There Is a Limit: The Story of the West Bank). Jerusalem: Keter, 1983 (Hebrew).

Har-Even, A. "Haim Itakhnu Yakhasei Eimun?" (Are Relations of Confidence Possible?) In *Bein Sikun Lesikui* (Between Threat and Hope), ed. A. Har-Even, 7-42. Jerusalem: Van Leer Institute, 1980 (Hebrew).

——, ed. *Bein Milhama Lehesderim: Hasikhsukh Haisraeli-Aravi Leahar 1973* (Between War and Arrangements: The Arab-Israeli Conflict after 1973). Tel Aviv: Zmora-Beitan-Modan, 1977 (Hebrew).

——, ed. *Bein Sikun Lesikui* (Between Threat and Hope). Jerusalem: Van Leer Institute, 1980 (Hebrew).

Harkabi, Y. *Haamana Hapalestinait Vemashmauta* (The Palestinian Covenant and Its Meaning). Jerusalem: Information Center, 1977 (Hebrew).

——. "Haideologia Haaravit Beyakhas Laconflict" (The Arab Ideology toward the Conflict). In *Emdat Haaravim Basikhsukh Haisraeli-Aravi* 57-110

——. *Hapalestinayim: Mitardema Lehitorrerut* (The Palestinians: From Quiescence to Awakening). Jerusalem: Magnes, 1979 (Hebrew).

——. *Tmurot Basikhsukh Haisraeli-Aravi* (Changes in the Israeli-Arab Conflict). Tel Aviv: Dabir, 1979 (Hebrew).

——. *Tokhnit Hapeula Haaravit Neged Israel* (The Arabs, Plan of Action against Israel). Jerusalem: Academon, 1975 (Hebrew).

——, ed. *Arav Veisrael: Hakhlatot Hamoatzot Haleumiot Hapalestinayot (3-4)* (Arabs and Israel: Decisions of the Palestinian National Councils). Tel Aviv: Am Oved, Truman Institute, 1975 (Hebrew).

——, ed. *Arav Veisrael: Kovetz Tirgumim Mearavit (1)* (Arabs and Israel: A Compendium of Translated Texts from Arabic). Tel Aviv: Am Oved, 1975 (Hebrew).

——, ed. *Emdat Haaravim Basikhsukh Haisraeli-Aravi* (The Arabs' Position in the Israeli-Arab Conflict). Tel Aviv: Dabir, 1970 (Hebrew).

Holborn, L. W. "The Palestine Arab Refugee Problem." In *The Arab-Israeli Conflict,* ed. J. N. Moore, 152-66. Princeton, N.J.: Princeton University Press, 1977.

Inbari, P. *Meshulash al Hayarden: Magaim Khashayim Bein Artzot Habrit, Yarden Veashaf* (Triangle on the Jordan: Secret Contacts between the U.S., Jordan and the PLO). Jerusalem: Kane, 1982 (Hebrew).

Izhar, M. *Artzot Habrit Vehamizrah Hatikhon* (The U.S. and the Middle East). Tel Aviv: Am Hasefer, 1974 (Hebrew).

——. "Bekhirot Laeeryot Beyehuda Veshomron: Hebetim Politiim" (Elections to the Municipalities in Judea and Samaria: Political Aspects). *Medina, Memshal Veyakhasim Beinleumiim* 5 (1974):119-26 (Hebrew).

Johnson, N. *Islam and the Politics of Meaning in Palestinian Nationalism.* London: Kegan Paul International, 1981.

Jureidini, P. A. and Hazen, W. E. *The Palestinian Movement in Politics.* Toronto: Lexington Books, 1976.

Kama, D. "Hasikhsukh, Lama Vead Matai?" (The Conflict: Why and Until When?). Tel Aviv: Shakmuna, 1975 (Hebrew).

Kazziza, W. W. *Revolutionary Transformation of the Arab World.* New York: St. Martin's Press, 1975.

Khalidi, W. *Conflict and Violence in Lebanon: Confrontation in the Middle East.* Cambridge: Harvard Studies in International Affairs, 1979.

Lanir, T. *Meuravut Israelit Belevanon* (Israeli Interference in Lebanon). Tel Aviv: Tel Aviv University, 1980 (Hebrew).

Lesh, A. M. *Arab Politics in Palestine 1917-1930,* London: Cornell University Press, 1979.

Le Gac, D. *Au Nom de la Palestine.* Paris: Denoel, 1975.

Lentin, R. *Sikhot im Nashim Palestinayot* (Discussions with Palestinian Women). Jerusalem: Mifras, 1982 (Hebrew).

Litany, Y. "Leadership in the West Bank and Gaza." *Jerusalem Quarterly* 24 (1980):99-109.

Lustick, I. "Israel and the West Bank after Elon Moreh: The Mechanics of De Facto Annexation." *The Middle East Journal,* Autumn 1981, 35/4: 557-77.

Maoz, M. *The Palestinian Guerrilla Organizations and the Soviet Union.* Jerusalem: Harry S. Truman Research Institute, 1975.

———, ed. *Yadei Hamaarakha Haaravit Beisrael al Reka Milkhemet Yom Kippurim* (The Goals of the Arabs' Combat against Israel in the Context of the Yom Kippur War). Jerusalem: Hebrew University of Jerusalem, Center for the Study of the Israeli Arabs and the Israeli-Arab Relations, 1974 (Hebrew).

Mari, S. "Higher Education Among the Palestinians." In *The Palestinians and the Middle East Conflict,* ed. G. Ben-Dor. Ramat Gan: Turtledove, 1976:433-48.

Miller, L. B. "America and the Palestinians: In Search of a Policy." In *The Palestinians and the Middle East Conflict,* ed. G. Ben-Dor. Ramat Gan: Turtledove, 1976:281-90.

Mishal, S. "Anatomya Shel Bekhirot Munitsipaliot" (The Anatomy of Municipal Elections). *Hamizrakh Hakhadash* 4 (1974):63-67 (Hebrew).

———. "Jordanian and Israeli Policy in the West Bank." In *The Hashemite Kingdom of Jordan and the West Bank,* ed. A. Sinai and A. Pollack. New York: American Academic Association for Peace in the Middle East, 1977:210-22.

———. "Ashaf Verayon Hamedina Hapalestinait" (The PLO and the Idea of the Palestinian State). In *Habaya Hapalestinayit: Sugiot Nivkharot* (The Palestinian Problem: Selected Aspects), Tel-Aviv: Tel-Aviv University Press, 1982:27-45.

———. *The PLO Under Arafat—Between Gun and Olive Branch.* New Haven: Yale University Press, 1986.

Moore, J. N., ed. *The Arab-Israel Conflict: Readings and Documents.* Princeton: Princeton University Press, 1977.

Mosely, L. A. *Arab Politics in Palestine, 1917-1939.* Ithaca, N.Y.: Cornell University Press, 1979.

Nakhleh, E., ed. *A Palestinian Agenda for the West Bank and Gaza.* Washington, D.C.: American Enterprise Institute, 1980.

Neman, Y. "Atzmaut, Bitakhon Veshtakhim" (Independence, Security and Territories). In *Sefer Eretz Israel Hashlema* (The Book of the Greater Land of

Israel), ed. A. Ben-Ami. Tel-Aviv: Greater Israel Movement, 1977 (Hebrew): 175-85.

Nevo, J. *Abdallah Vearaviei Eretz-Israel* (Abdallah and the Arabs in the Land of Israel). Tel Aviv: Tel Aviv University, Shiloah Institute, 1975 (Hebrew).

———. "Yakhas Araviei Eretz-Israel Layishuv Hayehudi Velatnua Hatzionit" (The Palestinian Arabs' Attitude toward the Jewish Settlement and the Zionist Movement). In *Tsionut Vehasheela Hayehudit* (Zionism and the Jewish Question). Jerusalem: Zalman Shazar Center, 1979 (Hebrew).

Neyer, Y. "The Emergence of Arafat." In *The Palestinians: People, History and Politics*, ed. N. Curtis, Y. Neyer, and A. Pollac, 129-130. New Brunswick: Transaction Books, 1975.

Nissan, M. *Israel and the Territories: A Study in Control.* Ramat Gan: Turtledove, 1978.

O'Ballance, E. *Arab Guerrilla Power, 1967-1972.* London: Archon Books, 1974.

Okhana, A. *Ashaf, Hairgun Umatarotav* (The PLO: The Organization and Its Aims). Jerusalem: The Information Center, n.d. (Hebrew).

O'Neil, B. E. *Armed Struggle in Palestine: A Political and Military Analysis.* Boulder, Colo.: Westview Press, 1978.

———. "Towards a Typology of Political Terrorism: The Palestinian Resistance Movement." *Journal of International Affairs* 22, no. 1 (1978):17-42.

Perlmutter, A. "A Palestinian Entity." *International Security* 5, no. 4 (1981):111-19.

———. "Types of National Movements, Progressive and Fascist." In *The Palestinians and the Middle East Conflict*, ed. G. Ben-Dor, 485-504. Ramat Gan: Turtledove, 1978.

Pirhi, D. "Midvarav Umiktavav Shel David Pirhi Zal" (From the Writings and Speeches of the late David Pirhi). In *Eser Shnot Shilton Israeli Beyehuda Veshomron* (Ten Years of Israeli Rule in Judea and Samaria), ed. R. Israeli, 147-206. Jerusalem: Magnes, 1980 (Hebrew).

Porat, Y. *Mimehumot Lemerida: Hatnua Haleumit Hapalestinayit, 1929-1939* (From Riots to Revolt: The National Palestinian Movement, 1929-1939). Tel Aviv: Am Oved, 1978 (Hebrew).

———. *Tsmikhat Haleumiut Haaravit-Hapalistinayit, 1919-1929* (The Emergence of Arab Palestinian Nationalism, 1919-1929). Tel Aviv: Am Oved, 1978 (Hebrew).

Quandt, W. B. "Political and Military Dimensions of Contemporary Palestinian Nationalism." In *The Politics of Palestinian Nationalism*, ed. W. B. Quandt, F. Jabber, and A. M. Lesch, 43-154. Berkeley: University of California Press, 1973.

Rabin, J. "Yakhasim Istrategiim" (Strategic Relations). In *Bein Sikun Lesikui* (Between Threat and Hope), ed. A. Har-Even, 42-62. Jerusalem: Van Leer Institution, 1980.

Rabinovitch, I., and Tabor, O. "Retsifut Vetmurot Bemishtar Habaath Besuria: Mishtar Assad Besuria" (Continuity and Changes in the Baath Regime in Syria: the Assad Regime in Syria). *Skirot*, Shiloah Institute, Tel Aviv University, August 1974 (Hebrew).

Rabinovitch, I., and Zamir, H. *Milkhama Vemashber Belevanon, 1975-1981* (War and Crisis in Lebanon, 1975-1981). Tel Aviv: Kibbutz Hameukhad, 1982 (Hebrew).

Rubinstein, D. "Haitonut Haaravit Bashtakhim Hamukhzakim" (Arab Press in the Administered Territories). In *Sefer Hashana, Shel Haitonayim,* (The Yearly Book of the Journalists) 8-181, 1975 (Hebrew).

Safran, A. *Hebetim Geographiim Upsikhologiim Shel Hasikhsukh Haaravi-Israeli* (Geographic and Psychological Aspects of the Arab-Israeli Conflict). Haifa: University of Haifa, Jewish-Arab Center, 1976 (Hebrew).

Safran, N. *Medinat Israel Veyakhaseha im Artzot Habrit* (The Israeli State and Its Relations with the U.S.). Tel Aviv: Shocken, 1979 (Hebrew).

Said, E. Q. *The Question of Palestine.* New York: Times Books, 1979.

Sayigh, R. *Palestinians: From Peasants to Revolutionaries.* London: Zed Press, 1979.

Schiff, Z., and Yaari, E. *Israel's Lebanon War.* New York: Simon and Schuster, 1984.

Sela, A. *Habaath Hapalestinay* (The Palestinian Baath). Jerusalem: Magnes, 1984 (Hebrew).

Shafir. G. "Changing Nationalism and Israel's 'Open Frontier' in the West Bank." Tel Aviv University, 1984, mimeograph.

Shalev, A. *Kavei Hagana Beyehuda Veshomron* (Lines of Defense in Judea and Samaria). Tel Aviv: Center for Strategic Studies, 1983 (Hebrew).

Shamgar, M. "Legal Concepts and Problems of the Israeli Military Government: The Initial Stage," In *Military Government in the Territories Administrated by Israel 1967-1980: The Legal Aspects,* ed. M. Shamgar, 13-60. Jerusalem: Hebrew University of Jerusalem, 1982.

Shamir, S. *Mitsrayim Behanhagat Sadat* (Egypt under Sadat's Leadership). Tel Aviv: Dabir, 1978 (Hebrew).

Shamir, S.; Shapira, R.; Rekhess, E.; et al. "The Professional Elite in Samaria." In *The Palestinians and the Middle East Conflict,* ed. G. Ben-Dor, 461-83. Ramat Gan: Turtledove, 1976.

Shimoni, J. *Hatnua Haleumit Haaravit Beeretz Israel, 1918-1945* (The Arab National Movement in the Land of Israel, 1918-1945). Tel Aviv: Am Oved, 1947 (Hebrew).

———. *Medinot Arav: Pirkei Historia Medinit* (The Arab States: Chapters of Political History). Tel Aviv: Am Oved, 1977 (Hebrew).

Shkhoda, R. *Haderekh Hashlishit* (The Third Way). Jerusalem: Mifras, 1981 (Hebrew).

Sinai, A., Pollack A. (eds.) *The Hashemite Kingdom of Jordan and the West Bank.* New York: American Academic Association for Peace in the Middle East, 1977.

Stanley, D. "Fragmentation and National Liberation Movements: The PLO." *Orbis* 21/41 (1979):1033-55.

Susser, A. "The Palestinian Organization." In *Middle East Contemporary Survey,* ed. C. Legum, H. Shaked, and D. Dishon, 3:285-305. New York: Holmes & Meier, Shiloah Center, Tel Aviv University, 1979.

Teguer, J. "Hamered Haaravi Beshnat 1936 Beperspectiva shel Imut Yehudi Aravi Beeretz Israel" (The 1936 Arab Revolt in the Perspective of the Jewish-Arab Confrontation in Palestine). In *Tsionut Vehasheela Haaravit*

(Zionism and the Arab Question), 89-108. Jerusalem: Zalman Shazar Center, 1979 (Hebrew).

Teveth, S. *Klallat Habrakha* (The Blessing's Curse). Tel Aviv: Shocken, 1969 (Hebrew).

Vinter, J. "Maarekhet Hakhinukh Bashtakhim Hamukhzakim" (The Educational System in the Administered Territories). In *Eser Shnot Shilton Israeli Beyehuda Veshomron* (Ten Years of Israeli Rule in Judea and Samaria), ed. R. Israeli, 107-15. Jerusalem: Magnes, 1980 (Hebrew).

Weizmann, E. *Hakrav al Hashalom* (The Battle for Peace). Jerusalem: Eidanim, 1981 (Hebrew).

Yaari, E. *Fatah* (The Fatah). Tel Aviv: Levin-Epstein, 1970 (Hebrew).

Yariv, A. *PLO: A Profile.* Jerusalem: Israel Universities' Study Group for Middle Eastern Affairs, 1974.

———. "The European Community and the Palestinians." In *The Palestinians and the Middle East Conflict*, ed. G. Ben-Dor, 281-320. Ramat Gan: Turtledove, 1976.

———. "Yesodot Mediniut Habitakhon Shel Israel" (The Bases of Israel's Security Policy). In *Hasikhsukh Haaravi-Israeli* (The Arab-Israeli Conflict) eds. E. Gilboa and M. Naor, 295-304. Tel Aviv: Matkal Ed., 1981 (Hebrew).

Yariv, A. "The War in Lebanon: The Effects on Israel's Strategic Situation." *Memorandum no. 8*, February 1983, Center for Strategic Studies, Tel Aviv University.

Yodfat, A. Y. and Arnon-Ohanna, Y. *PLO Strategy and Tactics.* New York: St. Martin's Press, 1981.

Yost, C. W. "The Arab-Israeli War: How It Began." In *The Arab-Israeli Conflict: Readings and Documents*, ed. J. N. Moore. Princeton: Princeton University Press, 1977.

4. *IDF PUBLICATIONS (IN HEBREW)*

Adir, M. "Hashpaat Milkhemet Yom Hakippurim al Hakhashiva Haistrategit Haaravit" (The Influence of the Yom Kippur War on Arab Strategic Thought). *Skira Khodshit* 8-9 (1975):5-18.

Dishon, D. "Hazira Habein Aravit Bemivtza Sheleg" (The Inter-Arab Stage during the Sheleg Operation). *Skira Khodshit,* June 1982.

El-Peleg, "Al mediniuta shel Israel Beyosh" (About Israel's Policy in Judea and Samaria). *Skira Khodshit,* May 1982.

Elran, M. "Hamizrakh Hatikhon, Mabat Leatid" (The Middle East: A Look at the Future). *Maarakhot* 270-71 October (1979):37-42.

Gazit, S. "Bameh Shone Ashaf?" (In What Is the PLO Different?). *Skira Khodshit,* July 1980.

———. "Hashtakhim Hamukhzakim: Khamesh Shanim" (The Administered Territories: Five Years). *Dapei Meda,* November 1971.

———. "Hashtakhim Hamukhzakim: Mediniut Vemaas" (The Administered Territories: Policy and Acts). *Maarakhot* 204 (1970):1-39.

Gilbert, M. *Atlas Hasikhsukh Haaravi-Israeli* (Atlas of the Arab-Israeli Conflict). Tel Aviv: Ministry of Defense, 1980.

Harkabi, Y. *Fatah Baistrategia Haaravit* (The Fatah in the Arab Strategy). Tel Aviv: Maarakhot, 1969.

———. *Yesodot Hasikhsukh Haisraeli-Aravi* (Foundations of the Israeli-Arab Conflict). IDF: Education and Information, February 1971.

Levita, J. "Tsad Nosaf Leyetsirat Yakhasei Gomlin Takinim" (Another Step toward Normal Reciprocal Relations). *Skira Khodshit*, January 1972.

Maoz, M. "Tahalikhim Vemegamot Bashtakhim" (Processes and Tendencies in the Territories). *Skira Khodshit*, May 1980, 3-9.

Moshe, X. "Haganat Hakhof Mipnei Khadirat Klei Shayt" (The Defense of the Shore against Maritime Infiltration). *Maarakhot* 283 July (1982):51-54.

Rabinovitch, I. "Milkhemet Yom Hakippurim Vehayakhasim Habein Araviim (The Yom Kippur War and the Inter-Arab Relations). *Maarakhot* 236 (May 1974):5-12.

Rakhnich-Kigner, H. "Yakhasii Memshal Reagan im Ashaf Lenokhakh Hamaarakha Belevanon" (The Reagan Administration's Relations with the PLO as a Result of the Operation in Lebanon). *Skira Khodshit*, June 1982.

Shteinberg, M. "Tfisat Hamaavak Hamezuyan, Bereiyat Hairgunim Hapalestinayim" (The View of Armed Struggle among the Palestinian Organizations). *Maarakhot* 283 (July 1982):2-6.

Shtendel, U. "Araviei Israel Bein Patish Vesadan" (The Israeli Arabs between Hammer and Anvil). *Skira Khodshit*, February 1982.

Soker, J. "Shmone Shnot Memshal Israeli Bashtakhim" (Eight Years of Israeli Administration in the Territories). *Skira Khodshit*, July 1975, 7-9.

Stempler, S. "Mashmaut Hatzlakhatan Shel Habekhirot Beshomron" (The Meaning of the Success of the Elections in Samaria). *Skira Khodshit*, April 1972, 32-33.

Yariv, A. "Omek Istrategi: Hashkafa Israelit" (Strategic Depth: An Israeli View). *Maarakhot* 270-71 (October 1979):21-26.

———. "Tmikhat Artzot Arav Baterror Haaravi" (The Support of Arab Terror by Arab States). *Skira Khodshit*, July 1980, 19-20.

Zayd, I. "Hagana Merkhavit Vehagana Ezrakhit Bamilkhama Baterror" (Territorial and Civilian Defense in Anti-Terror Warfare). *Maarakhot* 270-71, October 1979:270-71.

5. DOCUMENTS AND OTHER SOURCES OF INFORMATION

a. General

The Palestinian Problem: The Background Data. Israeli Center for Information, Jerusalem, March 1975.

Kanowsky, E. Interview on the economy of the Arab countries and the Israeli-Arab conflict, February 1975. In *The Negotiations about the Instituting of Autonomy (April 1979-October 1980)* Tel-Aviv: Shiloah Institute, 1981.

b. Views of Guerrilla and Antiguerrilla Strategies

The Jewish View

Ministers about the Territories. Debates of Labour Party Cabinet Members, at the secretary of the Israeli Labor party on October 5, 1972, November 9 and 21, 1972, December 12, 1972.

Milson, M. Interview, in *Maariv*, June 3, 1980.

——. Interview, Palo Alto, Calif., October 15, 1984.

Yariv, A. Interview, Tel Aviv, May 13, 1983.

The Arab View

A la Tsaf of the Executive Bureau of the PFLP. Interview, September 22, 1979 (from IDF sources).

Basam Shaqaa, Muhammad Milhim, Amnon Alentsar. Interview, *Aluton*, March 7, 1980 (from IDF sources).

Chat with an Arab journalist in the territories. *Al-Dustur*, February 18, 1980 (from IDF sources). *Publications from Arab Newspapers*, Tel-Aviv: The Shiloah Institute (Hebrew),

Syrian comments. *Al-Tura*, April 28, 1982, 2-3 (from IDF sources).

c. Guerrilla Activities, Organizations, and Relations

IDF Spokesman. *A Guide to Terror Organizations*. November 1978.

IDF, Education and Training. *Guerrilla Organizations*. 1974.

IDF. "Lebanon and Guerrilla Organizations." *Dapei Meda*, October 10, 1969.

IDF Spokesman. *Major Terror Actions (June 12, 1967-September 12, 1980)*, August 1981.

IDF. *The PLO: A History of Blood*, 1982. General Headquarters.

IDF, Education and Training, "The PLO in Lebanon." *Daguesh*, February 1983.

IDF Spokesman. *The PLO and International Terror*. March 1981.

IDF. "Hijackings." *Dapei Meda*, January 11, 1970.

IDF Spokesman. *PLO Ties with the USSR and Other Eastern Bloc Countries*. September 1981.

IDF Spokesman. *Libyan-PLO Relations*. September 1982.

Information Briefing. *The Saudi Arabian-PLO Connection*. Information Center, Jerusalem, June 1981.

d. In the Territories

Details about the PNF in the Territories. *Al-Nahar* (Beirut), May 30, 1974.

Details about the PNF in Gaza. *Shaon Falestin*, April 1, 1980.

Bir Zeyt University. *Report on How Israeli Military Order No. 854 Affects Higher Education in the West Bank*, Bir Zeyt University, Public Relations Office, October 1982.

The Civilian Authorities: Files on "Universities," "Academic Freedom," "Communists in Judea and Samaria," "Facts, Miscellaneous."

"The Activity of the Palestinian-Jordanian Committee," a report (October 19, 1979).

e. Anti-Guerrilla Activities

Israel, Two Years after the War. IDF Headquarters, Education, 1969.
The Administered Territories, 1971-1972. Ministry of Defense, 1973.
The Administered Territories, 1972-1973. Ministry of Defense, 1974.
The Administered Territories, 1973-1974. Ministry of Defense, 1975.
Israel, Coordinator of Government Operations in Judea and Samaria, Gaza District, Sinai, Golan Heights. *A Thirteen-Year Survey (1967-1980).* Israel, January 1, 1981.
"Arab Terror and the Fight against It." *Daf Lamasbir,* Center for Information, no. 17, 1972.
IDF Spokesman. *Sheleg and Lebanon.* 1983.
IDF Education. *The Sheleg Operation.* 1982.
IDF Spokesman. *The Jordanian Line.* 1980.
Moshe, Interview. An Officer on the West Bank (1984).
X, Interview. A Senior Officer, on the Israeli-Lebanese border (1984).

6. REPORTS AND ARTICLES IN ISRAELI DAILIES (HEBREW)

Al-Hamishmar (Left-Wing Mapam)

Amitai, Y.: August 8, 1980 (Hotam: 10).
Banko, A.: August 22, 1980 (Hotam: 3-2).
Kapeliuk, A.: April 4, 1980.
Shur, I.: December 25, 1980: 2.
Symposium: September 19, 1980: 5 and 10.

Davar (Labor Party)

Beilin, Y.: December 3, 1976 (Hashavua: 16, 17).
El-Peleg, T.: October 10, 1980: 16.
Gazit, S.: March 19, 1982: 13.
Lindus, I.: November 28, 1979: 7.
Milson, M.: January 1, 1982: 8, 13, 24; January 8, 1982 (Hashavua).
Negbi, M.: June 12, 1980: 9.
Rubinstein, D.: September 30, 1971; November 17, 1978; February 15, 1980: 13; March 29, 1980: 5; May 23, 1980: 11; August 19, 1980: 5; September 2, 1980: 5; September 2, 1980: 14, 15.
Yari, E.: March 21, 1976.

Haaretz (Left-of-Center, Independent)

Bareli, T.: June 4, 1982: 15; September 2, 1982: 9; November 18, 1981: 7; March 14, 1983: 8; April 21, 1983: 1; June 19, 1983.
Eilon, A.: March 12, 1982: 13; February 26, 1983: 13.

Feinberg, N.: October 9, 1977; 9.

Golan, M.: March 30, 1982: 11.

Habakuk, Y.: October 26, 1978; December 7, 1980: 20-21; January 2, 1981; December 19, 1983.

Hadad, A.: June 5, 1972: 15; January 1, 1980.

Litani, Y.: December 31, 1978: 9; January 30, 1980: 9; March 14, 1980; June 25, 1980: 9; December 5, 1980; December 12, 1980: 15; November 30, 1981: 9; January 1, 1982: 9, 11; March 29, 1982; January 18, 1982; March 15, 1982.

Manzur, A.: November 3, 1980.

Maor, M.: January 13, 1981: 9.

Pedhatzur, R.: May 13, 1983: 12, 13.

Schiff, Z.: February 8, 1980; December 12, 1980:13; May 10, 1982.

Maariv (Right–Wing Independent)

Bitzur, Y.: March 25, 1980: 3.

Cohen, A.: June 27, 1980.

Goldstein, D.: June 13, 1980: 24.

Lavi, T.: November 10, 1978: 23.

Tsuriel, J.: July 23, 1982.

Ynov, E.: June 8, 1979; January 20, 1980; November 19, 1980.

Zahur, E.: July 20, 1982.

Yediyot Akharonot (Right–Wing Independent)

Shaked, R.: June, 7, 1983; June 12, 1983; July 5, 1983.

Index

About the Author

ELIEZER BEN-RAFAEL is Senior Lecturer and Chairman of the Department of Sociology, Tel Aviv University. He has previously been associated with Hebrew University, Harvard University, and the Ecole des Hautes Etudes, Paris. He is the author of *The Emergence of Ethnicity: Cultural Groups and Social Conflict in Israel* (Greenwood, 1982) and *Social Aspects of Guerilla and Anti-Guerilla Warfare.*